Mad Rulers and Worthy Sons

A Translation and Analysis of the Newly Excavated *Zhouxun*

by

Andrej Fech

Three Pines Press
St. Petersburg, FL 33713
www.threepinespress.com

© 2023 by Andrej Fech

All rights reserved. No part of this book may be
reproduced in any form or by any means, electronic or
mechanical, including photocopying, recording, or by any
information storage and retrieval system, without permission
in writing from the publisher.

9   8 7 6 5 4 3 2 1

First Three Pines Press Edition, 2023
Printed in the United States of America

⊗ This edition is printed on acid-free paper that meets
the American National Standard Institute Z39.48 Standard.
Distributed in the United States by Three Pines Press.

Cover art: "Tang Ming Huang Instructing the Prince," painting by unidentified artists, probably of the Ming dynasty. Metropolitan Museum of Art, New York, acc. no. 51487. Public Domain.
Cover Design by Brent Christopher Wulf.

Library of Congress Cataloging-in-Publication Data

Names: Fech, Andrej, 1973- translator, editor.
Title: Mad Rulers and Worthy Sons : a Translation and Analysis of the Newly
   Excavated Zhouxun / by Andrej Fech.
Other titles: Zhou xun. English | Translation and Analysis of the Newly
   Excavated Zhouxun
Description: First Three Pines Press edition. | St Petersburg, FL : Three
   Pines Press, 2023. | Includes bibliographical references and index.
Identifiers: LCCN 2023000137 | ISBN 9781931483728 (paperback)
Subjects: LCSH: China--History--Zhou dynasty, 1122-221 B.C.--Sources. |
   China--Kings and rulers.
Classification: LCC DS747.33 .Z46 2023 | DDC 931/.03--dc23/eng/20230104
LC record available at https://lccn.loc.gov/2023000137

Contents

Acknowledgments	iv
Preface	v

Part One: Discussion

1. Discovery and Publication	1
2. The Protagonists	13
3. Textual Organization	23
4. Rhetorical Strategies	33
5. Philosophical Concepts	41
6. Wider Context	62

Part Two: Translation

1. First Month	77
2. Second Month	88
3. Third Month	99
4. Fourth Month	105
5. Fifth Month	111
6. Sixth Month	119
7. Seventh Month	130
8. Eighth Month	136
9. Ninth Month	143
10. Tenth Month	149
11. Eleventh Month	155
12. Twelfth Month	165
13. Intercalary Month	173
14. The Day after the La-Festival	180
Conclusion	202
Bibliography	205
Index	225

Acknowledgments

The present book could not have been written without the generous support of several people whom I would like to thank at this juncture.

First and foremost, my heartfelt thanks go to Philip J. Ivanhoe. In June of 2017, PJ invited me to give a talk on power transfer in the *Zhouxun* at the Center for East Asian and Comparative Philosophy at the City University of Hong Kong. Later, he kindly offered to host a reading group to discuss my proposed translation and interpretation of the text. I greatly benefitted from our numerous weekly meetings in 2018.

I am equally indebted to another participant to this group, Eirik Harris. In addition to the reading group, I am grateful to him for our discussions on the intellectual tenets of the work as well as numerous translation issues. Working together with PJ and Eirik gave me an invaluable opportunity to learn from their expertise in interpreting ancient Chinese texts.

I also would like to extent my thanks to Yuri Pines with whom I had an opportunity to discuss the *Zhouxun*. During our meeting, Yuri kindly agreed to look over the translation and provided valuable insights into the interpretation of the manuscript.

Furthermore, I am grateful to Sarah Allan and Andrew Seth Meyer for their elucidating suggestions on some thematic issues surrounding the *Zhouxun* at the Society for the Study of Early China 2017 annual conference. Andrew West has my gratitude for creating fonts for some rare variant graphs found in the *Zhouxun*, thus making it possible to create a Word file of the entire manuscript.

While I have incorporated many suggestions from these scholars into my work, all the mistakes remain mine.

Finally, I would like to thank the University Grants Committee, Research Grants Council in Hong Kong, which supported this research as the ECS project entitled: "'Elevating the Worthy' and 'Mandate of Heaven' in the Late Warring States Period" (HKBU22613218). In the course of the project, I received assistance from Wang Jue, to whom I am also grateful.

Preface

This book analyses the newly excavated manuscript *Zhouxun* and provides a first translation into a Western language. There are many reasons why the investigation of this work is important. The *Zhouxun* is a lengthy text which was lost at some point in its transmission, probably already during the Han dynasty. Naturally, the study of such a text helps us gain a fuller picture of the intellectual landscape of early China. But what makes the investigation of this text particularly rewarding is the fact that it provides a unique view of early Chinese history, from the times of the legendary Yao to the mid-Warring States period.

The text espouses the view that the transfer of power in ancient China was carried out based both on hereditary and meritocratic principles. That is, sons were chosen to inherit their fathers based on their abilities and not their position within the lineage hierarchy stipulated by ritual. The *Zhouxun* depicts Chinese history to the effect that political succession has been ever since regulated solely by the incumbent ruler's assessment of his progenies' performance. In its abandonment of the fundamental rule of primogeniture, the *Zhouxun* appears to support the political aspirations of royal family members who were traditionally excluded from power transfer, such as rulers' younger sons and sons by concubines. I came to see this trait as reflecting the events in the state of Qin just before the unification of the Chinese states.

Another intriguing feature of the *Zhouxun* is that a work with the same title and scope—in fourteen chapters—is mentioned in the Daoist section of the earliest extant catalogue of the imperial library, the *Hanshu* "Yiwenzhi." I agree with those scholars who claim that this catalogue entry refers to the same text as the extant *Zhouxun*. Firstly, it is highly unlikely that two different texts with the same basic characteristics existed and, secondly, some thoughts expressed in the extant copy can, indeed, be found in central Daoist classics.

That said, the *Zhouxun* lacks the main features associated with Daoist philosophy, introducing neither a Dao-based cosmology nor characteristic political practices, such as nonaction, nor specific cultivation techiques. On the contrary, it demonstrates several traits that are emphatically non-Daoist, such as frequent quotations from the *Odes*, the mainstay of Confucian or Ru education. There are two ways to explain this idiosyncrasy. Either the *Zhouxun* bears witness to a long-forgotten tradition within the Daoist school to which we now have access, or the work was included into the Daoist section based on the few matches it had with Daoist tenets to categorize ancient lore according to the standards of the Han dynasty. In either case, the investigation of the manuscript can enhance our understanding of early Daoism. In the former situation, we gain a fuller knowledge of its different branches, while in the latter scenario, we learn how Daoism was perceived by early imperial historiographers.

Part One

Discussion

Chapter 1

Discovery and Publication

The *Zhouxun* 周馴（訓）or *Instructions of the Zhou* is part of the Peking University collection (*Beijing daxue cang Xi Han zhushu* 北京大學藏西漢竹書), a group of bamboo-slip manuscripts dated to the Western Han and donated to the institution in 2009 (Beijing daxue chutu wenxian yanjiusuo 2011, 49).[1] In addition to the *Zhouxun*, the corpus also contains a copy of the *Laozi* 老子, the *Zhao Zheng shu* 趙正書 (The Book of Zhao Zheng), *Wang Ji* 妄稽, *Fan Yin* 反淫 (Contra Immoderation) and some other texts (Foster 2017, 168).

As the texts were illegally retrieved by a private party, the circumstances of their discovery and curation remain unknown. Hence, the Peking University manuscripts, alongside the Shanghai Museum and Tsinghua University collections, can be characterized as "looted" artefacts. As such, they present scholars with a series of concerns.

Among the most serious ethical problems is the fact that the purchase of looted manuscripts raises the concern of complicity of academics in practices of grave desecration by encouraging a black market in stolen artefacts (Goldin 2013a, 153–160). As for scholarly issues, not being able to study manuscripts in their original archeological environment gives us only a limited picture of their function and purpose.[2] Finally, regardless of how genuine a particular looted document might appear to be, we simply have no means of proving that it is actually not a forgery, at least when using conventional practices of manuscript authentication.[3] In the case of the Peking University collection, the suspicion of forgery was raised against the *Laozi*, its most prominent text (Xing 2016). Even though this suspicion has been persuasively refuted (Foster 2017, 167–239; Staack 2017), the mere fact that it could be raised is indicative of the problematic status of looted manuscripts.[4]

---

[1] The title is recorded on the back of the third slip of the manuscript (Han 2015, 250). Some passages in this book are based on my previous work on the *Zhouxun* (Fech 2018 and 2020).
[2] For the arrangement and function of texts in early Chinese graves, see, for instance, Lai 2015.
[3] As Kern 2019, 46 has pointed out, forgers might even use blank bamboo slips which are abundant in ancient graves, to make their creation pass the carbon-14 dating test. The only solution to that problem would be testing the ink characters are written in.
[4] Similar concerns are expressed by Vermander 2022, 83.

Being aware of these issues, I believe that not investigating the available, albeit looted, manuscripts would be equally detrimental, given the valuable information they contain, even in their fragmented state. The study of the texts from the Shanghai and Tsinghua collections, has, for instance, changed our understanding of early Chinese historiography and philosophy in many ways. Likewise, the study of the Peking university manuscripts, in general, and the *Zhouxun*, in particular, has the potential to provide new evidence about early China.

The *Zhouxun* was published in the first volume of a two-volume collection containing some Peking University manuscripts in September 2015. In addition to the high-resolution photographs of the slips' frontside, drawings of their rear side are also provided, elucidating the position of the verso lines. Furthermore, the volume contains a transcription of the text, a commentary by the editors and parallel passages from other texts. Transcription is presented based on the presumed original structure of the *Zhouxun* (Beijing daxue chutu wenxian yanjiusuo 2015, 121–122; hereafter cited as *Beida Mss*). The second volume of that collection also contains an article by Han Wei, the most comprehensive analysis of the various features of the manuscript to date.

Transcription

The Beida version of the *Zhouxun* features 211 bamboo slips measuring 30.2–5 cm in length and 0.8–1 cm in width, which were bound with three threads. When fully written, most slips contain twenty-four characters.[5] These parameters distinguish it from most other manuscripts from this collection.[6]

As with most excavated materials, the manuscript of the *Zhouxun* contains almost no punctuation. That is, except for the characters themselves, the only visible markings on the surface of the slips are: dots (•), placed on the top of the slips to signify the beginning of a new textual unit (in most cases, chapters, but, sometimes, smaller sections); repetition marks (=), placed after a character on the right edge of the slip to indicate that it should be read twice at this juncture, and, finally, lines applied to the verso of the slips.[7]

The published transcription, however, contains several additional elements. Most importantly, the editors have added punctuation, based on their

---

[5] *Beida Mss*. 121. There are only nine exceptions in the whole manuscript, which are slips 78, 104, 110, 133, 134, 145, 147, 189 and 194. Among them, slips 110, 133 and 147, containing twenty-seven characters each, conclude chapters 8, 10 and 11 respectively. Therefore, it stands to reason that, in this case, the copyists tried to avoid the situation when a bamboo slip is inscribed only with three characters, which would have happened had they followed the regular pattern of inscription.

[6] For the *Laozi*, see Han 2011, 67; for the *Zhao Zheng shu*, see Zhao H. 2011, 64; for the *Wang Ji*, see He J. 2011, 75.

[7] For a discussion of the function of verso lines, see Staack 2015.

3 / Chapter 1

understanding of the text. As I show below, their interpretation of the text structure and, consequently, the use of punctuation can be challenged in a number of cases. Furthermore, the number of bamboo slips is indicated after the respective last character written thereupon, as in, for instance, *bu li xiao ren* 不立孝仁 126. Accordingly, *ren* 仁 is the last character on slip 126. To be able to identify each individual graph, the combination of two numerals will be used in this book: the slip number slash (/) the number indicating the character's position on the slip. For instance, because slip 126 is inscribed with twenty-four graphs, the character *ren* appearing at its end has the individual number of 126/24. In addition, the published version contains the following symbols:

1) ( ) for phonetic loan characters or graphic variants;
2) 〈 〉 for writing errors;
3) 【 】 for lacunae which can be reconstructed with a high degree of certainty based on the internal logic of a passage or other considerations. For instance, the beginning of chapter 4 is transcribed in the published version as: 【・維歲四月更旦之日，龏（共）大子朝，周昭文公自身貳（敕）之，用茲念也。曰：】. This shows that, although the passage is now missing, there is a good reason to assume that originally it appeared at that particular juncture in the text.
4) ☐ for lacunae where the number of characters can be estimated;
5) ⋯⋯ for lacunae where the character number cannot be estimated.

One is able to read the transcription of the manuscript only after having familiarized oneself with the symbols introduced above.

The Scope

The recovered version comprises 211 bamboo slips brushed with 4882 characters and eighty-nine repetition marks.[8] At the same time, the manuscript concludes with the count: "Grand total: 6000 (characters)" (*dafan liu-qian* 大凡六千) (slip 211/14–17). Consequently, it seems that about 1118 characters, i.e., almost 19 percent of the original content, have been lost. This number roughly corresponds to forty-six slips (each accommodating twenty-four graphs), making the original scope of the present copy about 257 slips (for a slightly different estimate, see Han 2015, 249–250). However, the loss rate of 19 percent appears unusually

---

[8] The editors only provide an approximate scope of less than 5000 characters (Han 2011, 72). The number 4882 does not include the title of the work, the four characters contained in the overall count, or the seventeen characters situated on six the bamboo snippets (slips 212–217), which cannot be confirmed to belong to the *Zhouxun*.

high in the context of other Beida manuscripts, many of which have been recovered with only minor, if any, losses (Han 2011, 67). Indeed, an approximation of the original scope of this *Zhouxun* edition suggests that such an extensive loss was unlikely.

As the content analysis will show in detail below, the present copy of the *Zhouxun* comprised fourteen chapters. For the first thirteen, the number of missing slips has been already determined with a high degree of certainty, based on the pattern of verso lines, plot development, etc. It is only for the concluding chapter 14, the longest unit in the text, that the corresponding statistics are more difficult to estimate. The number of the extant slips and missing slips in each chapter (except for the last one) is as follows:

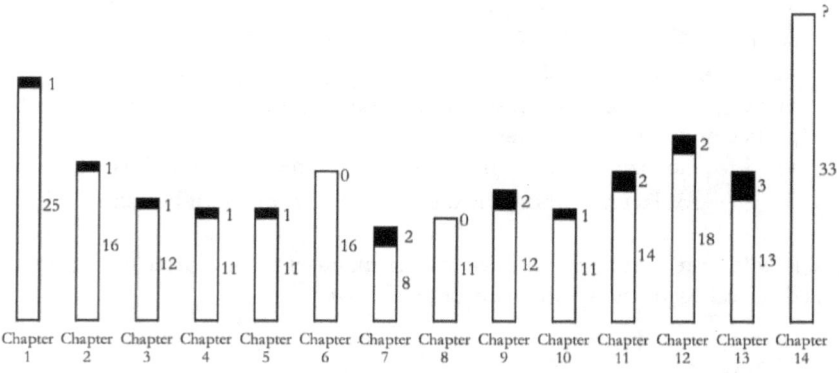

Ratio of Extant and Missing Slips

As can be seen, while the number of missing slips in a chapter never exceeds three, eight chapters have either no lacunae at all or lack only one slip. This chart can also help us approximate the initial number of slips for each chapter. Using it, we can calculate the mean percentage of missing slips for the first thirteen chapters. It is almost exactly 9 percent. The corresponding number of characters for this text selection would be then around 4558 (4150 extant graphs plus 408 extrapolated).

Now, if the initial scope of the *Zhouxun* really was around 6000 characters, then chapter 14 must have originally contained no less than 1642 characters or around sixty-eight slips. In this case, the chapter would be unique in regard to both its length and the degree of its damage (48 percent). But if we apply the just obtained ratio of 9 percent to its remnants, we get 804 characters (732 extant plus 72 extrapolated). Consequently, the overall number of graphs in the text could be estimated to have been around 5362 (4558 plus 804), that is, about 638 characters (26 slips) fewer than recorded in the overall count.

While small-scale inaccuracies in the word count were common in the manuscript culture of early China (Zhang X. 2006, 175), divagations as significant as this were rare and demand explanation. Chen Jian (2015) conjectures that part of the *Zhouxun*'s final count might have referenced some "independent units" which, while being included in an earlier version, were left out of this copy. I argue that the tally could instead refer to a group of texts. To begin with, excavated materials contain examples of word tallies, which, while appearing to relate to one text only, provide statistics for several.[9] Also, the notion "grand total" is used in some manuscripts to designate a total word count for several accounts.[10] The concluding statement in the *Zhouxun* is written in a different style than the text proper (Han 2015, 250). In view of this, it is entirely possible that the number 6000 indicated the scope of the texts, which the author of this record believed to constitute a distinct group (either thematically, or in terms of their origin or for other reasons). However, given the nature of the Beida collection, it cannot be determined which other text(s) formed a group together with the *Zhouxun* (or whether they were ever part of this corpus).[11]

Palaeographic and Linguistic Characteristics

The calligraphic style of the *Zhouxun* is the clerical script of the type "Silkworm's Head and Swallow's Tail" (*cantou yanwei* 蠶頭燕尾), which was found to be closest to the calligraphy of the Dingzhou Bajiaolang 定州八角廊 slips (Yan 2011a, 71). Because the latter were discovered in a grave whose occupant passed away in 55 BCE, it stands to reason that the available copy of the *Zhouxun* was produced some time prior to that, probably during the last years of Han Wudi (r. 140–87 BCE).[12]

Numerous characters in the *Zhouxun* deviate in some way from their (current) standard form. Based on the transcription of the work, the number of these

---

[9] The Mawangdui text *Zhao Li* 昭力 is concluded with a word tally of six thousand characters which, given the small scope of this text, must have also referred to the preceding *Mu He* 繆和 (Liao M. 2008, 347).
[10] In the group of Mawangdui texts dubbed "Zhanguo zonghengjia shu" 戰國縱橫家書 (Documents of the Strategists in the Warring States), this notion indicates the total number of characters used in five historical anecdotes, thus separating them from other texts in the collection (Mawangdui Hanmu boshu zhengli xiaozu 1976, 82, and Blanford 1991, 198n12).
[11] None of the Beida manuscripts contains about 640 characters to constitute a unit measuring 6000 characters together with the *Zhouxun*. On the list of all Beida manuscripts and their respective scopes, see Beijing daxue chutu wenxian yanjiusuo 2011, 54.
[12] Su Jian-Zhou 2017, 233 calls the reign period Taishi 太始 (96–93 BCE) as the most likely date of origin for the Peking University version.

variants is approximately 472. Consequently, to be recognizable to modern Chinese readers, about 10 percent of the text requires interpretation of different degree of sophistication. This is a very low percentage compared to other early manuscripts, especially those from the pre-imperial period. Moreover, the editors identified only twelve writing errors among the variants.

This implies that the present manuscript was produced at a time when written language had already acquired a high degree of stability. That this process was not yet completed can be seen in those (around a dozen) cases where one and the same character was written differently.[13] Sometimes, different variants of the same character can even be found in adjacent sentences (see, for instance, *du* 猶 (44/14) and *du* 獨 (45/12) in ch. 3). The fact that they were not corrected to adhere to the same standard suggests that divergent graphic representations were considered legitimate. A small number of characters in the *Zhouxun* appear to function as phonetic loans for other characters (for example, *wǎŋ* 皇 (71/1) for *hwaŋh* 況, *tsiauk* 爵 (102/10) for *tsiauk* 雀, *grên* 閒 (158/22) for *krâns* 諫, *boŋ* 逢 (163/13) for *phuŋ* 豐). Their appearance points to the possible role of orality in the transmission of the *Zhouxun*. While all these phenomena were very common among early manuscripts, the uniformity of the graphic representation of language in the present text speaks to a rather late date of production.

The linguistic analysis of the work suggests, however, that at least some parts of it existed already in the pre-imperial period. For instance, Han Wei identifies four linguistic phenomena that were no longer common during the Qin and Han dynasties (2015, 253–255). They are: 1) the expression *yongbi* 庸必 announcing a rhetorical question: "is it really…?"[14]; 2) the expression *weiwu* 唯毋 in the meaning of "if"; 3) the interchangeable use of characters *yi* 以 and *er* 而; 4) the use of character *shu* 述 in the adverbial meaning of "then; thereupon."

Han Wei also shows evidence for Qin- and Han-related modifications of the text. Accordingly, the influence of the Qin writing system on the *Zhouxun* is likely to be seen in the occasional use of the character *tai* 泰 instead of the homophone *da/tai* 大. Moreover, the fact that the word for "state" is expressed only by means of the character *guo* 國, while the synonymous *bang* 邦 is completely

---

[13] On the gradual standardization of writing in early China, see Galambos 2004, 189–194.
[14] This argument is problematic insofar as *yong* 庸 appears throughout the *Zhouxun* as part of the rhetorical question marker *qi yong* 其庸, which indeed can be attested in some pre-imperial works, such as the *Zuozhuan* (He L. 1989, 367). However, the excavated fragments of the *Wenzi* 文子—most likely, created during the first decades of the Han dynasty—show that *qi yong* was used well into the Former Han (Hebei sheng wenwu yanjiusuo Dingzhou Hanmu zhujian zhengli xiaozu 1995, 30, slip 0837). On the Han origin of the *Wenzi*, see Wang B. 1996, 1911; Zhang F. 2007, 125; van Els 2018, 43–47.

absent from the text, speaks to the scribes' conscious effort to avoid the naming taboo of the Han dynasty founder, Liu Bang 劉邦 (?–195 BCE).[15]

Su Jian-Zhou, while agreeing with the Zhanguo origin of most parts of the *Zhouxun*, adduces further evidence for modifications which aimed to adapt the text to the new political and linguistic realities of the early imperial era (2017, 247–252). Most remarkably, Su maintains that some parts of the *Zhouxun*—the evidence provided contains several phrases from chapters 3 and 5—could have been created only during the Qin and Han dynasties (2017, 252–256). One of the relevant terms is *chengdan* 城旦 "earth pounder convicts" from chapter 5, which signifies one of the harshest sentences in the legal system of Qin and Han, as corroborated by a wealth of excavated legal documents (Yates 2002, 283–331; Barbieri-Low and Yates 2015, 415n27). What makes this case particularly interesting is that the likelihood for *chengdan* to replace another term is rather low, given its close integration into the rhyme pattern[16] of the passage where it appears (68/23–69/17):

Rhyme

越之【68】城旦	元	Yue's earth pounder convicts
發冢於干（邗），	元	dismantle graves in Han,
吳既為孟（虛），	魚	Wu is nothing but wasteland now.
其孰衛〈衛〉闔廬？	魚	Who will defend Helü?

The conclusion seems justified that this entire stanza must have been created after the introduction of *chengdan* into the Qin penal system.[17] At the same time, however, the exact date of its introduction is unknown and thus we cannot rule out the possibility that this punishment was inherited from the legal codex of the state of Qin.[18] In any case, the mention of this term in the *Mozi* 墨子, possibly proving its existence in the pre-imperial period[19], cannot be taken lightly.

Another potentially revealing term in this context is the "single-piece manuscript" (*du* 牘) in chapter 13 (167/9). Thies Staack estimates that it first occurred due to "lexical changes directly following the Qin unification" in 221 BCE (2018, 282). In the Liye textual materials, its earliest appearance can even be traced back

---

[15] For these and other examples, see Han 2015, 255–256. The naming taboo for "Bang" is observed in most Peking University manuscripts.
[16] Here and below rhyme groups are identified based on Schuessler 2009 and rhyming characters are placed in boxes.
[17] Su Jian-Zhou 2017, 256 refers here to Chen Jian's view.
[18] For the influence of the state of Qin's law on the legal system of the Qin dynasty, see Chen Z. 1963, 30.
[19] *Mozi* "Linghao" 號令 (Sun Y. 2001, 599). For the creation time of the work, see Graham 1993, 337–338.

to a specific date: July 26, 217 BCE (Staack 2018, 245–95, 280). At the same time, Staack acknowledges that this term appeared in such transmitted sources as the *Zhuangzi* and *Zhanguo ce*, i.e., books that are traditionally associated with the Warring States period (2018, 279n111). Therefore, the evidence based on the use of the term *du* cannot be regarded as irrefutable.

The linguistic characteristics of texts may also reflect the geographic specifics of their origin. For instance, the predominant use of particle *ji* 及 in the meaning of "and" is often seen as a reliable indicator for affiliation with the state of Qin, while the preference for the synonymous *yu* 與 is associated with other territories, such as Chu 楚 or the "three Jin" (*San Jin* 三晉) (Wu H. 2019, 198–199; Pines 2020, 45). Unfortunately, the general validity of this rule is called into question by several notable deviations.

For instance, the impressive compendium compiled in Qin, the *Lüshi chunqiu* 呂氏春秋, gives a clear preference to *yu* 與 over *ji* 及 when conveying the meaning of "and" (132 versus 14 occurrences) (Yin 2008, 353, 359). In the *Zhouxun*, for its part, the *yu/ji* ratio as conjunctions is eight to zero occurrences (Su 2017, 245–246). However, in view of the situation with the *Lüshi chunqiu*, the geographic significance of this ratio remains unclear.

To conclude, the linguistic evidence yields a rather complex picture according to which different parts of the *Zhouxun* can be linked to both the pre-imperial and early imperial periods of Chinese history. However, given manifold uncertainties, the data reviewed allows only for approximate conclusions. This is especially true of assumptions regarding the geographic provenance of the work.

The Setting

The setting of the *Zhouxun* is established in the two standardized expressions which appear in the beginning and at the end of each individual chapter.

The first thirteen chapters employ the same opening formulas which provide the following details:

維歲 [X] 月更旦之日，龔（共）大子朝，周昭文公自身貳[20]之，用茲念也。曰：

---

[20] The editors interpret character *er* 貳 as a graphic variant of *te* 貣, which is then determined as a loan for the phonetically close word *chi* 敕, "to warn, to caution" (*Beida Mss.* 124n4). However, as a transitive verb, *er* means "to help," "to assist," "to increase." This is true of the *Zuozhuan* (He L. 1989, 121) as well as the Mawangdui medical texts (Harper 1997, 428, 432). Therefore, I maintain that it there is no need to treat it as a graphic variant or phonetic loan of another character. I choose the verb "enjoin" to convey the meaning of "attaching" instructions to Prince Gong to his benefit.

> It was on the first day of the [X] month of the year, when Crown Prince Gong came to court. Lord Zhaowen of Zhou personally enjoined him with these (following) reminders. He said:

Accordingly, on the first day (*gengdan* 更旦) of the thirteen months—twelve regular months of the year plus an intercalary month (*runyue* 閏月)—a protagonist called Prince Gong 龔 or 龏 (1/9), came to the (geographically unspecified) court of another protagonist, Lord Zhaowen of Zhou 周昭文公, to receive instructions. The identity of the protagonists will be discussed in the next section, but here suffice it to say that, according to historical records, they lived in the second half of the 4th century BCE. The time setting of their meetings is reminiscent of the (idealized) ancient practice of "announcing the month" (*gao-yue* 告月), when a king used the audiences which took place during the first day of the month to announce to his subordinates and regional rulers the activities appropriate for a certain month.[21] This event was also embedded into the practice of ancestral worship (Schaab-Hanke 2010, 202n31).

Furthermore, the way of recording their meetings is reminiscent of how audiences (and other royal activities) are represented in numerous bronze inscriptions and early transmitted texts.[22] The great emphasis placed on the fact that Lord Zhaowen delivered his instructions personally (*zishen* 自身) is not trivial, given that most royal speeches were proclaimed in the name of Zhou kings by ritual officers, called "the scribe of the interior" (*neishi* 內史) in the ritual system of Zhou.[23] Officials were also usually in charge of creating the documents presented during audiences.[24] Emphasis on the personal delivery of instructions appears to underscore their great importance and, as we will see below, a certain degree of distrust towards officials.

The mode of instructing Prince Gong is depicted as "enjoining." But the instructions themselves are referred to as *nian* 念, translated here as "reminders."

---

[21] This event was also called *gaoshuo* 告朔, *shishuo* 視朔, or *tingshuo* 聽朔 (Durrant, Li and Schaberg 2016, 1232n964). For a discussion of this ostensibly ancient practice based on the *Shiji* chapter "Lishu" 歷書, see Schaab-Hanke 2010, 201–203.

[22] See, for example, the inscription on the "Greater Cauldron of Yu" 大盂鼎 as translated and discussed in Cook and Goldin 2016, 32–34. For the transmitted texts, see the "modern script" chapter "Duofang" 多方 of the *Shangshu* (Gu and Liu 2005, 1610).

[23] See *Zhouli* "Chunguan zongbo" 春官宗伯 (Sun Y. 2015, 2561–2570). See also Li F. 2003, 121 and Kern 2010b, 78–79. The expression *Wang ruo yue* 王若曰, prominent in bronze inscriptions and some chapters of the *Shangshu*, is interpreted by some scholars to the effect that while these speeches were attributed to the kings, they were delivered by court officials (Chen M. 1985, 163, 166–167). Therefore, the translation of the expression as "His majesty seemingly said" seems appropriate (Allan 2012, 553–554).

[24] Cook and Goldin 2016: 303, *celing* (*ming*) 冊令 (命).

In modern Chinese, this meaning is conveyed by the related character *shen* 諗, which is a composite of the semantic determinative "word" (*yan* 言) and *nian*. However, it is possible that the connotation of "reading out loud" (in modern Chinese: *nian* 唸) was likewise present in the notion of *nian*, as the admonition that had to be intoned (Behr and Führer 2005, 20–21).

The ending of the first thirteen chapters is constructed in a similarly standardized manner:

已學（教）²⁵大子用茲念，斯乃受（授）之書，而自身屬（囑）之曰：女（汝）勉毋忘歲 [X] 月更旦之馴（訓）。

Having instructed the crown prince with these reminders, [Lord Zhaowen] gave him the text [of his speech] and personally cautioned him, saying: "Strive not to forget the instructions from the first day of the [X] month of the year."

The ending also reflects the well-recorded practice of giving written copies of speeches delivered by the monarch or his officials to the addressees of these speeches upon the conclusion of the audiences.²⁶ As can be seen, the last sentence contains Lord Zhaowen's direct speech. As this short speech was made after the script with the relevant instruction was given to Prince Gong, we can conclude that the latter did not receive a written transcript of this last admonition.

Accordingly, if we assume that the encounter between the two protagonists did, indeed, take place, we have to distinguish between the document that was pre-prepared for Prince Gong's instruction, and given to him at the end of the meeting, and the document that contained the transcript of the entire encounter, including the last address to be stored in the archive.²⁷ The emphasis on the personal delivery of instruction is repeated here. However, this time, this educational endeavor is described with the verb *shu* 屬, in the meaning of caution (*zhu* 囑). We also encounter here the notion featuring in the title of the work, namely, "instruction" (*xun* 訓). As such, the *Zhouxun* belongs to one of the six types of documents collected in the *Shangshu* 尚書 (Nylan 2001, 125).

In chapter 14, both framing formulas are modified. It opens:

---

²⁵ In the published version, there is a comma after the character *xue* 學.
²⁶ Chen M. 1985, 163; Li F. 2003, 120–121; Allan 2012, 555. Interestingly, in its meaning "(to) double" *er* 貳 refers to the duty of the "scribes of the interior" to produce copies of documents which they presented during audiences. See *Zhouli* "Chunguan zongbo" (Sun Y. 2015, 2569–2570). For a brief discussion of the notion *er* as a copied version of documents, see Kuszera 2017, 140n99.
²⁷ For this practice, see Allan 2012, 555.

- 維歲冬（終）享駕（賀）之日，龏（共）大子朝，周昭文公自身貳之，用茲念也。曰：【205】
- It was on the day of the year end's food offering ceremony, when Crown Prince Gong came to court. Lord Zhaowen of Zhou personally enjoined him with these (following) reminders. He said:

Evidently, the hitherto common formulaic phrase the "first day of the [X] month" ([X] *yue gengdan zhi ri* 月更旦之日) is replaced through the expression the "day of the year end's food offering ceremony" (*suizhong xianghe zhiri* 歲終享賀之日). The religious connotations of this ceremony were more pronounced than that of the gatherings on the first day of a month (Bodde 1975, 52).

The ending of the chapter demonstrates an even greater degree of divergence from the established pattern:

210/4 已學（教）大子以六王五柏（伯）之念，斯乃受（授）之書，而自身屬（囑）之【210】曰：女（汝）勉毋忘臘之明日親（新）歲之馴（訓）。大凡六千【211】

Having instructed the crown prince with the reminders of the six kings and five hegemons, [Lord Zhaowen] gave him the text [of his speech] and personally cautioned him, saying: "Strive not to forget the new year's instructions from the day after the La-sacrifice." Grand total: six thousand [characters].

As can be seen, this instruction concerned the examples of the six kings and five hegemons (*liuwang wuba* 六王五伯) and was delivered on the day after the La-sacrifice (*lazhi mingri* 臘之明日) of the new year (*xinsui* 新歲). We thus see that chapter 14 is unique among the textual units of the *Zhouxun*, in that it appears to refer to two different dates in its framing formulas: it opens with "the day of the year end's food offering ceremony" and closes with the "day after the La-sacrifice" of the new year. At the same time, it appears to refer to the same event. This peculiarity appears to manifest the authors' intention to create a sense of transition between the past year and the new year. In this way, Lord Zhaowen's instructions were shown to retain their significance and validity even after the beginning of the new cycle of twelve (or thirteen) months. This transitional role distinguished this chapter from the rest of the text.

Through the type of information contained in its framing formulas, the *Zhouxun* can be associated with the genre of documents.[28] Indeed, there are

---

[28] For a discussion on the characteristics of documentary literature and other examples among the excavated texts, see Krijgsman 2017, 310–311,

several representatives of documentary literature, both transmitted and excavated, that show close affinity to the manuscript under investigation.²⁹ Among them, the *Shangshu* chapter "Guming" 顧命, the *Baoxun* 保訓 and, to a lesser extent, *Xizhe junlao* 昔者君老 deserve special mention. The *Zhouxun* shares with these works the setting of father-ruler imparting instructions upon his heir.

However, the other three sources place the royal instruction in the most dramatic of circumstances, just before the passing of the king. That is, they regard the transmission of the teaching as a unique one-time event that could not be performed at other times. The *Zhouxun*, in contrast, views regular educational activities as an essential part of royal responsibilities. The role of written text also differs in all these works. While the *Xizhe junlao* makes no mention of written transmission (Cook 2017, 227–228), "Guming" views text as a tool enabling the transmission of the king's charge to the heir via the officials (Meyer 2017a, 129). The *Baoxun* is not clear as to who produces the physical copy of the instructions but treats it as a makeshift tool to replace the conventional oral way of admonition (Krijgsman 2019, 97).

The *Zhouxun* presents several anecdotes where rulers personally produce and recite the manuscripts to their successors. Considering this, it would not be too farfetched to assume that Lord Zhaowen was also the author of his instructions and the creator of the physical copy. After listening to his father's instruction, Prince Gong and other potential successors noted in the *Zhouxun* receive the written copy to further study and reflect on it in a private setting.

Another major difference between the *Zhouxun* and the three mentioned works is that, for the late Zhanguo readers, Lord Zhaowen and Prince Gong were almost contemporaries, belonging to the recent past (see below), while the latter feature Kings Wen, Wu, Cheng as well as unnamed ideal rulers of high antiquity. By focusing on a contemporaneous ruler using the frame and the topic conventionally applied to ancient monarchs, the *Zhouxun* presents a certain challenge to the documentary tradition. As I argue below, this challenge consists in the attempt to reformulate the conventional power transfer paradigm in response to the meritocracy discussion. In order to better understand the nature of this challenge, I address the question of the identities of Lord Zhaowen and Prince Gong, as well as their relationship, in the next section.

---

[29] When applying the typology of texts in the transmitted compilations of Documents, as developed by Grebnev 2017, 255–261, the *Zhouxun* can be characterized both as a text with "template-based contextualization" as well as "writing-informed characterization."

Chapter 2

The Protagonists

The frame of the *Zhouxun* has Prince Gong attend Lord Zhaowen's court at the beginning of each month and on other significant dates of the year. This is reminiscent of the obligation regional lords had to pay regular visits to their superiors. At the same time, the title Crown Prince seems to imply that the said person was related to Lord Zhaowen as his son and designated successor.

The text proper confirms the validity of this interpretation and shows that the frame was not just a later addition. On the one hand, Lord Zhaowen is portrayed as treating Prince Gong as his son and heir apparent in several chapters. On the other, this sovereign is reported to be based in the city of Chengzhou 成周, while the residence of Prince Gong is said to be in the Ruyi 鄏邑 "City of Ru" (mostly called Jiaru 郟鄏 in the transmitted sources). The following excerpt from chapter 2 says:

37/11 爾有蓐（鄏）邑，而成周之人不為女（汝）民，其【37】何以守國？
38/4
You have the City of Ru, but if the people of Chengzhou are not your people, how will you preserve the state?

This fragment implies that Prince Gong was already in possession of the City of Ru at the moment of the instruction, while the prospect of inheriting Lord Zhaowen's position implied for him (additionally) obtaining the rule over Chengzhou (see also Han 2015, 259–260), the most crucial step for which was to win the allegiance of its population. The notion of the state (*guo*) mentioned here appears to refer to the state of Zhou, which includes both territories surrounding the cities of Ru and Chengzhou.

This view of the domain of Zhou is also implied in chapter 11, where Lord Zhaowen says:

144/20 今女（汝）無孝而【144】難聽親，則周唯（雖）小國，其庸可得有？
144/13
Now, (if) you are not filial and dislike listening to your father, then, although Zhou is a small state, how could you obtain it?

Accordingly, Prince Gong's becoming a sovereign over Zhou was contingent on his ability to demonstrate filial piety (*xiao* 孝) and to heed his father's instructions (*tingqin* 聽親). But his right to rule over the City of Ru does not seem to be at stake.

The quoted passages appear to suggest that the *Zhouxun* operated with the notion of the Zhou as a unified political entity. At the same time, Chengzhou and Ruyi (as well as the related territories) are said to have been separately ruled by Lord Zhaowen and Prince Gong. Considering this and in view of the tropes mentioned in the two framing formulas, Prince Gong appears as ruler over an independent allotment (with the capital in Ruyi) within the larger territory of Zhou, ruled by Lord Zhaowen. In the context of Zhou regulations regarding enfeoffment of offspring, as well as related stories in chapters 3 and 10, this suggests that Prince Gong was not heir apparent based on the rule of primogeniture (Chen X. 1992, 89).

As has been shown, the domain of Zhou appears to have been under the overall rulership of Lord Zhaowen, who resided in Chengzhou. This raises the question about the role of Zhou kings in the *Zhouxun*, who were the nominal rulers of the "All-under-Heaven" (*tianxia* 天下) until the demise of the dynasty in 249 BCE. Given the conspicuous silence about Lord Zhaowen's relationship to the Zhou "Sons of Heaven" (*tianzi* 天子), it seems that he was indeed regarded as the highest political authority in the domain.

As for their personal character traits, Prince Gong is presented as someone who is not yet worthy of the throne, highlighting the necessity of his education (chs. 2, 6, 8, 10, 11, 12 and 13). Lord Zhaowen, on the other hand, is described as the ruler (of a small state) concerned with moral excellence, attempting to inculcate high moral values in his successor using the examples of the virtuous rulers of the past (see Fech 2018, 157–158).

In the following, I investigate how the two protagonists and the political situation of the late Zhou dynasty are portrayed in the transmitted sources.

Transmitted Sources

Accounts found in the received works are strikingly different from the *Zhouxun* in regard to several crucial points. First, it is a well-documented historical fact that, in the second half of the fourth century BCE (during Lord Zhaowen's rule), the Zhou dynasty was no longer politically united but was split into two independent states: the West and the East Zhou, with capitals in the cities of (Jia)ru

郟鄏 and Chengzhou.[1] Moreover, the received texts contain no account of the encounters between Lord Zhaowen and Prince Gong. While persons so identified (with varying degrees of certainty) can be found in several books, they are not portrayed as father and son, and it is even uncertain whether these "Lord Zhaowen" and "Prince Gong" were contemporaries. These discrepancies call into question the historicity of the *Zhouxun* narrative. Yet, regardless of the issue of historicity, it is still advisable to investigate the appearances of Lord Zhaowen and Prince Gong in the transmitted literature, for it might help us to determine the reasons for their appearance as protagonists in the manuscript under investigation. Their occurrences are summarized in the table below.[2]

Table 1: Protagonists of the *Zhouxun* in the Received Literature

	Lüshi chunqiu 呂氏春秋	*Zhanguo ce* 戰國策	*Huainanzi* 淮南子	*Shiji* 史記
Lord Zhaowen of Zhou	Chapters: "Yu da" 諭大 and "Wu da" 務大 Name: Lord Zhaowen of Zhou 周昭文君 Interlocutor: Du He 杜赫	Chapter: "Dong Zhou" 東周 Name: Ruler of Zhou 周君 Interlocutor: Du He	Chapter: "Daoying xun" 道應訓 Name: Lord Zhaowen of Zhou Interlocutor: Du He	
	Chapter: "Baogeng" 報更 Name: Lord Zhaowen of Zhou Interlocutor: Zhang Yi 張儀	Chapter: "Dong Zhou" Name: Lord Wen of Zhou 周文君 Interlocutor: Lü Cang 呂倉		

---

[1] Franke 2001, 191; Li X. 1985, 17; Wu R. 1995, 137–338; Li F. 2006, 65–66. On the identical location of Jiaru and the modern-day city of Luoyang, see Franke 2001, 191 and Yang B. 1995, 1476.
[2] In addition to these sources, Lord Zhaowen is also mentioned in the *Hanshu* chapter "Gujinren biao" 古今人表 as belonging to the "lower" section of the "middling" group (*zhongxia* 中下). *Hanshu* 20.946.

Prince Gong		Chapter: "Dong Zhou"		Chapter: "Zhou benji" 周本記
		Name: Prince Gong 共太子 Father: Unnamed Ruler of the East Zhou		Name: Prince Gong 共太子 Father: Lord Wu of the WestZhou 西周武公 (r. 4th c. BCE)

An individual called "Prince Gong" 共太子 can be found in the parallel accounts of the *Zhanguo ce* and *Shiji*. Even though the character denoting the name of this protagonist, is different from the name of the *Zhouxun* protagonist, i.e., Gong 龏/龔, they could be related as phonetic loans. Therefore, it is possible that we are dealing with one and the same person. Both the *Zhanguo ce* and *Shiji* agree in describing Prince Gong as a designated successor to the throne, who predeceased his father. Consequently, the bereaved father was faced with the necessity to choose a successor from among other (initially less obvious) candidates.[3] However, in the *Zhanguo ce* (1.24), the sovereign is an unnamed ruler of the East Zhou, while the *Shiji* identifies him as Lord Wu of the West Zhou 西周武公 (r. 4th c. BCE).[4] The latter account corresponds to the information about Prince Gong dwelling in the City of Ru (West Zhou) given in the *Zhouxun*; as such, the account of the *Shiji* appears more plausible.[5] The received texts contain no further information on this protagonist.

As regards Lord Zhaowen, I have argued elsewhere, only the narrative in the "Baogeng" chapter of the *Lüshi chunqiu* among the different strands of information available in the received texts (see Table 1) shows affinity to his idealized portrayal in the *Zhouxun* (Fech 2020b, 214–215). Therefore, to keep the discussion focused, in the following, I only analyze his appearance in this chapter.

This chapter contains the most comprehensive and extolling account of Lord Zhaowen in the received literature. Here, he is presented as a ruler who

---

[3] *Shiji* "Zhou benji" 4.161; *Zhanguo ce* 1.24: "Zhou Gong Taizi si" 周共太子死 (Fan X. 2006, 69; Crump 1970, 23). The two sources also correspond in reporting that, eventually, a new heir apparent was installed with the direct interference of the foreign power of Chu 楚.
[4] *Shiji* 4.161; Nienhauser 1994a, 79: 西周武公之太子死，有五庶子，毋適（嫡子）立。 "After his Heir, Gong, died, Duke Wu of West Chou had five sons by his concubines, but no more sons by his queen to be installed as Heir."
[5] Han 2015, 264 maintains that the *Zhanguo ce* editor might have modified the identity of Prince Gong's father to comply with the *Zhouxun*.

became "prominent" due to his unreserved respect for and support of the "worthy" (xian 賢) shi 士.⁶ To exemplify this point, the chapter offers a narrative where this ruler reportedly extended gracious treatment to the aspiring political advisor Zhang Yi 張儀 (?–310 BCE) at a time when the latter was still a relatively unknown man. After becoming prime minister of Qin, Zhang Yi repaid Lord Zhaowen for his kind treatment by making him respected by the rulers of the far larger and mightier states. The story goes as follows:

> 張儀，魏氏餘子也，將西遊於秦，過東周。客有語之於昭文君者曰：「魏氏人張儀，材士也，將西遊於秦，願君之禮貌之也。」昭文君見而謂之曰：「聞客之秦。寡人之國小，不足以留客。雖游然豈必遇哉？客或不遇，請為寡人而一歸也，國雖小，請與客共之。」張儀還走，北面再拜。張儀行，昭文君送而資之，至於秦，留有間，惠王說而相之。張儀所德於天下者，無若昭文君。周，千乘也，重過萬乘也，令秦惠王師之，逢澤之會，魏王嘗為御，韓王為右，名號至今不忘，此張儀之力也。(Chen Qiyou 2001, 902)

Zhang Yi was a "minor son" of the house of Wei. When travelling west to Qin, he passed through East Zhou. A retainer spoke to Lord Zhaowen about [Zhang Yi], saying: "Zhang Yi of the house of Wei is a talented *shi* and he is travelling west to Qin. I hope your lordship will treat him with courtesy." Lord Zhaowen received him in an audience and said to him: "I have heard that you are going to Qin. My own state is small and insufficient to keep you. But, even though you are leaving [for Qin], can you really be sure to be given an opportunity [to implement your policies]? Should you not be given such an opportunity, then I would like to ask you to return as a favor to me and, even though my state is small, I will be willing to share it with you." Turning to go, Zhang Yi bowed twice facing north. When he departed, Lord Zhaowen saw him off and provided him with supplies. Zhang Yi arrived in Qin and, after some time, King Hui was pleased with him and made him prime minister. Of those whom Zhang Yi treated with kindness, none equaled Lord Zhaowen. Zhou had one thousand chariots, yet Zhang Yi treated it with more respect than a state with ten thousand chariots. He made King Hui of Qin regard Lord Zhaowen as his teacher. When they met at Fengze, the king of Wei served as Lord Zhaowen's driver and the king of Han as his guard on the right. Even today his reputation has not been forgotten. This is due to Zhang Yi's influence.⁷

---

⁶ Chen Q. 2001, 901; Knoblock and Riegel 2000, 352. It is mainly based on the "Bao geng" chapter that Lord Zhaowen is sometimes identified as the most prominent and able person among the ruling elite of the late Zhou dynasty (Wu R. 1995, 147).

⁷ Compare translation in Knoblock and Riegel 2000, 354.

The historicity of this adulatory account is very doubtful. According to the *Shiji*, the meeting at Fengze 逢澤 took place in 342 BCE, long before Zhang Yi assumed the prime minister position in Qin (328 BCE).[8] Moreover, Sima Qian 司馬遷 suggests that the meeting was organized to pay respects to the king of Zhou, the "Son of Heaven," for bestowing the status of "hegemon" (*ba* 伯) upon Lord Xiao of Qin 秦孝公 (361–338 BCE), King Hui of Qin's father, in 343 BCE. Thus, presenting Lord Zhaowen as the main beneficiary of the Fengze meeting was inaccurate for several reasons. His fame in Qin and his position as "teacher" of King Hui of Qin, likewise, appear highly questionable.

The dubious historicity of this account only underscores that some authors involved in the creation of the *Lüshi chunqiu*, especially the "Baogeng" chapter, held Lord Zhaowen in high esteem. While it is unclear when this story was created, its inclusion into the compendium already shows that some intellectuals of the period attempted to elevate his standing. Interestingly, the similarity between this chapter and the *Zhouxun* also includes an apparent neglect for Zhou kings. In the next section, I address the possible reasons for this view against the background of available historical sources. To this end, I attempt to reconstruct the succession of Zhou kings, as well as of the rulers of the West Zhou and East Zhou. Doing this will help determine the familial relationship between Lord Zhaowen and Prince Gong.

The *Zhouxun* and Zhou Disintegration

The *Shiji* reports that the polity of the West Zhou was established by King Kao 考 (r. 440–426 BCE), who granted this territory as a fief to his brother, the future Lord Huan 桓公 of West Zhou (r. ?–415 BCE) (*Shiji* 4.158; Wu R. 1995, 133–134). It was during the rule of Lord Huan's grandson, Lord Hui 惠公 (r. 366–? BCE) that the East Zhou emerged. However, there are conflicting records of how the state of East Zhou was founded. According to the *Shiji*, Lord Hui allocated this polity to his youngest son to "serve the king" (*feng wang* 奉王). This was the first ruler of the East Zhou, Lord Hui 惠公 of East Zhou (r. 366–360 BCE) (*Shiji* 4.158). However, the *Hanfeizi* 韓非子 presents a very different account according to which the first East Zhou sovereign was not the son, but the younger brother of Lord Hui of West Zhou, who rebelled against his sibling and established the polity of the East Zhou on conquered territory.[9] The difference

---

[8] *Shiji* "Qin benji" 秦本紀 (5.203; Nienhauser 1994a, 110–111). See Yang K. 2001, 431.
[9] *Hanfeizi* "Nei chu shuo xia" 內儲說下 (Wang X. 2003, 254; Liao 1959, 19) and "Nan san" 難三 (Wang X. 2003, 902; Liao 1959, 176). Also, the *Lüshi chunqiu* "Xian shi" 先識 (Chen Q. 2001, 956; Knoblock and Riegel 2000, 374–376) speaks about the formation of the West and East Zhou in terms of political split and disintegration. It is possible that the foreign powers

between the two accounts concerns a number of points: the familial ties of the East Zhou founder to Lord Hui of West Zhou (son versus brother), the foundational story of the East Zhou (enfeoffment versus rebellion), and the relationship between the two states (amiable versus belligerent).

After the division of the Zhou domain, the city of Chengzhou, the long-term seat of political power and authority of the Zhou dynasty, became the capital of the East Zhou and the Zhou kings were effectively left with no territory of their own. The East Zhou rulers made the most of the predicament and impotence of the "Sons of Heaven," exploiting their weak position for their own political goals (Wu R. 1995, 143–144). A similar pattern of appropriating the highest authority of the Zhou kings became manifest in the West Zhou, after the last Zhou ruler, King Nan 赧 (r. 314–256 BCE), decided to move his seat there (*Shiji* 4.160; Wu R. 1995, 138). The narratives in the *Zhouxun* and the "Baogeng" chapter of the *Lüshi chunqiu*, which do not even mention Zhou kings, may be seen as reflecting their dire situation and hapless state.

Based on the available sources, the complex relationship between the three strands of Zhou aristocracy can be presented in the following way:

Table 2: Political Split During the Last Two Centuries of Zhou Dynasty

West Zhou (Capital: Jiaru)	Zhou Kings "Sons of Heaven"	East Zhou (Capital: Chengzhou)
	King Ding 定 (r. 468–441 BCE)	
Founder: Lord Huan 桓公 (r. 440–415 BCE)	King Kao 考 (r. 440–426 BCE)	
	King Weilie 威烈 (r. 425–402 BCE)	
Lord Wei 威公 (r. 414–367 BCE)	King An 安 (r. 401–376 BCE)	
	King Lie 烈 (r. 375–369 BCE)	
Lord Hui 惠公 (r. 366–? BCE)	King Xian 顯 (r. 368–321 BCE)	**Founder:** Lord Hui 惠公 (r. 366–360 BCE)
		?

---

of Zhao 趙 and Wei 魏 actively participated in this conflict. See Yang K. 2001, 583–584. For overall analysis, see Wu R. 1995, 135–136.

?	King Shenjing 慎靚 (r. 320–315 BCE)	Lord Zhaowen 昭文公[10] (r. c. 342–c. 314 BCE)
Lord Wu 武公 (r. 314–?) (Prince Gong)	King Nan 赧 (r. 314–256 BCE)	?
Lord Wen 文公 (r.?–256BCE)		
		Ruler of the East Zhou (r. ?–249 BCE)

Accordingly, while the succession of the last Zhou kings can be reconstructed seamlessly, the situation in the East and West Zhou does not yield an equally clear picture. For instance, it seems unlikely that Lord Wu 武公 (r. 314–?) inherited the West Zhou throne directly from Lord Hui given the substantial temporal gap between their reigns. Therefore, the existence of an unknown West Zhou ruler between Lord Hui and Lord Wu is likely (Wu R. 1995, 137). Also on the East Zhou side, it is sometimes assumed that there was a ruler between the reigns of Lord Hui and Lord Zhaowen.[11] It is also unclear as to how many sons, if any, Lord Zhaowen had and how many generations of East Zhou rulers there were between his reign and the demise of this state in 249 BCE. Some of these uncertainties have a direct bearing on the relationship between Lord Zhaowen and Prince Gong.

Different scenarios are possible here. If the founder of the East Zhou, Lord Hui, was the youngest son of the eponymous ruler of the West Zhou (as claimed in the *Shiji*) and there were no other rulers than those mentioned in the table, then Lord Zhaowen was Prince Gong's cousin. But if, following the *Hanfeizi*, we determine the East Zhou founder as the youngest brother of Lord Hui of the West Zhou while all other parameters remain the same, then Lord Zhaowen was Prince Gong's uncle once removed. It remains doubtful if these two individuals could have met because of the apparent temporal gap between them. Adding other members in the left and right columns would only increase the distance in their familial relationship. This shows once again that the *Zhouxun*'s view of its protagonists as father and son, provided the authors had these two historical actors in mind, is not supported by available sources.

---

[10] According to Liang Yusheng 梁玉繩 (1716–1798), Lord Zhaowen's personal name was Jie 傑. Wang Liqi maintains that Lord Zhaowen was the son of Lord Hui of East Zhou (Wang and Wang 1988, 574).

[11] Lin Zhipeng 2015, 196 identifies this sovereign as Lord Wu 武公 of the East Zhou, who supposedly occupied the throne between the years 359 and 339 BCE.

Summary

Based on the above we see that while the *Zhouxun* accurately reflects some aspects of the political situation of the period, such as, for instance, the weakness of the Zhou kings, it appears to present a distorted picture when speaking about the political unity of the Zhou domain as well as the father-son ties between Lord Zhaowen and Prince Gong. There have been several attempts to address these inconsistencies to render the *Zhouxun* narrative coherent with the political realities of that era. To begin with, Lin Zhipeng points out that, according to the *Shiji*, the West and East Zhou started being ruled separately (*fen zhi* 分治) only under King Nan of Zhou (r. 314–256 BCE). Consequently, during Lord Zhaowen's time, the political division of the Zhou was not yet completed (2015, 195). Yet, it is not clear how this new situation of being "ruled separately" around 314 BCE was different from the preceding state of affairs, when the two polities of the West and East Zhou simultaneously existed on Zhou soil, with their respective capitals and ruling elite. It is telling that the main deviation that we find in the received sources regarding these two states concerns the degree of their hostility toward each other and not the fact of their existence. As for the complex issue of the Lord Zhaowen-Prince Gong relationship, Han Wei (2015, 264) suggests that their encounters did indeed take place, even though Prince Gong was heir apparent to Lord Wu of the West Zhou. To briefly restate Han's argument, Prince Gong reached out to Lord Zhaowen seeking political support and advice. Later, records of their conversations were utilized by the authors of the *Zhouxun* but were transformed into father-son meetings to enhance the educational value of the work and to address the then poignant issue of power transfer.[12] Although Han takes great pains to account for the complex interstate realities of the day, his interpretation remains rather hypothetical.

As just shown, attempts to reconcile the plot of the *Zhouxun* with available historical information did not yield convincing results. Before more compelling evidence emerges, it therefore seems plausible to assume that, rather than being actual historical records, Lord Zhaowen's speeches to Prince Gong were literary creations. In this case, however, we need to explain the reasons behind their introduction. Several possibilities exist here. Considering Lord Zhaowen's "fame" among some intellectual groups in pre-imperial China, emphatically demonstrated in the "Baogeng" chapter, it seems plausible that some members of these groups would feel inclined to use his reputation to further their own ideas. Besides, the figure of Lord Zhaowen was suitable to make several distinct ideological points. For instance, by presenting him as the main political authority in Zhou, the authors could have aimed at emphasizing the impotence of the Zhou

---

[12] Yan Buke (2011a, 73) is even more affirmative in promoting the historical accuracy of the *Zhouxun*.

kings, as well as the bankruptcy of some notions associated with them, such as the theory of "Heavenly Mandate," which never appears in the text. In place of these outdated principles, Lord Zhaowen embodied new guidelines crucial for establishing an orderly society and maintaining power, such as the idea of "worthiness" (*xian* 賢). The alleged connection of Lord Zhaowen to the state of Qin, also stated in the "Baogeng" chapter, is worth deliberating upon as will be shown below.

As for Prince Gong, given his obscurity, it is difficult to estimate just how much the authors of the *Zhouxun* knew about the historical figure and what aspects of his life were decisive for singling him out as the protagonist of the work. Several interpretations are possible here too. For instance, he could have been chosen simply because he was known as a "crown prince" who, having predeceased his father, was not destined to become a ruler. As such, he might have become firmly linked to the position of crown prince, symbolizing the prototypical heir apparent, as it were. But it is entirely possible that other considerations mentioned in the pertinent accounts of the *Shiji* and the *Zhanguo ce* played a role too, such as, foreign influence in the issue of heir selection or the juxtaposition of Prince Gong with the "loved" (*ai* 愛) sons of Lord Wu. The validity of these assumptions cannot be verified and so we need to state that the reasons behind Prince Gong's appearance as Lord Zhaowen's successor remain unclear.

Chapter 3

Textual Organization

Lord Zhaowen's instructions to Prince Gong consist of three main elements. First, there are general "theoretical" instructions (in short: TI), making up the entirety of chapter 1 and the beginning of chapter 12. In keeping with the admonishing character of the text, they start with the negative imperative "must not" (*bu ke (yi)* 不可（以）).

Then, there are "historical" accounts, which invariably start with the formula "in the past" (*xi* 昔) and appear in all chapters but the first. Based on their formal characteristics, these accounts can be divided into "speeches," that is, royal monologues directed at the potential successor, and "narratives" which, unlike the former, contain dialgogues between different actors and tell a story involving them. Speeches (in short: X_S) feature in only three chapters, while narratives (in short: X_N) constitute the main content of most chapters.

Finally, most historical accounts are contrasted with references to the present, which invariably start with the character *jin* 今 (now; today). In some chapters, Lord Zhaowen uses this formula to address Prince Gong as in "Now, you" (*jinru* 今汝). I use the abbreviation J_R to refer to this type of speech. In other chapters, the formula "Now, I" (*jinwo* 今我) (in short: J_W) is used to express Lord Zhaowen's concerns. Chapter 11 stands out in that Prince Gong is directly addressed twice: using "Ah, well" (*wuhu* 嗚呼) in the beginning and "Now, you" at the end of the chapter.

These three main constitutive elements are imbedded in the fabric of the chapters and make an appearance in different combinations. The theoretical instructions stand out from the rest of the text through their rigid form and their circumvention of the dichotomy of past and present. Most accounts of the "past" are followed by brief concluding statements (in short: S) which provide certain interpretations of historical events.

While most summaries are formulated using no specific rules, there are also two standardized expressions. The first (S_1) is: "this is what X expresses in saying Y" (*ci X zhi suo wei Y* 此 X 之所謂 Y), where X stands for an authoritative source and Y signifies notions or ideas capping a story (chs. 4, 6, 7, 9). The second (S_2) is: "and so, X is Y" (*gu X zhe Y ye* 故 X 者 Y 也). Here, X describes a particular accomplishment of an exceptional character, while Y is the main reason why they achieved it (chs. 10–13). In chapters featuring "personal admonitions" of Prince

Gong, these summaries serve as important bridges between the "past" and "present."

Finally, most of Lord Zhaowen's instructions are concluded by rhetorical questions (RQ). The most frequent standardized formula (RQ$_1$) is: "how can (one) not… " (*huke yiwu* 胡可以毋). Usually necessitating a more proactive involvement of the addressees (Yuan Ai 2022), rhetorical questions in the *Zhouxun* underscore that instructions were delivered to Prince Gong for his reflection and deliberation. Yet they also convey a sense of admonition.

Represented in a table, different constitutive parts of Lord Zhaowen's speeches look as follows:

Table 3: Chapter Structure of the *Zhouxun*

Ch.	Structure						
1	11(+1?) TI						
2	X$_S$	X$_S$	S		J$_R$		RQ
3	X$_N$		S				RQ$_1$
4	X$_N$		S + S$_1$				RQ$_1$
5	X$_S$						
6	X$_N$		S$_1$				J$_R$
7	X$_N$		S$_1$				RQ$_1$
8	X$_N$				J$_W$		
9	X$_N$		S$_1$				RQ$_1$
10	X$_N$		S$_2$		J$_R$		RQ
11	*Wuhu*	X$_N$	S$_2$		J$_R$	X$_N$	RQ
12	4 TI	X$_N$	S$_2$	X$_N$	S$_2$	J$_R$	RQ
13	X$_N$		S$_2$		J$_W$		RQ
14	11 X$_S$ (+J$_R$?)						

As can be seen, Lord Zhaowen's instructions vary in regard to their complexity. While some contain only a few constitutive elements (chs. 5, 8), others have a rather sophisticated structure (chs. 11, 12). Chapters 4, 7, and 9 show identical patterns of organization, while chapters 10 through 13 resemble each other in utilizing similar elements. The two groups constitute distinctly recognizable clusters within the text. These differences might point to the heterogeneous nature and different origin of the materials they contain. Yet, being thus arranged, these variegated sources have been made to serve the sole purpose of educating Prince Gong.

The three main constitutive properties of Lord Zhaowen's instructions operate differently in how they claim truth and create authority. The validity of theoretical instructions is based on logical reasoning (to be elucidated later) and is presented as unrelated to time and, in most cases, tradition. This may possibly explain why this content is introduced at the very beginning of the text, implying its superiority to the knowledge derived from historical accounts. The "ancient" lore obviously claims validity through its connection to the illustrious monarchs of antiquity and their ministers.

While there is a certain degree of thematic overlap between these two types of instructions—for instance, the emphasis on "leniency" (*kuan* 寬) in chapters 7 and 12—they are not organized in strict correspondence, which is characteristic of some pre-Qin and early Han books.[1] Thus, in the *Zhouxun*, historical and philosophical truths claim their validity individually and are not derived from each other. The actions of "today," however, can be justified only insofar as they emulate the authoritative "past." It is thus small wonder that, in his appeals to Prince Gong, Lord Zhaowen mostly reformulates points broached in his discussion of an idealized past.

Chapter Order

Chapters 2 to 14 contain a wealth of historical references.[2] Their main protagonists (sixteen altogether) are usually exemplary rulers of the past or (in ch. 9 only) famous ministers. The earliest of them is the legendary ruler Yao 堯 and the latest, separated from Lord Zhaowen only by some fifty years, is Lord Xian of Qin 秦獻公 (r. 384–362 BCE). By selecting Yao as the earliest monarch, the *Zhouxun* resembles the *Shangshu* but, at the same time, it covers a larger span of Chinese history, reaching well into the Warring States period. In a table, the main protagonists of each chapter are as follows:

---

[1] See, for instance, the six "Chushui" 儲說 chapters in the *Hanfeizi* 韓非子, which are divided into the more theoretical "scriptures" (*jing* 經) and illustrative "explanations" (*shuo* 說). See Schaberg 2011, 400–401. In the same work, there are also the chapters "Jie Lao" 解老 and "Yu Lao" 喻老, applying the exegetic strategies of philosophical reasoning and illustrative example to the *Laozi*. See Queen 2013, 197–256.
[2] For a comprehensive analysis of historical anecdotes and their role in philosophical texts, see Schaberg 2011, 394–414.

Table 4: Main Protagonists of the Historical Accounts

Ch.	Main Protagonists	Period/State
2	1.) Cheng Tang (ca. 1600 BCE) and Tai Jia 2.) Yu (ca. 2070 BCE) and Qi	Shang Xia
3	King Wen of Zhou (*d.* 1047 BCE) and his sons	Zhou
4	King Zhao of Chu (r. 515–489 BCE)	Chu
5	King Goujian of Yue (r. 496–465 BCE)	Yue
6	Lord Wen of Jin (r. 636–628 BCE)	Jin
7	Lord Mu of Qin (r. 659–621 BCE)	Qin
8	Lord Wen of Jin	Jin
9	Zhao Dun (?–601 BCE)	Zhao
10	Marquis Wen of Wei (r. 424–387 BCE) and his sons	Wei
11	1.) Lord Xian of Qin (r. 384–362 BCE) and his sons 2.) Yao and Shun	Qin Pre-dynastic
12	1.) King Cheng of Zhou (r. ca. 1042–1021 BCE) 2.) Lord Huan of Qi (r. 685–643 BCE)	Zhou Qi
13	Zhao Jianzi (?–476 BCE) and his sons	Zhao
14	1.) Yao and Dan Zhu/Shun 2.) Shun and Shang Jun/Yu 3.) Yu and Qi 4.) Cheng Tang and Tai Jia 5.) Chang (King Wen) and Fa 6.) Fa (King Wu) and Song (King Cheng) 7.) Lord Mu of Qin and unnamed heir 8.) King Goujian of Yue and unnamed heir 9.) Lord Huan of Qi and unnamed heir	Pre-dynastic Pre-dynastic Xia Shang Zhou Zhou Qin Yue Qi

As can be easily recognized, this sequence is idiosyncratic in starting with the Shang dynasty (and not with Yao or, at least, the preceding Xia). It is also apparent that different chapters feature a varying number of protagonists. Below, I will demonstrate that Lord Zhaowen's unusual depiction of early Chinese history results from a combination of temporal, topical and geopolitical factors.

To begin with, the policies and lineages associated with the listed individuals differ in regard to the frequency of their appearance, yielding respectively:

Three times: Zhou dynasty (chs. 3, 12, 14); State of Qin (chs. 7, 11, 14); State of Jin (chs. 6, 8, likely 14).

27 / Chapter 3

Twice: Xia dynasty (chs. 2, 14); Shang dynasty (chs. 2, 14); State of Qi (chs. 12, 14); State of Chu (chs 4, likely 14); State of Yue (chs. 5, 14); Zhao lineage (chs. 9, 13).

Once: State of Wei (ch. 10).

The inclusion of Zhao and Wei appears to reflect the political realities of the Warring States period, which witnessed the gradual ascendancy of the two states. The absence of the relatively weak and marginal states of Han 韓 and Yan 燕 from this record might speak to the same point (Lewis 1999a, 594, 596). Among the three most frequently mentioned polities, Zhou and Qin still existed as the alleged meetings between Lord Zhaowen and Prince Gong took place. The prominence of the two states might not be coincidental given the setting of the *Zhouxun* and the alleged prominence of Lord Zhaowen in Qin.

Considering the importance of the annalistic form of historiography in early China (Van Auken 2016, 6), the approximate timeline of the events discussed by Lord Zhaowen in the course of his instructions will be examined next. It could be represented in the following way:

Timeline of Events Recorded in the *Zhouxun*

Setting the last chapter aside for the time being, a strictly chronological presentation of events can be shown for each individual polity. That is, the appearance of the early Zhou sovereigns, King Wen and King Cheng, in chapters 3 and 12 respectively corresponds to the chronological order of their rule. The same is true of chapters 6 and 8, which deal with Lord Wen of Jin before and after his ascension to the throne of the state of Jin. Chapters 7 and 11 (featuring Lord Mu and Lord Xian of Qin), and chapters 9 and 13 (portraying Zhao Dun and Zhao Jianzi) adhere to the same principle of chronological organization.

There are also several obvious examples of non-chronological arrangements that demand explanation. First, the events described in chapters 4 and 5 both precede the occurrences dealt with in chapter 6. This inconsistency can be resolved by pointing out that these two chapters deal with "kings" (*wang*), that is, King Zhao of Chu and King Goujian of Yue. As such, they are consistent with the previous chapters (2, 3), which also feature kings, and are different from most of the subsequent chapters, which feature representatives of lower ranks, such as "lords" (*gong*), "marquises" (*hou*) etc. The first five historical narratives (chs. 2-5) all concern kings. Therefore, it seems that in this case the chronological order of presentation was abandoned in favor of the principle "kings first," and, quite possibly, in order to present the two polities from the South-Eastern fringes of Chinese civilization together.

Other examples show that a chronologically inconsistent presentation of events took place to make a point. For instance, chapters 2 and 11 each present two historical accounts in reversed temporal order, by mentioning Cheng Tang prior to Yu and Lord Xian of Qin prior to Yao, respectively. To explain this peculiarity, it should first be noted that, in both chapters the second, more ancient, account evidences the earliest occurrence of a specific political practice.

In chapter 2, it is the transfer of power to a "worthy" son, heralding the establishment of the first hereditary dynasty (Xia), while chapter 11 mentions the first example of demoting an unworthy heir apparent and, instead, transferring power to a worthy minister. In these two cases, references to the past were made to achieve opposite goals. In chapter 2, the goal is to show the continuity between the past and the present in regard to establishing worthy sons. For its part, chapter 11 points out the impractical character of the ancient practice of enthroning a worthy minister given the realities of the day. Inverted chronology played an important role in making this point and was by no means coincidental. The reviewed examples show that "Lord Zhaowen's" treatment of historical precedents was simultaneously informed by chronological, thematic, and geopolitical considerations.

Chapter 14, as the concluding formula suggests, originally contained the instructions of the six kings and five hegemons. The extant Beida fragments of the chapter can indeed be divided into eleven thematic sections, while containing references to nine rulers. Hence, it stands to reason that two of the opening fragments featuring the names of the respective monarchs have been lost. Among the nine mentioned sovereigns, we find Yao, Shun, Yu, King Tang, King Wen, and King Wu, who indeed were referred to as the six kings in early China.[3]

---

[3] For the six kings in the *Lüshi chunqiu*, see Chen Q. 2001, 606n9.

Therefore, it seems that what is missing here are parts of information about the two hegemons. In my view, the hegemons in question are Lord Wen of Jin (r. 636–628 BCE), and, rather surprisingly, King Zhao of Chu (r. 515–489 BCE).[4] I come to this conclusion in view of the generally consistent portrayal of the same individuals in different chapters of the *Zhouxun*. Since the two passages with missing opening sections show close parallels to the depictions of these two rulers in chapters 4 and 6, it is very likely that the list of the five hegemons originally included, in order of their seniority, Lord Huan of Qi, Lord Mu of Qin, Lord Wen of Jin, King Goujian of Yue and King Zhao of Chu. This list is unique among other combinations of the five hegemons circulated in early China, in that it includes King Zhao of Chu.[5]

With the exception of Shun, all sovereigns featured in chapter 14 also appear as the main protagonists in chapters 2 through 12 (note that King Zhao of Chu and King Goujian of Yue are treated as "kings" in chapters 4 and 5). Intriguingly, these characters' instructions as recorded in the last chapter appear to have taken place prior to words and actions of theirs as depicted elsewhere. To give an example, in chapter 5, King Goujian is shown to deliver a final speech from his deathbed, while in chapter 14 he is portrayed as travelling in his state of Yue, i.e., enjoying good health.

Moreover, in some case, these instructions seem to be causally connected to events from other chapters. For instance, King Wen's admonitions of his heir Fa in chapter 14 and the latter's ascension to ruler over *tianxia* in chapter 3 are described using similar terms. This peculiarity can be explained with reference to the "transitional" nature of chapter 14, which became clear in the analysis of the two introductory formulas of the *Zhouxun*. Accordingly, this chapter can be viewed both as marking the end and the beginning of the book. Therefore, there is no contradiction in the fact that the content of this final chapter temporally and logically precedes occurrences recorded in the rest of the *Zhouxun*.

Some representatives of the six kings and five hegemons are also portrayed to instruct their successors outside of chapter 14. As a result, there are two educational accounts of Yao and Shun (chs. 14, 11), Yu and Qi (chs. 14, 2), Cheng Tang and Tai Jia (chs. 14, 2) as well as King Goujian of Yue and his unnamed heir (chs. 14, 5). In this case, the antecedence of chapter 14 may imply that it contained instructions for individuals before they were established as successors,

---

[4] This view is different from the positions proposed by Han 2015, 253, and Chen J. 2015. These scholars name King Helü 闔廬 of Wu (r. 514–496 BCE) as the last missing hegemon. However, even though King Helü is called hegemon in chapter five, it is very unlikely that he was included among the five hegemons in chapter 14, because all other hegemons appear as exemplary individuals in separate narratives (in chs. 5, 6, 7, 12). The same goes for King Zhao of Chu, whose behavior is praised in no uncertain terms in chapter 4.
[5] For the different lists of the five hegemons, see Khayutina 2006, 22. See also, Durrant, Li and Schaberg 2016, 722n68.

whereas other chapters referred to the events that took place after this issue was settled.

Despite the similarity of the imparted content, the text never uses the same notion twice when describing the didactic efforts of individual powerholders. That is, if chapter 14 speaks of "enjoining," then the corresponding account elsewhere is sure to employ a different term, for instance, "to say" (*wei* 謂). In any case, the fact that several monarchs were presented exclusively in educational contexts appears to stress the crucial importance of rulers' persistent personal involvement in the cultivation of their successors.

Unlike the six kings and five hegemons, several individuals make only one appearance in the *Zhouxun*. These are Jin minister Zhao Dun (?–601 BCE), Marquis Wen of Wei (r. 424–387 BCE) and his son Ji 擊, the future Marquis Wu of Wei 魏武侯 (r. 395–370 BCE), Lord Xian of Qin (r. 384–362 BCE) and the head of the Zhao lineage, Zhao Jianzi 趙簡子 (?–476 BCE) and, his son, Zhao Xiangzi 趙襄子. This selection may reflect the political realities of the late Zhanguo period, during which the states of Zhao and Qin were particularly strong. The stories involving the representatives of Wei, Qin and Zhao (chs. 10, 11, 13) are common in espousing the demotion of the eldest son in favor of a younger brother. Therefore, the text might suggest that the political ascension of these powers was connected to their dismissal of the rule of primogeniture.

The account of Lord Xian of Qin in chapter 11 is unique among the other individuals outside of the scope of the six kings and five hegemons in juxtaposing him with the greatest paragon of morality among ancient Chinese rulers, Yao. This juxtaposition is not coincidental. Rather, Yao's counterintuitive appearance in the end of chapter 11 (and not in the beginning of chapter 2) serves to highlight the greatness of the Qin ruler, to which I will say more later.

Finally, the topical arrangement of the chapters as presented above adheres to a certain pattern. Represented in a table, the main tropes are as follows:

Table 5: Thematic Macrostructure of the *Zhouxun*

Ch.	Main Topic
1	Ways of handling the ministers and cautions against them
2	Worthiness as the main precondition for rule
3	Establishing a worthy heir brings great success to a polity
4	Kindness to the populace of the capital pays off in a difficult moment
5	Annihilation of a state because of the establishment of an inept heir
6	Ascension to the throne due to the people's support
7	Victory in a war due to the support of the population
8	Annihilation of a state because of inept rulership

31 / Chapter 3

9	Kindness to the *shi* pays off in a difficult moment
10	Establishing a worthy heir brings great success to a polity
11	Worthiness as the main precondition for rule
12	Ways of handling the ministers / ministers are indispensable
13	Establishing of a worthy heir brings great success to a polity
14	Instructions of the six kings and five hegemons

The first twelve chapters, which correspond to the constituent months of the regular year, can be arranged into two halves (chs. 1-6 and 7-12) that mirror each other thematically. Chapters 1 and 12, 2 and 11, 3 and 10, 4 and 9, 5 and 8, 6 and 7 show similarities in content and, at times, form. Presented in a graph, this symmetrical arrangement can be shown as follows:

Thematic Chapter Arrangement

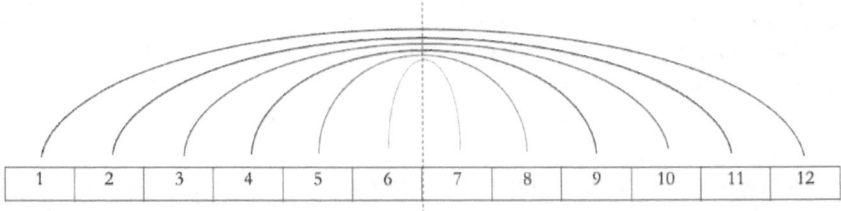

I contend that it is justified to consider the first twelve chapters as a separate overarching unit as I do here. After all, the twelve months, to which they correspond, constitute the unchanging elements of the year, whereas the intercalary month is introduced only occasionally. Possibly, this is the reason why the content of chapter 13 has a close parallel in chapter ten. Because if its moral message were unique, it would have been lost during a twelve-month year.

As shown, the specific selection of the ancient rulers and the order of their treatment demonstrate a certain interpretation of history and serves to emphasize particular thematic points. Dealing with the past belongs to the argumentative strategy of the text. In addition to this, Lord Zhaowen employs several specific rhetorical strategies to increase the persuasive power of his instructions. These will be analyzed in the next section.

Chapter 4

Rhetorical Strategies

The language of *Zhouxun* shows a high degree of sophistication in employing different rhetorical devices. Some of them appear only sporadically, while others can be found throughout the text. In the present section, I analyze them in the following order: chain argument, rhymes, parallelism, rhetorical questions and, finally, quotations from other (authoritative) sources.

Chain Argument. In a chain argument or anadiplosis, the last part of a sentence is repeated in the beginning of the subsequent sentence. This rhetorical figure belongs among the most common tools of persuasion in ancient China (Harbsmeier 1998, 282). In the *Zhouxun*, it appears only in Lord Zhaowen's "theoretical" instructions from chapter 1 and the beginning of chapter 12. One admonition from the opening chapter says, for instance:

13/10 為人君者，不可以信讒，信讒則苛民。苛民則正（政）乳（亂）。正（政）乳（亂）[13] 則民移，民移則國空虛，國空虛而城不守。主欲毋危，其得已乎？14/24

A ruler must not believe slander. If he believes slander, he will be harsh to the people. If he is harsh to the people, his rule will be chaotic. If his rule is chaotic, the people will move away. If the people move away, the capital will be empty and weak. If the capital is empty and weak and its walls unprotected, then, though the sovereign wishes to avoid peril, can he achieve it?

Such an arrangement of the argument has the advantage of establishing close causal relationships between its individual units. Its persuasiveness is based solely on its formal characteristics and does not require other elements, such as references to ancient lore. However, it is also evident that spontaneous conversation hardly develops in this manner. The formal rigidity of these lines speaks against the possibility of them being conversation records, even though speeches exchanged during court audiences "were comprehensively rewritten in order to make them more 'correct'" (Falkenhausen 2011, 269).

Rhymes. Extensive use of rhyme is common in several chapters of the *Zhouxun*. For instance, chapter 5 depicts King Goujian of Yue as admonishing his heir in a passage that contains as many as thirty-four rhymed (mostly tetrasyllabic) lines. And chapter 6 is built of several rhymed sections covering an impressive seventy-two (likewise mostly tetrasyllabic) lines in length. Unlike many other examples of tetrasyllabic rhymed passages, which express some general, abstract ideas and "bland" truths (Schaberg 2015, 103), these two examples refer to concrete historical events, individuals, and places. They constitute intriguing examples of historical narratives couched in rhyme. The use of rhyme is also prominent in chapters 2, 8, 12, 13 and, most noticeably, 14. However, unlike chapters 5 and 6, the rhymed passages in these chapters contain fewer historical references. In general, rhyme appears to be especially prominent in "speeches," amplifying their admonishing character.

The *Zhouxun* contains several examples of the so-called irregular rhymes. The most frequent of them include combinations of the rhyme groups *you* 幽 / *xiao* 宵 (chs. 6, 8), *zhen* 真 / *geng* 耕 (chs. 2, 6, 11), *zhen* 真 / *yuan* 元 (chs. 2, 10, 12), *zhi* 之 / *zhi* 脂 (chs. 2, 8, 14), *zhi* 之 / *ge* 歌 (chs. 2, 8, 14) and *zhi* 之 / *zhi* 職 (chs. 6, 8, 11, 14). While some of these combinations, such as *zhen* / *geng*, are often determined as particular to the southern Chinese dialects (Luo and Zhou 2007, 81), these few examples alone are insufficient to prove the southern provenance of the *Zhouxun*. After all, the most eminent Qin compilation, the *Lüshi chunqiu*, also abounds in the examples of *zhen* / *geng* rhymes as well as many other "southern" rhyme combinations (Zhang S. 2008, 409).

Parallelism and Symmetry of Argument. Rhymed passages in the *Zhouxun* often contain contrasting information that can be arranged in two juxtaposed strands. For instance, this is how the founder of the Shang dynasty, (Cheng) Tang, advises his alleged heir Tai Jia in chapter 14 (slips 184–186):

Introduction:

| 1 | 湯謂太甲曰： | | Tang said to Tai Jia: |

Negative Ramifications:

2	爾不畏天，	真	"If you do not stand in awe before Heaven,
3	其安得見日？	質	how will you get to see the sun?
4	爾不事神，	真	If you do not serve the spirits,
5	將予汝疾，	質	they will inflict diseases upon you.
6	身病而體痛，	東	With ailing body and aching limbs,
7	豈能有瘳？	質	how could you be helped?

Rhetorical Strategies / 34

Positive Ramifications:

8	爾能畏天,	真	If you are able to stand in awe before Heaven,
9	則壽命永長。	陽	your life will be long.
10	爾能事神,	真	If you can serve the spirits,
11	則無疾殃。│	陽	you will suffer neither diseases nor calamities.
12	禍災不至,	質	With neither misfortune nor disasters looming,
13	國安而身利。	脂	your state will be at peace and your body will stand to gain."

As can be seen, Cheng Tang shows two opposite scenarios to Tai Jia, the one entailing ailment and demise, and the one leading to personal health and stability in the domain. The distinct rhyme combinations help create a sense of the fundamental difference between these two scenarios. By presenting the consequences of one's actions in this radical way, Cheng Tang implies that there is no alternative for Tai Jia but to comply with these instructions, that is, to stand in awe before Heaven.

Lord Zhaowen's admonitions of Prince Gong are often constructed in a similar fashion, as this example from chapter 6 (84/12–87/10) shows:

Positive Ramifications

1	今汝能慈孝,		Now, if you are able to be compassionate and filial,
2	尊仁貴信,	真	to honor humaneness and value trustworthiness,
3	余雖未爾立,│		then, even though I haven't established you,
4	而身自令,	耕	you will ensconce yourself.
5	余雖已終,		So when I am near my end,
6	至于季年,	真	reaching my final years,
7	眾之立汝也,		the masses will establish you
8	若日之必出,		as certainly as the sun will rise,
9	猶將│戴天。	真	[treating you] as Heaven above them.

Negative Ramifications

10	爾遠信仁		But if you distance yourself from trustworthiness and humaneness
	而不能慈孝,	宵	and are not able to be compassionate and filial;

11	惡學憎善		If you despise learning, loathe goodness
	而不聽教導,	幽	and do not heed teachings and counsels;
12	余雖身置|汝,		then, even if I personally install you,
13	人將代汝,		others will replace you,
14	民莫而肯好。	幽	and none among the people will like you.

Even though the formal parallelism between the two strands is less apparent here than in the above case, Lord Zhaowen still employs semantic opposition to argue that the only sensible way of action for Prince Gong is to be "compassionate and filial" and to "respect humaneness and value trustworthiness." The difference between the respective end-rhymes (zhen 真 and you 幽) underscores their semantic contrast.

Rhetorical Questions. I have already pointed out that rhetorical questions conclude most chapters of the *Zhouxun*. They are also characteristic of the entire content of the work, including chain argument passages, "ancient" speeches, as well as pleas to Prince Gong. Even a "folk song" about the ignominious treatment of King Helü's grave from chapter 5 includes a series of rhetorical questions. In most cases, this figure is constructed by means of the multifunctional particle *qi* 其. My data analysis shows that 39 from a total of 122 occurrences of *qi* in the *Zhouxun* mark rhetorical questions (32 percent). This is a very high percentage compared to the *Zuozhuan* (He L. 1989, 357) or, to take a more contemporaneous text, the *Lüshi chunqiu* (Yin 2008, 310–311). In fact, the use of *qi* 其 in rhetorical questions is so prominent in the *Zhouxun* that we find it there in several very uncommon combinations with other question particles, such as *qian* 其安 (eight times), *qihu* 其胡 (eight times) or *qiyong* 其庸 (four times).

The text also uses another rhetorical question particle, *qi* 剀 (豈). However, it mostly appears in the ancient royal speeches invoked by Lord Zhaowen. The 豈/其 ratio in those speeches is roughly 15 to 14, whereas in his own instructions, the same ratio is only 3 to 24. Evidently, the usage of either *qi* 豈 or *qi* 其 was one of the main linguistic tools that the authors used to create a sense of separation between the "antiquity" and "present" times. This is surprising insofar as *qi* 其 is usually regarded as the more "ancient" particle (Pines 2002, 218). I can only interpret this fact to the effect that, given Lord Zhaowen's characteristic use of *qi* 其 in combination with other particles, *qi* 豈 appeared as a preferable option to mark the other's (ancient) speech.

Rhetorical Strategies / 36

Quotations. Frequent quotations from other sources to bolster the argument constitute another rhetorical strategy of the *Zhouxun*.[1] In the recovered version, the most frequently explicitly quoted source are the Documents, which appear eight times under the general designation *shu* 書 and once as a Document of Zhou (*Zhoushu* 周書) in chapter 2. With seven marked mentions, the Odes occupy the second position. Like the Documents, they appear under the generic term *shi* 詩, with the exception of a reference to the "Daya" 大雅 section in chapter 11. The next frequently invoked literary genre are the proverbs (*yan* 諺), which are quoted five times. Beyond this, there is a reference to a text called *Pengzu* 彭祖 (ch. 1) and two to an unspecified saying (ch. 12).

From twenty-four direct references to these five types of sources, twenty are made by Lord Zhaowen, while Lord Huan of Qi (chs. 12 and 14) and, most likely, King Zhao of Chu (chs. 4 and 14) refer to two sources each. In chapters 5 and 8, *shi* (as words in a song) and *shu* (as writings) play a central role in the anecdotes containing them as expressions of general sentiment and/or principles to be taken into consideration by a wise ruler. However, their appearance in the text is not framed by the formulas that Lord Zhaowen usually employs to connote authoritative sources. The distribution of the marked quotations throughout the *Zhouxun* is uneven, as can be seen in the table below:

Table 6: Marked Quotations in the *Zhouxun*

Ch.	*shu*	*shi*	*yan*	"heard" sayings	Titled Sources
1		3 (Mao 26, 195, 288)	3		*Pengzu*
2	1 = *Zhoushu*				
3					
4		1 (Mao 254)			
5					
6	1				
7	1				
8					
9	1	1 (Mao 7+235)			
10	1				

---

[1] For analysis of the quoted sources in the manuscript, see Han 2015, 279–289 and Kusano 2019. For some notable investigations of the *shi* and *shu* quotations in excavated materials, see Riegel 1997; Liao M. 2001a and 2001b; Kern 2005b and 2005c; Staack 2010.

Chapter Four

11		1 = "Daya" (Mao 256)			
12				2	
13			1		
14	1	1 (Mao 254)	1		
Total	9	7	5	2	1

Accordingly, chapter 1 stands out by featuring ten such references. Chapter 14 contains three, and chapter 9 has two. In most other chapters, only one quote appears, while chapters 3, 5, and 8 contain no references to authoritative sources.

As just mentioned, in the last two chapters, linguistic articulations of higher principles in the form of *shi* and *shu* play an important role in the storyline of the anecdotes recounted. One thus cannot escape the impression that the absence of marked quotations in these chapters might be connected to the respective plots. As it seems, chapter 3 is rather unique in that is has no appeals to textual authority in any of its parts. This is astonishing insofar as this chapter deals with the foundation story of the Zhou dynasty, that is, the period of time which came to be renowned for its refined culture and the various practices of inscribing the shared cultural memory of the Zhou aristocracy onto various materials.

None of the nine *shu* citations in the *Zhouxun* has a counterpart in the transmitted anthologies of the Documents. This seems to support the view of "the *Shangshu* traditions which is fluid and dynamic, rather than fixed and static, the work of small textual communities rather than one general readership across the face of China" (He and Nylan 2019, 59).[2] At the same time, *shu* quotations employ a limited number of archaisms, which is common to many other excavated manuscripts from the pre-Qin and early imperial times.

The linguistic distinction between the quoted content (representing ancient lore) and the quoting text is, thus, less pronounced than in most transmitted Han sources. This early and less conspicuous mode of integrating *shu*-quotations in the greater body of the text could have been, indeed, determined by the authors' hope to "have their arguments receive a good response and wider reception" (He and Nylan 2019, 45). This view is consistent with the political realities of pre-Qin China. It was not until the imperial period, when archaizing speech in the (often imagined) style of early *shu* grew in significance as one of the officially sanctioned ways to invoke the authority of the past to pursue the political agenda of the day, that the heavy use of archaisms became a prominent feature of the *Shangshu*.[3]

---

[2] On the loose and heterogenous nature of the early *shu*, see also Schaberg 2001, 72–80 and Kern 2005b, 317–318.
[3] On the early imperial support of the *shu*, see Schaberg 2017, 354–355.

In contrast to *shu*, all *shi* quotations in the *Zhouxun* have counterparts in the transmitted *Shijing*. The poems are, in order of their appearance, "Bozhou" 柏舟 (Mao 26), "Xiaomin" 小旻 (Mao 195), "Jingzhi" 敬之 (Mao 288) (all in ch. 1), "Ban" 板 (Mao 254) (ch. 4), "Tuju" 兔罝 (Mao 7), "Wenwang" 文王 (Mao 235) (ch. 9), "Yi" 抑 (Mao 256) (ch. 11) and "Ban" (Mao 254) (ch. 14). These poems appear in all four sections of the *Mao Shi*. It seems the authors have deliberately attempted to provide a selection of poems that would be representative of the entire anthology. This, on the other hand, corroborates the traditional view (now also supported by the Anhui university manuscript) that the formation process of this canonical collection of poems must have been completed well before the foundation of the Qin empire.[4]

Interestingly, in five cases, the *shi*-lines open with reduplicatives: *genggeng* 耿耿, *zhanzhan lingling* 戰戰淩淩 (both in ch. 1), *jiujiu* 赳赳 and *jiji* 濟濟 (both in ch. 9) and, also, *wuhu* 於乎 (ch. 11). Given that there is a total of sixteen quoted *shi*-lines in the *Zhouxun*, reduplicatives appear in 31 percent of all *shi*-lines. This is significantly higher than the relevant ratio in the transmitted *Shijing*, which is 9 percent (Mazanec 2018, 21). Reduplication is often understood as evidencing the "musical" or "performative" nature of the Odes (Kern 2000, 80; Cook 2011, 316).[5] But in the *Zhouxun*, this stylistic feature, rather than emphasizing the musicality of the Odes,[6] effectively sets the poetic lines apart from the rest of the text, possibly highligting their elevated status.

Most of the proverbs employed in the *Zhouxun* consist of two-line sayings characterized by parallelism in structure and juxtaposition in meaning. The semantic opposition is underscored through rhymes. Thematically, they contain more imagery coming from the natural world and human craft. While *shi* and *shu* originally emerged as part of royal sacrifices, banquets, speeches, and ritual performances (Kern 2009, 182–188; Allan 2015, 272–276), proverbs—a fundamentally oral linguistic form—were not associated with any specific religious practices, educational activities or any set of writings. Instead, they expressed "observations, judgments, or wisdom about commonly shared experience and values, using familiar images and tropes" (Rohsenow 2001, 151). Proverbs could substantiate truth claims while taking a stand outside of a specific intellectual tradition. In the *Zhouxun*, they play an important role as a necessary means to facilitate

---

[4] The appearance of the Anhui University manuscript provides the strongest evidence to date for the existence of the "Guofeng" section of the poetic canon during the Warring States period (Huang D. 2017, 58). For more on the Anhui University collection of the Odes, see Xu Z. 2017. For the translation of six poems from this collection and their comparison with their transmitted counterparts, see Shaughnessy 2021.

[5] On the semantic connotations of reduplicatives, see Smith 2015.

[6] On the emancipation of the Odes from musical performance in the *Zuozhuan* and some chapters of the *Lunyu*, see Van Zoeren 1991, 35–44. For use of poetry in diplomatic encounters, see Lewis 1999b: 156–158 and Li Wai-yee 2014.

the development of argument or the overall assessment of an issue. They also appear as a necessary educational tool in chapters 1 and 13. There, they express the minimal moral requirements that a throne contender must master.

Finally, in chapter 12, there are two references to sayings which the respective protagonists claim to have heard (*wen zhi* 聞之). These two passages stand out through the length and complexity of their structure. They constitute independent textual units comprising several argumentative steps.

Depending on the context of their appearance, whether the passage is a piece of argumentative persuasion, anecdote, or personal address to Prince Gong, the role of explicitly marked quotations changes. In a piece of argument-based persuasion, they are generally used to substantiate Lord Zhaowen's claims and to enhance the lucidity of his reasoning. In historical anecdotes, their role consists mostly in capping a story under a specific notion, thus demonstrating the significance of that story in the traditional value system. Finally, in his personal appeals to Prince Gong, Lord Zhaowen uses quotations to show that the demand of character cultivation and reformation that he persistently directs at his heir is firmly encoded in the authoritative lore.

There are several formulaic expressions with which "external" material is imbedded in the larger textual context. The most basic is "and so, X says Y" (故 X 曰 Y), where X stands for a relevant source and Y signifies the quoted text. This simple yet decisive formulation underscores the final character of the saying following it. It evidently functions as a summary of the ideas previously expressed in the text (Wagner 2015, 49, 40n33). In the *Zhouxun*, it is applied only to the *shi* (chs. 1 and 9) and *shu* (ch. 1).

This basic formula is extended by adding either the line "does it (not) give expression to this case?" (其此之謂乎？) or the line "it gives expression to this" (此之謂也)." Intriguingly, the former is applied to *shu* (three times in ch. 1 and once in ch. 2) as well as the *Pengzu* (ch. 1), whereas the latter is used only in combination with *shi* (twice in ch. 1). It seems that, the authors were striking a more assertive tone in their hermeneutic approach to the Odes.

Another common formulaic expression is "This is what X expresses in saying Y" (此 X 之所謂曰 Y 者也). This formula appears seven times and works in combination with *shi* (ch. 4), *shu* (chs. 6, 7, 9, 10) and proverbs (twice in ch. 1). It is used to summarize historical narratives as well as to elucidate the meaning of the preceding argument.

While most passages contain only one marked quotation, in four cases we find quotation "clusters" featuring several sources. These are combinations of: 1) a proverb and a Document (ch. 1); 2) a proverb and two Odes (ch. 1); 3) a Document and two Odes (ch. 9); and 4) an Ode and a Document (ch. 14). By combining several "authoritative" sources, the authors not only provide a larger body of evidence to substantiate their exemplifications, but also effectively interpret the quoted materials by means of each other. Consequently, they treat the wisdom encapsuled in the different linguistic forms—written (*shu*), sung, performed (*shi*), and oral (*yan*)—as having equal validity.

By demonstrating comprehensive command of different types of knowledge associated with the Documents, Odes, proverbs, etc., Lord Zhaowen emerges as a figure possessing a deep understanding of the world and its various cultural and physical phenomena. Moreover, he appears as a figure who is able to pass authoritative judgements on different historical events; often, with the help of quotations. As such, he assumes a role similar to that of the "Gentleman" or "Confucius" in the *Zuozhuan* (Lewis 1999b, 168).[7] Their affinity is further underscored by the use of similar quotation practices,[8] which are markedly different from those one finds in another early Chinese historiographic work, the *Guoyu* 國語.[9] As will be discussed further below, the *Zhouxun* might have been indeed created in an environment where the *Zuozhuan* (or materials that came to be incorporated therein) was known.

As shown above, the macro- and micro-level organization of the *Zhouxun* as well as its linguistic and rhetorical characteristics demonstrate a high degree of deliberation. Evidently, this work represents an example of a masterfully crafted literary composition. Thus, the assumption seems justified that that the *Zhouxun* was produced in a single creative effort.[10] It is very likely that, in this process, already existing material was used and, if necessary, modified to fit the conceptual framework of the book. Yet, this mode of textual production was predominant in early China.[11]

---

[7] Lord Zhaowen resembles "Confucius" in presenting a consistent interpretation of historical events (Henry 1999, 147–149). However, with regard to explicit quotations (of *shi* and other sources), he is closer to the "Gentleman," who resorts to quotations more frequently than "Confucius" (for the former, see Mao 2011, 234–235; for the latter Henry 1999, 132).

[8] The formula "gives expression to (this)" ((其是)之謂) is very common in the exegetic endeavors of the "Gentleman" as directed at *shi* and *shu*. For examples, see Mao 2011, 235–240.

[9] On the *Guoyu*'s date and relation to the *Zuozhuan*, see Chang, Boltz and Loewe 1993, 263–264. On *shi* and *shu* quotations in the *Guoyu*, see Zhang J. 2020, 99–109.

[10] Han 2015, 254 maintains that the *Zhouxun* consists of four layers that were created at different times, chapters 1 to 12 (the earliest part), then chapter 13, then the so-called "small chapters" (*xiao zhang* 小章) and finally the chapter associated with "the day of the year end's food offering ceremony." On the other hand, Su Jian-Zhou 2017, 256 claims that the two framing formulas of the *Zhouxun* were added to the rest of the text only during the Han dynasty.

[11] On the composite nature of early Chinese texts and independent building blocks as their basic constituents, see Boltz 2005, 57–61. Any attempt to establish the original version or *urtext* runs counter to convention in early China, where versions of a text were transmitted and modified by different actors and yet regarded as equally "authentic" (Hein 2019, 55–58).

Chapter 5

Philosphical Concepts

The main goal of Lord Zhaowen's educational endeavor is to inculcate into Prince Gong the correct principles of governance, making him a worthy contender to the throne. Because, according to the main premise of the *Zhouxun*, a ruling family will be able to retain and strengthen its position only when power is transferred to a worthy individual. More precisely, only a worthy successor will be effective in "protecting the state" (chs. 1, 2, 3, 6, 12), "protecting sacrificial offerings" (chs. 10 and 13), and, ideally, "capturing other states" (ch. 14).

Conversely, the text is adamant that an inept ruler will "lose" and "destroy" his domain (chs. 3, 6, 10, 11, 12, 14). When losing his state, a powerholder does not only suffer personally but, what is much worse, he directly harms his ancestors, by discontinuing sacrificial offerings (chs. 3, 5). Therefore, in a sense, Lord Zhaowen's motivation to establish a worthy successor is based on his personal interest to create permanent conditions for receiving sacrificial offerings after his own departure to the netherworld.

This underscores the crucial importance of power transfer. This issue is addressed in no less than eight chapters, which can be divided into two types. The first group (chs. 2, 5, 11, 14) contains examples of how some of the most illustrious rulers of antiquity admonished their successor to strive to obtain moral excellence lest they are demoted. In general terms, these chapters establish as historical tradition that early monarchs regarded the personal education of their offspring as their natural and, perhaps, most important responsibility. On the other hand, the second group (chs. 3, 6, 10) provides accounts of the prosperous states where succession was settled based exclusively on the heir' abilities, ignoring all the conventional selection criteria. To emphasize this point, the individuals discussed in these chapters are younger sons of their fathers.

Chapter 13 stands out by combining both elements: the ruler's instruction to his progeny as well as a demonstration of the great results obtained upon the installation of a worthy successor. This chapter appears to be particularly important as its narrative of a sovereign educating his sons by means of a written text mirrors the encounters between Lord Zhaowen and Prince Gong.

Otherwise, the two groups of chapters appear to be complementary. While the former show the absolute necessity of elevating a worthy successor and demonstrates the ways of achieving worthiness through education, the latter claim that any "worthy" son, when given a chance, will vastly expand the influence of his domain. The arrangement of the two types of chapters in the text is as follows:

Table 7: Power Transfer in the *Zhouxun*

Ch.	Relevant Topic
1	———
2	Admonitions of the Heir Apparent
3	Benefits of Installing a Worthy Successor
4	———
5	Admonition of the Heir Apparent
6	Benefits of Installing a Worthy Successor
7	———
8	———
9	———
10	Benefits of Installing a Worthy Successor
11	Admonition and Demotion of the Heir Apparent
12	———
13	Admonition and Benefits of Installing a Worthy Successor
14	Admonitions of the Heir Apparent

The two types of chapters dealing with the issue of power transfer appear in the *Zhouxun* side by side. This arrangement seems by no means accidental and was, most likely, intended to reinforce the author's rejection of any criteria for determining succession other than worthiness.

Main Notions

Worthiness is the most frequently used term in the text; it also appears in nine different chapters. Therefore, the entire text may be regarded as an instruction on how to become a worthy ruler and even those chapters which do not mention this term directly, can be seen as elucidating its meaning.[1]

As for the various other values and principles discussed in the context of worthiness as a means of consolidating power, the following table provides an overview:

---

[1] For a detailed discussion, see Fech 2018, 158.

Table 8: Main Notions in the *Zhouxun*

Ch	xian 賢	de 德	xiao 孝	ren 仁	ci 慈	hui 惠	zhi 智	dao 道	shan 善	hui 慧	sheng 聖	kuan 寬	ai 愛	ti 悌	ming 明	shen 神	gui 鬼	li 禮	yi 義
1	1	1					3		1		1				2				
2	1	1	1	1		1		2			1	1		1	1				1
3	4		1								1						1		
4		3																	
5			1						1				1						
6		2	3	5	3	1	2		1	1				1					
7		1				1					1								
8	1			1				2											
9		3											1						
10	6		2	2	1				2										
11	4	1	1			1													
12	2					2	1					2							
13	3		1	1	1									1					
14	4	4	1	1	3	1		4	1	1	1		1			3	2	1	1
Ttl	26	16	11	11	8	7	6	6	5	4	4	4	3	3	3	3	2	2	2

This makes it clear that the *Zhouxun* chapters differ significantly in regard to the "density" of the terms discussed. Chapter 4 highlights the importance of only one notion, chapter 9 has two, while chapters 7 and 8 each have three. On the other hand, there are also chapters with more diversified philosophical content. For instance, chapter 14 features fifteen different notions and principles, chapter 2 has eleven, and chapter 6 has ten. In general, the eight chapters dealing with the issue of power transfer tend to be much denser with regard to the use of philosophical nomenclature.

However, in most cases, philosophical concepts are given no definitions and their mutual relationship is not further specified. Chapter 6, for instance, does not make any attempt to elucidate what constitutes *de* 德, *ren* 仁, *xiao* 孝, *hui* 惠, how these virtues might be cultivated, what difficulties one may face when developing them, what their relationship to human dispositions is, or whether they are interconnected.[2] This apparent lack of coherent treatment certainly reflects the fact that, in most cases, different notions and virtues are ascribed to

---

[2] See, for example, *Lunyu* "Xue er" 學而 (Cheng Shude 1990, 13): 孝弟也者，其為仁之本與！ "Might we not say that filial piety and fraternal respect constitute the root of humaneness?"

different historical actors appearing in the anecdotes. Therefore, while by widely operating with ethical norms and philosophical concepts the authors demonstrate their familiarity with the main intellectual debates of the time, one does not find an elaborate edifice of thought in the *Zhouxun*.

Based on their standard definitions as well as the respective context of their appearance in the text, philosophical notions can be subsumed under the following headings, presented here in the order of their prominence:

— Moral virtues involving kind and magnanimous treatment of the people, especially subordinates: *de* 德 "virtue(-inspired gratitude)," *ren* 仁 "humaneness," *hui* 惠 "kindness," *kuan* 寬 "leniency," *ai* 愛 "love"—42 times;
— Moral virtues connoting loving and respectful relations within family: *xiao* 孝 "filial piety," *ci* 慈 "parental love/compassion," *ti* 悌 "brotherly piety"— 22 times;
— Intellectual virtues involving wisdom and perspicacity: *zhi* 智 "wisdom," *hui* 慧 "intelligence," *sheng* 聖 "sagacity," *ming* 明 "clairvoyance"—17 times;
— Possession of the (proper) Way, *dao* 道—6 times;
— Goodness with connotations of excellence: *shan* 善 "goodness"—5 times;
— Reverence towards ghosts (*gui* 鬼) and spirits (*shen* 神)—5 times;
— Proper ways of action and correct decorum: *li* 禮 "propriety" and *yi* 義 "righteousness"—4 times.

When considering these categories against the background of the main concern of the *Zhouxun*, which is securing and maintaining political power, it becomes evident that in the authors' eyes the best way to achieve this end was to extend kind and good treatment to the population. For, as is shown in chapters 4, 7, 9, 11, the people always reciprocate kindness with unwavering support. On the other hand, the ruler is doomed when treating the people harshly (*ke* 苛) (ch. 1).

The importance of developing caring and loving relations with one's family also comes impressively to light from the above.[3] These family-relevant virtues appear exclusively in the chapters dedicated to the transfer of power. It is also significant that "filial piety" and "brotherly piety" connote ideal behavior towards family members who occupy a higher position in the intrafamilial hierarchy than oneself.[4] This is markedly different from the first group of virtues,

---

[3] For the function of family as "the radical locus for human growth" in early Chinese thought, see Ames 2003, 171–172.
[4] *Ci* seems to be an exception as it usually denotes "the love of someone above towards someone below" (Svarverud 1998, 213–214). On the more egalitarian, and presumably later, meaning of *ci* as "compassion," see *ibid.*, 257–258.

almost exclusively associated with the top-down mode of interaction.⁵ The above suggests that, prior to becoming a sovereign, an aspiring ruler needs to be able to submit oneself to the will of his more senior family members. This demand appears sensible in the *Zhouxun*, where Prince Gong is expected to comply with Lord Zhaowen's demands for reformation. Interestingly, another prominent virtue associated with the subordinate strata of society, "loyalty" (*zhong* 忠), does not feature in the text. Being a cardinal ministerial virtue (Svarverud 1998, 204–205; Sou 2013, 12), its absence seems to signal that the *Zhouxun* did not intend to target ministers, but rather junior family members, i.e., male offspring.

The next prominent topic concerns correct discernment and judgement. While employing several relevant notions, the text does not address this issue in a systematic way. As it was the case with moral virtues, no strategies for developing one's intellectual abilities are presented. However, chapters 1 and 12 identify one's emotional involvement as the main hindrance to the objective assessment of a situation. Accordingly, a worthy ruler should be able to keep his "likes and dislikes" (*xi nu* 喜怒) under control. Moreover, there is an appeal to "moderate desires" (*jie yu* 節欲) in chapter 13.

The notion of the Way (*dao* 道) as it appears in the *Zhouxun* is devoid of any cosmological connotations, referring instead to compliance with correct principles of action. In this regard, the text differs from most Daoist classics which operate with the basic assumption that the Way forms the origin and regulating principle of the world. Nor does the text present notions characteristic of the main Daoist classics, such as "naturalness" (*ziran* 自然), "non-action" (*wuwei* 無為), "dark virtue" (*xuan de* 玄德) etc.⁶ Therefore, it can be concluded that the nomenclature of the *Zhouxun* is by no means specifically Daoist.⁷

The religious worship of ghosts and spirits clearly plays a subordinate role appearing only in the concluding chapter 14. The mention of the practice in this chapter appears logical given its ascription to the year end's festival, whose main activity consisted in offering sacrifices to the spirits. Therefore, it seems rather far-fetched to view their appearance as evidence for a Mohist influence on the *Zhouxun*.⁸ Reverence towards spirits is identified as the main precondition for obtaining longevity (*shou* 壽) and good health.⁹

---

⁵ Humaneness, at least in the definition of the *Shuowen jiezi* 說文解字, was equated to treating people as one's parents (*qin* 親). Svarverud 1998, 283. For further details, see *ibid.*, 282–289.
⁶ For a discussion of the main Daoist terms, see Liu X. 2015, 71–110.
⁷ On Daoist connotations of worthiness, see Fech 2020a.
⁸ Han 2015, 272–273. Early Confucianism also contains several "religious" elements as communicating with "the spiritual and the numinous" was deeply integrated "into the fabric of state, family, and personal life" (Sommer 2003, 216).
⁹ For a discussion of "demonological therapy" in early Chinese medicine, see Unschuld 2010, 34–45.

Finally, Table 8 shows that considerations of the proper ways of action and correct decorum occupy only a marginal position. Their marginality can be interpreted as signaling the rejection of some conventional standards and practices. Indeed, as will be shown below, the *Zhouxun* rejects the fundamental rule of primogeniture.

In addition to these points, the *Zhouxun* (in chapter 14) also shows the conviction that there is a clear correspondence between the management of the self/body (*shen* 身) and the state. Accordingly, only a ruler with a well-regulated way of life will be able to order a state. However, we find no instructions as to the exact way of action in this regard. Some sporadic references to health discourse appear in chapters 1 and 12 where the orderly (*zhi* 治) and balanced (*ping* 平) state of *qi* 氣 is proclaimed as influencing one's longevity.[10]

These are some main characteristics of a worthy ruler and/or throne contender. Such an individual is believed to succeed in solidifying his personal power and extending it beyond the borders of his state. On the other hand, an inept ruler is doomed to lose his domain. The political failure of a monarch is often described in terms of getting "replaced" (*dai* 代), a topic broached in chapters 1, 2, 6, 8, and 14. As discussed in the *Zhouxun*, replacement mostly results from subordinates' subversive activities, while military conquest through another polity is addressed less frequently.

The Role of Subordinates

The bulk of philosophical notions and anecdotes in the *Zhouxun* deal with the importance of treating subordinates correctly. The prominence of the ruler-subordinate relationship can be seen in nearly every chapter of the text as reflected in the following table:

Table 9: Notions of Subordination

Ch.	*min* 民	*chen* 臣	*ren* 人	*zhong* 眾	*shi* 士	*baixing* 百姓	*xia* 下	*guan* 官	*shuren* 庶人	Named Aides
1	6	9	1				3	1		
2	6	1	3	1		2				

---

[10] On the correlation between the political and medical realms in early China as well as the importance of balance, see Unschuld 2010, 67–72.

47 / Chapter Five

3										Hong Yao
4	3		4							
5	1			1						
6	4	4	1	3		1	1			
7			4						1	
8										Jiufan
9				5						
10										
11	1	2			1					
12	2	2		2		1				Guan Zhong
13	2									
14	6	1	1	1						
Ttl.	31	19	14	7	6	5	4	1	1	3

As shown here, the text employs several notions when referring to subordinates, the most prominent of which are the "people" (*min* 民) and "ministers" (*chen* 臣).

The "people," alongside the related terms of "hundred surnames" (*bai xing* 百姓) and "masses" (*zhong* 眾), refers to the population group who are said to change their position toward powerholders depending on the latter's ethical dispositions. That is, they are said to support magnanimous sovereigns, while leaving or opposing those who take restrictive measures. The people's support is understood either as eager willingness to subordinate themselves to the ruler or, more dramatically, as readiness to sacrifice their lives to protect the ruler or the state. As such, the people constitute the very foundation of sovereign power.

The notion of ministers is more complex. To begin, three prominent aides in early China, Hong Yao 閎夭, Jiufan 咎犯, and Guan Zhong 管仲—the only ministers mentioned by name—are shown to have been instrumental in the successes of the Zhou dynasty as well as the states of Jin and Qi. It is small wonder that the ability to correctly assess ministerial performance, to identify "worthy" ministers (*xianchen* 賢臣) and use their counsel belongs among the main qualifications of a "worthy" ruler. Such a powerholder heeds his aides "remonstrations" (*jian* 諫) (chs. 12, 13), does not cover up his "mistakes" (*guo* 過) (ch. 12), and does not "believe slander" (*xin chan* 信讒) (chs. 1, 12).

In contrast to this positive treatment, the opening chapter of the *Zhouxun* mainly depicts the "ministers" and "subordinates" (*xia* 下) as a source of mortal danger for powerholders, who are looking for ways to overthrow the latter and establish themselves at the top of the state. To successfully deal with this threat, the ruler is advised to keep his emotions to himself, to correctly judge every situation, to conceal his thoughts from subordinates and feign ignorance. Evidently, ministers can be both advantageous and harmful to a powerholder. Both the ability to utilize ministers' talents (ch. 12) and the aptitude to effectively protect oneself against their encroachments (ch. 1) are associated with the notion of "wisdom" (*zhi* 智). The two aspects of wisdom are juxtaposed mainly in chapters 1 and 12.

Such ethical categories as kindness and magnanimity, which are said to ensure the people's full compliance show no effectiveness when applied to ministers. Simply put, while the main means of dealing with the people is kindness, in his interaction with ministers a ruler is advised to rely on his wisdom. It thus seems that the authors were promoting varying strategies towards different social strata. In this way, strategies of espousing kindness, on the one hand, and feigning ignorance as well as resorting to subterfuge, on the other, are no longer contradictory. A differentiated approach to subordinates is, indeed, reflected in other passages of the manuscript, for instance, in the story about Lord Mu of Qin in chapter 7 (97/11–98/1): "When ruling gentlemen, be upright to elicit their virtue. When ruling men of low rank, be lenient to exhaust their strength."

Transfer of Power

The authors of the *Zhouxun* regard power transfer as the most crucial and unpredictable component in the political life of a state. Accordingly, the only way to ensure the longevity of a ruling family is to bestow power to a worthy successor. For these authors, worthiness should take precedence over all other selection criteria for heirs.

One of the most illuminating accounts of the *Zhouxun* stressing the importance of worthiness tells of an event surrounding the establishment of the Zhou dynasty which is part of chapter 3. There, the successes of the Zhou are explained solely through King Wen's decision to choose a worthy successor, while considerations such as the nobility of the maternal lineage (*gui* 貴), or seniority (*zhang* 長) or personal emotional attachment (*ai* 愛) are dismissed. The difference of this approach from conventional practices becomes evident when we compare it to stipulations on the matter recorded in the *Zuozhuan*:

> 大子死，有母弟，則立之，無，則立長。年鈞擇賢，義鈞則卜，古之道也。
>
> When the heir apparent dies, if he has a full younger brother, he should be established as heir. If not, then the oldest among the lord's sons should be established. If the sons are of the same age, the worthy one is chosen. If they are equally dutiful, then divination is used. This was the way of the ancients.[11]

---

[11] *Zuozhuan*, Xiang 31.4 (Yang B. 1995, 1185; Durrant, Li and Schaberg 2016, 1277). All references to the *Zuozhuan* are based on Yang Bojun's edition of the work and translation by

Chapter Five

And furthermore:

> 昔先王之命曰 「王后無適，則擇立長。年鈞以德， 德鈞以卜。」王不立愛，公卿無私，古之制也。
> In times past, the command of the former kings said, "When there is no legitimate heir by the queen, then choose and establish the eldest as heir. When sons are of equal age, go by their virtue. When they are of equal virtue, go by divination." A king does not establish his heir on the basis of personal preference, and lords and ministers should be without personal bias. That was the system of old.[12]

This indicates that the "way of the ancient" stipulated that the eldest son by the principal wife should be established as the heir apparent. That is, succession should be decided based on considerations of seniority and nobility. Personal abilities, called here virtue, feature only in the third position.[13] The *Zhouxun* corresponds with the "system of old" solely in the rejection of personal preference.

The rejection of the cardinal rule of primogeniture[14], evidenced above, also features prominently in chapters 6, 10, 11, and 13, dealing with the states of Jin, Qin, Zhao, and Wei. There, the eldest sons have been ignored or dismissed as successors in favor of the rulers' younger progeny. In most cases, this decision is identified as the very reason for the political ascension of the respective polities.

Durrant, Li and Schaberg, 2016. Henceforth, when quoting from these two works I will reference page numbers only in the mentioned order.

[12] *Zuozhuan*, Zhao 26.9, 1478; 1667.

[13] A similar position is expressed in the *Gongyang zhuan* "Yin Gong" 隱公 1 (Li X. 2000, 15–16; Adapted from Miller 2015, 7–8): 立適以長不以賢，立子以貴不以長。桓何以貴？母貴也。母貴則子何以貴？子以母貴，母以子貴。 "Sons of the principal wife are established based on seniority and not worthiness, sons of concubines are established based on nobility and not seniority. So why was Huan considered noble? Because his mother was noble. Why is the son considered noble if the mother is noble? The son is noble because the mother is noble; the mother is noble because the son is noble."

[14] Hsu 1999, 566: "In theory, the *zongfa* system provided for the succession of the Zhou kings and the rulers of the various states by primogeniture. In each generation, the eldest son took his place in the 'principal lineage' (*da zong* 大宗)."

Abdication Stories

Abdication accounts present one of the most interesting phenomena in the philosophical discourse of pre-Qin China.[15] These stories generally promoted the idea that the main prerequisite to be a ruler consists in one's talents (worthiness), irrespective of one's social standing and they are largely understood to reflect the increased social mobility of the late Chunqiu and Zhanguo periods. Yet, inheritance of the rule determined solely by meritocratic principles was highly impractical in a society where changes in one's social standing had direct ramifications for one's ancestors and it soon came to be rejected by several thinkers. In general, we can, following Yuri Pines, distinguish between three positions regarding the praxis of abdication in the received philosophical literature of the predynastic era: "support," "qualified support," and "rejection."[16] In this classification scheme, the *Zhouxun* occupies the second position, because, while confirming the historicity of abdication, it presents a unique view of this process, focusing on the dismissal of the inept sons rather than elevation of worthy commoners.

Yao's Abdication

The earliest instance of abdication, at least, according to the *Shangshu*, took place between Yao and Shun.[17] This is how the *Zhouxun* describes this momentous event in the opening of chapter 14:

206/1 昔堯之所愛子曰丹朱，不好兹（慈）孝，龔（繁）樂以愉（淪）。堯欲其賢，而弗能【206】教海（誨）乃廢弗立，而吳（虞）舜受是置。於是為篇曰：子而能兹（慈）仁，則以代【207】其身。為其無親，則不若以國予世之賢人。【179】 [18]

In the past, the son whom Yao loved was Dan Zhu, who was fond neither of compassion nor filial piety and embellished music with excessive emotions. Yao wanted him to become worthy, but was unable to instruct him. Therefore, he dismissed [Dan Zhu], not establishing him. Instead, Yu Shun received this position. Thereupon, [Yao] composed a script [addressing

---

[15] For some influential discussion of the topic, see Gu 1982, 127–133; Graham 1991, 64–67; Pines 2005a, 245–293; Pines 2013a, 167–185; Allan 2015, 17–20. For my earlier analysis of this aspect of the *Zhouxun*, see Fech 2018.

[16] Pines 2005a, 271. Sarah Allan 2015, 19 discriminates between three different claims regarding abdication legends in the transmitted texts. Accordingly, Yao, 1) abdicated power to Shun; 2) could not have abdicated power to Shun, and 3) Shun forced the rule from Yao. In this classification, the *Zhouxun* takes the first position.

[17] "Yao dian" 堯典 (Gu and Liu 2005, 1–391).

[18] By placing slip 179 at this juncture, I follow Chen Jian (2015).

Shun] that said: "If you can be compassionate and humane, then I will use [you] to replace him. If he treats his father unlovingly, then it is better to give the state to a worthy of the age."

As can be seen, Shun plays here only a secondary role and none of the complex details of his family background and ascension to power, while recorded in other sources, are presented.[19] His marginality shows that the focus of the *Zhouxun* is on the relation between a father-ruler and a son-heir. It is clear that had Dan Zhu been able to change his ways, Shun would have never been invested with power.

The *Zhouxun* is the first (and so far, the only) among the excavated texts with abdication accounts to ever mention Dan Zhu. By calling the latter Yao's favorite son, the manuscript also diverges from the transmitted sources, in which we can hardly find any signs of fatherly affection toward him.[20] The list of Dan Zhu's flaws presented above is quite lengthy, including not liking compassion and filial piety, as well as embellishing music.[21] That is, he appears as the antipode to Shun who is usually depicted as a paragon of worthiness, filial piety, and kindness, as well as a regulator of music.[22]

This judgment of Dan Zhu, as severe as it appears at first glance, is much more lenient than in the transmitted sources, where he is routinely accused of

---

[19] See, for example, *Shiji* "Wudi benji" 五帝本 (1.31–38; Nienhauser 1994a, 8–16). Allan (2016, 37–45) maintains that, in the transmitted literature, the character "Shun" resolves the conflict between the principles of virtue and heredity by taking the middle ground. The *Zhouxun*, however, seems to treat him solely as the epitome of virtue.

[20] *Shangshu* "Yao dian" 堯典 (Gu and Liu 2005, 64; Adapted from Karlgren 1950b, 3): 放齊曰：「胤子朱啟明。」帝曰：「吁！嚚訟可乎？」 "Fangqi said: 'Your heir Zhu is intelligent and clairvoyant.' The emperor said: 'Alas; he is insincere and quarrelsome: will he do?'" In the *Shiji* 1.20; Adapted from Nienhauser 1994a, 8, Yao is recorded to give a similarly negative assessment of his son: 堯曰：「誰可順此事？」放齊曰：「嗣子丹朱開明。」堯曰：「吁！頑凶，不用。」 "Yao said, "Who can manage the affairs of my position?" Fangqi said, "The Heir, Dan Zhu, is open and bright." Yao said, "Oh, he is obstinate and mean; I do not want to use him."

[21] The same expression is also found in the *Yanzi chunqiu* 晏子春秋 "Jing Gong yu fei shizi Yangsheng er li Tu. Yanzi jian" 景公欲廢適子陽生而立荼晏子諫 (Wu Z.1982, 39; Milburn 2016a, 180): 古之明君，非不知繁樂也，以為樂淫則哀，非不知立愛也，以為義失則憂。是故制樂以節，立子以道。 "The enlightened rulers of antiquity were aware of the increasing complexity of music and they viewed the corruption of music as a tragedy. They were aware of the importance of establishing those whom you love, but they viewed any failure in justice as a source of great sadness. Therefore, the composition of music should proceed according to regulation, and the appointment of an heir should be done according to the Way."

[22] The story of Shun appointing master Kui 夔 to regulate music is recorded, among others, in the *Rongchengshi* (Li L. 2002, 273) and the *Shangshu* "Shun dian" 舜典 (Lau and Chen 1995, 2/3/18).

being "arrogant" (*ao* 傲) and "cruel" (*nüe* 虐)²³ and even as the worst human being of his time,²⁴ reminiscent of the last depraved rulers of the Xia and Shang dynasties, the infamous Zhou 紂 and Jie 桀.²⁵ The reason for this idiosyncratic lenience seems to be *inter alia* the result of calling Dan Zhu the favorite son of his illustrious father, for such a paragon of wisdom and morality as Yao could not possibly be portrayed as bestowing love upon an utterly evil and depraved man.²⁶ This has the interesting consequence that the text can no longer blame Dan Zhu's utter badness for his inability to reform, as it was often done in the received literature.²⁷ In fact, the *Zhouxun* is unusually outspoken about Yao's inability to reform his favorite son, coming closely to the position vigorously criticized by Xunzi 荀子 (ca. 300–ca. 230 BCE).²⁸ While such bluntness is unlikely to signal a critic of Yao, given his overall positive image in the *Zhouxun*, it can be interpreted in many different ways, including that behind the favorite sons there often were beloved consorts and concubines, whose families subjected the ruler to their influence. Such a man, representing an entire hostile clan, could not be reformed by definition. The point here, however, was rather that Yao, despite all the efforts undertaken to transform his beloved son, was eventually able to put aside his emotions and to make a "rational" decision in favor of Shun. As such,

---

²³ *Shangshu* "Gao Yao mo" 皋陶謨 (Gu and Liu 2005, 463; Adapted from Karlgren 1950b, 11): 無若丹朱傲，惟慢遊是好，傲虐是作。罔晝夜頟頟，罔水行舟。朋淫于家，用殄厥世。 "Do not be arrogant like Dan Zhu; negligence and pleasures, only those he loved, arrogance and oppression, only those he practiced, without (difference between) day and night he was obstreperous, without water he went in a boat, he formed a gang of cronies and was licentious in the house, thereby he cut off his succession."
²⁴ *Xunzi* "Zhenglun" 正論 (Wang X. 1988, 336; Knoblock 1994, 42): 朱象者、天下之嵬，一時之瑣也。 "Zhu and Xiang were perverse figures, the pettiest men of their day."
²⁵ Allan 2016, 86: "Jie and Zhòu Xin are not only creators of *luan*. [...] their bad character is frequently described in general terms, such as *bao* 暴 "violent," *nüe* 虐 "cruel," and *yin* 淫 "inclined to excess," "licentious." These are the same terms used to describe Dan Zhu, Shang Jun, and Qi, the bad sons of Yao, Shun, and Yu."
²⁶ On the inversion of moral character in the early stories about sage rulers and their depraved sons, see Lewis 2006, 80–85. In these stories, having a "criminal" son has become "a necessary attribute or hallmark of sagely status" (*ibid.*, 82)
²⁷ *Huainanzi* "Xiuwu xun" 脩務訓 (He N. 1998, 1330; Queen and Major 2010, 774): 沉湎耽荒，不可教以道，不可喻以德，嚴父弗能正，賢師不能化者，丹朱、商均也。 "Those, who indulged deeply in wine and sex, whose conduct was unrestrained, who could not be instructed by means of the Way or taught by the example of virtue, whom a stern father could not correct, whom a worthy teacher could not transform, were Dan Zhu and Shang Jun."
²⁸ *Xunzi* "Zhenglun" 正論 (Wang X. 1988, 336; Knoblock 1994, 42): 世俗之為說者曰：「堯舜不能教化。」是何也？曰：「朱象不化。」是不然也。 "A persuader's thesis common in the world today says: "Yao and Shun were incapable of teaching and transforming." How is this? They say: "[Dan] Zhu and Xiang were not transformed." This is not so."

the account of the *Zhouxun* was designed to emphasize that the exemplary rulers of the past did not establish successors based on their emotional attachment but solely on the candidates' "worthiness." At the same time, it was the ruler's direct responsibility to instill "worthiness" into the latter.

This "educational" focus might also explain why no other sons of Yao are mentioned in the *Zhouxun*, although, according to other sources, he had many more.[29] Because in this case Yao would appear either as having utterly failed in his attempts to educate (any of) his remaining sons or as having neglected the education of his progeny altogether. Both scenarios are damaging to Yao's elevated image. Obviously, the authors of the *Zhouxun* were attempting to create a version of the legend that would be consistent with their own agenda.

The text that Yao composed was most likely addressed to Shun, to serve in his moral betterment. This motif corroborates the *Zhouxun*'s view of written text as the main means of education. Yet, this was not the only instruction that Yao had communicated to Shun. Chapter 11 states:

145/14 昔堯貳舜曰：「置嗣無宜，以賢為【145】宜，立後無正，以賢為命。」146/9

In the past, Yao enjoined Shun, saying: "In installing one's heir, no [method] is appropriate, [other than making] worthiness your standard. In establishing one's successor, no [way] is orthodox, [other than making] worthiness your imperative."

This passage demonstrates Yao's continued efforts to instruct his successor (even though Shun was not his son). As such, it expresses the main concern of the *Zhouxun*'s authors, namely, that incumbent rulers should be personally responsible for the education of their successors to make the latter suitable for the throne. Yet, while this account is consistent with the rest of the text, it is highly peculiar in the context of other works of the period. Because, at least in the received pre-Qin literature, we find no records of Yao rendering Shun (more) worthy, but only of testing his (already present) abilities.

Shun's Abdication (Or did he abdicate?)

---

[29] *Lüshi chunqiu* "Qu si" 去私 1.5 (Chen Q. 2001, 56; Knoblock and Riegel 2000, 74): 堯有子十人，不與其子而授舜；舜有子九人，不與其子而授禹；至公也。"When Yao, who had ten sons, did not share the empire with them but passed it to Shun and when Shun, who had nine sons, did not share the empire with them but passed it to Yu, both acted with perfect impartiality." The account of the *Rongchengshi* is similar (Li L. 2002, 258): 堯有子九人，不以其子為後，見舜之賢也，而欲以為後。"Yao had nine sons, but he did not make his son successor. He observed Shun's worthiness and wanted to make him his successor." The *Shiji* (1.33) also mentions nine sons of Yao.

The second story involves Shun. Being an exemplary ruler, he is also portrayed as making worthiness the sole criterion determining his succession, in an account bearing close resemblance to that of Yao[30].

> 180/1 • 舜之所愛子曰商均，舜啟道（導）之，欲其能賢，學（教）之而不可，乃放遂〈逐〉【180】之，弗使王民。於是為篇曰：「父之愛子也，劓（豈）惡貴之？念予之國，恐【181】以祟之。夫亡國之人，劓（豈）將徒亡國而已？必失其身。」【182】
>
> • The son whom Shun loved was Shang Jun. Shun instructed and guided him, wanting to enable him to become worthy. But it was impossible to instruct him, and so [Shun] expelled and banished him, not letting him be king over the people. Thereupon, [Shun] composed a script that said: "When loving a son, will a father begrudge ennobling him (i.e., making him king)? [But] considering to give him the state, [the father] is afraid to curse him with it. Now, one who destroys a state, does he really destroy just the state? He will certainly lose his life [as well]."

Like Yao, Shun too is reported to have tried his best to make his beloved son, Shang Jun, and the only wished for successor, worthy of the throne. The complete absence of Yu from this account only underscores Shun's desire to establish his son as successor. However, Shun too failed to transform his son, who, in contrast to the received literature often depicting him (together with Dan Zhu) as the embodiment of evil,[31] is not given here any characterization. Just as it was the case with Dan Zhu, the reason for this less negative treatment in the *Zhouxun* seems, once again, to lie in the ostensible love of the virtuous father. As Shun reveals in his script, his love toward Shang Jun was also at play when he sent the

---

[30] Sarah Allan 2015, 18–19 points out that authors in ancient China tended to adopt one particular view towards all traditional abdication legends. A possible exception to this regularity can be found in the "Yao dian" and "Shun dian" chapters of the *Shangshu* which, while mentioning Yao's abdication to Shun, are silent about the latter's succession, as noticed by Martin Kern (2015, 145). Kern comes to the conclusion that this idiosyncrasy goes back to the imperial scholarly elite who, wishing to promote their interests, created the image of Shun who followed the hereditary principle of succession and, 151: "delegated much of his power, followed the advice of his subordinates, and abstained from personal activism driven by his own convictions."

[31] It is particularly in the *Lun heng* 論衡 that Shang Jun is often describes as "cruel" (*nue* 虐). See, for instance, *Lun heng* "Ben xing" 本性 (Huang H. 1990, 135; Adapted from Forke 1907, 385): 所與接者，必多善矣，二帝之旁，必多賢也，然而丹朱慠，商均虐，並失帝統，歷世為戒。"Those with whom the two might have mixed, were most excellent, and the persons forming the suit of the two emperors, were all most virtuous. Nevertheless, Dan Zhu was haughty, and Shang Jun brutal. Both lacked imperial decorum to such a degree, that they were set up as a warning to coming generations."

latter into exile. Not mentioned elsewhere, this particular event appears to be an appropriation of the motif of Shun banishing different people, such as his father, Gu Sou 瞽瞍,[32] his younger brother, Xiang 象,[33] and his former ruler, Yao.[34] The motivation behind sending his heir into exile was benign, for Shun is adamant that an incapable ruler will lead the state and himself into destruction. Even though Yu is absent from this passage, he is the most likely addressee of Shun's script, just like Shun was the recipient of Yao's writing.

Another similarity in the images of Yao and Shun as presented in the *Zhouxun* is that the latter is also portrayed as having only one son whereas, according to other sources Shun was blessed with multiple offspring.[35] Evidently, mentioning other sons would only exacerbate doubts on Shun's didactic abilities.

Interestingly, Yao and, rather hesitantly, Shun are the only champions of abdication in the account of the *Zhouxun*. The famous episode of Yu relinquishing power in favor of his minister Yi 益[36] is absent from this text and Yu's son, Qi 啟, is presented as his natural heir apparent. Therefore, we can characterize the *Zhouxun* as a text that, while recognizing the historical fact of merit-based transfer of power to worthy ministers, regarded it as a measure of last resort. The abdication stories in this manuscript were formulated to confirm the normalcy of power transfer within the ruling family, while at the same time rejecting the ruler's personal preferences as a criterion determining succession.

---

[32] See *Hanfeizi* "Zhong xiao" 忠孝 (Wang X. 2003, 467; Adapted from Liao 1959, 314): 瞽瞍為舜父而舜放之，象為舜弟而殺之。放父殺弟，不可謂仁。 "Gu Sou was Shun's father but Shun exiled him; Xiang was Shun's brother but Shun killed him. Who exiled his father and killed his brother, could not be called benevolent."

[33] See *Huainanzi* "Taizu xun" 泰族訓 (He N. 1998, 1409; Queen and Major 2010, 822): 故舜放弟，周公殺兄，猶之為仁也；文公樹米，曾子架羊，猶之為知也。 "Evaluate those who pursue by what they bring back; evaluate those who flee by where they end up. Thus, Shun banished his younger brother; the Duke of Zhou executed his older brothers, but they both alike were considered humane. Duke Wen [of Jin] planted rice. Zengzi yoked a goat, but they both alike were considered wise." *Shiji* "Huainan Hengshan liezhuan" 淮南衡山列傳 talks about Yao banishing his relatives (118.3080; Watson 1993, 328): 上聞之，乃嘆曰：「堯舜放逐骨肉，周公殺管蔡，天下稱聖。何者？不以私害公。天下豈以我為貪淮南王地邪？」 "When Emperor Wen heard of this, he sighed and said, 'The ancient rulers Yao and Shun exiled their own kin, and the duke of Zhou killed his brothers Guan and Cai, and yet the whole world calls them sages. This is because, whatever they did, they did not allow their personal feelings to interfere with the public good. Do the people of the empire now suppose that I acted as I did because I was greedy for my brother's territory?'"

[34] Fang and Wang 1981, 63: 舜放堯於平陽。 "Shun banished Yao to Pingyang."

[35] The *Rongchengshi* (Li L. 2002, 263): 舜有子七人，不以其子為後，見禹之賢也，而欲以為後。 "Shun had nine sons, but he did not make his son successor. He observed Yu's worthiness and wanted to make him successor."

[36] See, for example, *Shiji* "Xia benji" 夏本紀 (2.83).

Worthiness and Education

As has been shown above, in the educational philosophy of the *Zhouxun*, successors to the throne could become worthy by receiving instructions from their sovereign fathers. This philosophy is also reflected in the work's overall setting of Lord Zhaowen instructing Prince Gong. Chapter 13, recounting a story about Zhao Yang 趙鞅, also known under his posthumous title Zhao Jianzi, and his successor Zhao Xiangzi, offers a revealing example as to the authors' vision of the ruler's didactic activities and their notion of successful outcomes:

167/2 昔趙閒（簡）子身書二牘，而親自縣（擔）之。其書之言：「節欲而聽諫，【167】敬賢勿曼（慢），使能勿賤。為人君者能行之三者，其國必彌大，其民【168】弗去散（散）。」已縣（擔）茲書，右手把一以予柏（伯）魯，左手把一以予無郢（卹）。俱【169】……在，柏（伯）魯亡其書，令之口諷之而弗能得。無郢（卹）出其書於左袂，跪（跪）【170】而進之，令口諷誦之而習。閒（簡）子曰：「魯也，不智（知）好學之有賴也，不【171】智（知）從（縱）欲之日敗也，不智（知）自以為少而年已管（暮）也。不識之三者，其【172】安能守祭？」無卹好學而智（知）貴善言，孝弟（悌）茲（慈）仁而主令弗曼（慢）。令之【173】守祭，其使能使民毋去已罷（遷）。」乃立無卹以為泰（太）子。閒（簡）子已終，無【174】卹即立（位），述（遂）為賢主。175/7

In the past, Zhao Jianzi personally inscribed two wooden tablets and recited the contents by himself. His inscription read: "Moderate desires and heed remonstrations, respect the worthy and do not treat them contemptuously. Employ the capable and do not look down on them. If a ruler is able to carry out these three points, his state will certainly become ever greater, and his people will not leave him and disperse." After reciting this inscription, he took one copy into his right hand to give to Lu, the Elder, and took the other copy into his left hand to give to Wuxu. Both… … to remain. Lu, the Elder, lost his copy, and, when asked to recite it [from memory], was unable to do so. Wuxu [on the contrary] took his copy out of his left sleeve, kneeled down and presented it [to Jianzi]. When asked to recite and chant it, he turned out to be well versed in it. Jianzi said: "Lu, you do not realize that to love learning is advantageous. You do not realize that indulging in desires brings a speedy decline. You do not realize that, although you see yourself as young, you are already in your twilight years. How can someone who does not understand these three points protect our ancestral altars? Wuxu, you are fond of learning and realize that good words are to be valued. You are filial, brotherly, compassionate, humane and not neglectful of your ruler's orders. If I entrust you with the protection of our ancestral altars, you will be able to prevent people from leaving and moving away." Thereupon, he established Wuxu as crown prince. After Jianzi died, Wuxu ascended the throne, and thereupon became a worthy sovereign.

There are several points to take from this account. First, the instruction was carried out by means of written documents which the addressees were expected to keep to themselves for study after having been advised orally. The similarity of this account to other stories in the *Zhouxun* as well as the encounters between Lord Zhaowen and Prince Gong is clear. Secondly, in the anecdote, Zhao Yang attempted to educate both of his sons and determined his successor based on their responses. This appears to entail that the ruler should engage in instructing as many sons as possible to keep his options open and to be able to choose from a wide range of potential candidates.[37] Furthermore, in this narrative, the reason for choosing Wuxu was his excellence with regard to what we can call intellectual and moral merits. On the one hand, he remembered and recognized the value of Zhao Yang's adage, which constitutes his "love of learning" (*hao xue* 好學). On the other, Wuxu is said to have routinely demonstrated filial and brotherly piety, love and humanness. The connection between the two sets of virtues is not clarified, but, at least, in the case of filial piety we can assume that Zhao Xiangzi demonstrated it by memorizing his father's words. The free recitation of Zhao Yang's words also provides a reliable tangible criterium for assessing Zhao Xiangzi's talents. This trope might have been introduced to address a problematic issue as to how one may ascertain a candidate's real abilities.[38] Indeed, the question of sincerity when it comes to displays of moral excellence in the context of power transfer was frequently broached in early China.[39]

---

[37] Note that Mencius rejected the practice of fathers educating sons out of concern that it would jeopardize their relationship (Tu 1998, 125).
[38] *Baihu tong* 白虎通 "Feng gonghou" 封公侯 (Chen Li 1994, 148; Adapted from Tjan 1952, 419–420):《曾子問》曰：「立適以長不以賢何？以言為賢不肖，不可知也。」"The *Zengzi wen* says: "Why is the appointment of an heir from [among the sons of] the principal wife determined by seniority in age, and not by worthiness? It means that whether a man will prove to be worthy or unworthy cannot be known."
[39] For instance, Mo Di warns that throne contenders might just feign their abilities to receive rewards. See *Mozi* "Lu wen" 魯問 (Sun Y. 2001, 47; Johnston 2010, 709): 魯君謂子墨子曰：「我有二子，一人者好學，一人者好分人財，孰以為太子而可？」子墨子曰：「未可知也，或所為賞與為是也。釣者之恭，非為魚賜也；餌鼠以蟲，非愛之也。吾願主君之合其志功而觀焉。」"The Prince of Lu spoke to Master Mo Zi, saying: "I have two sons. One loves learning and the other loves dividing wealth among people. Which one should I make my successor?" Master Mo Zi replied: "It is impossible to know. It may be that they do what they do for reward and praise. The fisherman's bait is not a gift to the fish. Luring a

The educational model presented in the *Zhouxun* shows several characteristic elements. Traditionally, the instruction of the heir apparent was delegated to specific officials and lineage elders.[40] Direct fatherly guidance is frequently depicted as taking place in the context of "deathbed instructions," when the heir is summoned to receive his father's last will.[41] The *Zhouxun* also contains two such stories in chapters 5 and 11. However, this work greatly expanded the scope of father-rulers' educational responsibilities by rendering their didactic endeavors the only way to guarantee the successor's aptness for the throne. One possible explanation for this radical view could be the distrust towards officials, occasionally found in the *Zhouxun*. But it is also conceivable that the educational theme was introduced to give a ruler more freedom in determining his succession. In any case, Lord Zhaowen sees himself as the only person fit to instruct Prince Gong, as expressed in chapter 6:

88/24 非 [88] 我與而言，告女（汝）其然，它人其孰敢既出茲言？ 89/17
If not for me talking to you, telling you the way things are, would other people dare to utter these words?

To reiterate, the anecdotes from chapters 2, 5, 11, 13, and, above all, 14 strongly suggest that progeny instruction was practiced by all the illustrious rulers of the past. Consequently, the father-ruler image created in the *Zhouxun* includes some elements that were conventionally associated with tutors and ministers.

As for its content, early Zhou education mainly consisted of "lineage narratives," which included musical performance and elements of dance. Consequently, successful training involved "perpetual reenactment" of the foundational events of the Zhou dynasty (Cook 2011, 309). However, while indeed referring to the founders of the Zhou dynasty (and his predecessors) Kings Wen, Wu, and Cheng, Lord Zhaowen also invokes a number of exemplary rulers from different polities. Even the father-son pair, Zhao Yang and Zhao Wuxu, whose

---

mouse with a bait is not through love of the mouse. I wish the prince to take into account both their intention and achievement, and look at the matter."

[40] *Liji* "Wen Wang shizi" 文王世子 (Yang T. 2004, 252–254) depicts both different offices in charge of education as well as the Duke of Zhou's instructions of the young King Cheng. On the office of "Grand Tutor" 大傅, see Bielenstein 1980, 5. For the significance of officials for the education of crown princes, see Lewis 2005, 201; Sabattini 2009, 76 and Liao Q. 2018, 78.

[41] On the "postmortem" instructions of King Cheng's heir, Zhao 釗, through the latter's officers, see *Shangshu* "Guming" (Gu and Liu 2005, 1830; Karlgren 1950b, 72–73). For examples of "deathbed instructions" among the excavated texts, see the *Xizhe junlao* (Chen P. 2002, 246; for alternative transcription and interpretation, see Ji 2004, 269–271; Cook 2017, 226–228) and the *Baoxun* (Li X. 2010, 143; Allan 2015, 305). For a comparison between "Guming" and *Baoxun*, see Meyer 2017a, 135–138.

59 / Chapter Five

political successes were directly responsible for the demise of the state of Jin, and, with it, the established Zhou order, appear worthy of emulation. Various virtues ascribed to the characters appearing in Lord Zhaowen's instructions can be associated with Ru teaching.[42] Yet, unlike some prominent works of Confucian philosophy, which promoted education "for the sake of one's own full spiritual and moral development" (Chen L. 2016, 91), the *Zhouxun* maintains the necessity of self-cultivation to achieve the political goal of prolonging and consolidating one's rule over a domain.

The historical examples presented above suggest that while some successors were receptive to their fathers' or rulers' instructions (Shun, Yu, Zhao Xiangzi), others were not able to reform themselves as demanded (Dan Zhu, Shang Jun, Lu, the Elder). Yet, the *Zhouxun* offers no theoretical explanation of this discrepancy and we find no debate about types and gradations of people when it comes to learning abilities.[43] Even Dan Zhu, whose disposition appears to be indeed flawed from the outset, is depicted as someone potentially capable of improving. At the same time, however, in chapter 13, Lord Zhaowen acknowledges his and Prince Gong's inferiority to Zhao Jianzi and Zhao Xiangzi respectively with the following words:

176/4 今我不如趙閒（簡）鞅，而爾有（又）不及襄子無卹。厇（諺）曰：「搑（掩）雉【176】弗得，銀（更）順其風。」今而雖不能及趙襄子，曾不若厇（諺）？ 177/19

Now, I am inferior to Zhao Jian[zi] named Yang, and you are not as good as [Zhao] Xiangzi named Wuxu. [But] a proverb says: "If, when trying to catch pheasants, you fail, change [your approach] to suit their habits." Now, even though you are not as good as Zhao Xiangzi, can you really not accord with this proverb?"

If we take these words at face value and not as expressions of humility, they imply that there was a manifest and insurmountable difference between the two representations of the Zhao lineage and protagonists of the *Zhouxun*. This view presents various challenges. For instance, it is unclear how far an aspiring worthy was allowed to deviate from a role model. In other words, what is the difference between Prince Gong's inability to reach Zhao Xiangzi's level and Dan Zhu's inability to reform himself? No answer to such questions is given, and, therefore, the text seems simply to suggest that an earnest attempt to emulate the behavior

---

[42] On the main concerns and topics of Confucian self-cultivation, see Ivanhoe 2000, 1–37.
[43] See, for instance, *Lunyu* "Yang Huo" 陽貨 (Cheng Shude 1990, 1185; Slingerland 2003, 201): 唯上知與下愚不移。 "Only the very wise and the very stupid do not change." Tripartite gradation of students was also promoted in such Daoist works as the *Laozi*, *Zhuangzi* and *Wenzi*.

of ancient role models will suffice to qualify one for the throne. But if we consider filial piety as a prominent requirement for throne contenders, then, the frequent encouragements to "make effort" (*mian* 勉) to morally better themselves amount primarily to obedience and obeisance toward the father.

In the *Mengzi*, the aptness or ineptness of rulers' offspring is believed to be determined by the Heaven, as part of "Heaven's Mandate" theory (*tian ming* 天命).[44] In the *Zhouxun*, however, this foundational idea of the Zhou political order is missing, and the next section will address some possible reasons for this.

Worthiness and "Heaven's Mandate"

The complete absence of the concept of "Heaven's Mandate" constitutes one of the most salient characteristics of the *Zhouxun*. As shown in the fragment from chapter 3, our text saw the reasons for the ascendancy of the Zhou not in the obtainment of this mandate, but solely in King Wen's decision to establish (and, if we consider chapter 14, in his ability to raise) a worthy heir. This is very different from the conventional explanations of the Zhou's rise to supremacy found in manifold bronze inscriptions as well as the earliest chapters from the *Shangshu* and *Shijing*, based on the idea of the Mandate of Heaven.[45] The same applies to the founding stories of the Xia and Shang dynasties (Allan 2015, 13–14). Many traditional elements of the theory of Heaven's Mandate and the related idea of "dynastic cycle," such as the utter depravity and evilness of the last rulers of the preceding dynasties,[46] are likewise absent from the *Zhouxun*.[47] The focus is placed here solely on worthiness, which alone is deemed a sufficient precondition for rising to power regardless of the situation in other polities. Among the most successful states, our text mentions Wei (ch. 10) and Zhao (ch. 13), which is astonishing insofar as their recognition, alongside Han, as the official fiefs of *zhuhou* 諸侯 was tantamount to the ultimate collapse of the Zhou order.[48] Evidently, the *Zhouxun* had already detached itself from the conventional models of power legitimization. In view of this, it can be argued that the protagonist "Lord

---

[44] *Mengzi* "Wan Zhang shang" (Jiao 1987, 647; Lau 2003, 207): 舜、禹、益相去久遠，其子之賢不肖，皆天也，非人之所能為也。 "Shun and Yu differed from Yi greatly in the length of time they assisted the Emperor, and their sons differed as radically in their moral character. All this was due to Heaven and could not have been brought about by man."
[45] For the Mandate of Heaven in early sources, see Nylan 2001, 136; Li F. 2006, 157; Du 2007, 149–155; Kern 2010a, 23–24.
[46] *Shiji* "Xia benji" and "Yin benji."
[47] For "dynastic cycle," see Allan 2015, 10–15.
[48] *Shiji* "Zhou benji" (4.158; Nienhauser 1994a, 79): 威烈王二十三年，九鼎震。命韓、魏、趙為諸侯。 "In the twenty-third year of King Weilie, the Nine Tripods shook. The king appointed Han, Wei, and Zhao as feudal lords."

Chapter Five

Zhaowen" promoted a new set of (Zhou) principles, meant to replace ideas commonly associated with Zhou feudalism, and above all, the Mandate of Heaven.

This move is understandable given the bankruptcy of the idea of Mandate of Heaven at the alleged time of the *Zhouxun*'s composition. This notion began to change soon after its introduction during the Western Zhou. In addition to other things, its transformation involved a transition from the individual to the collective possession of the Mandate reflecting the growing number of Zhou rulers.[49] But by the time of the Warring States period, the notion became outright obsolete as it could no longer explain the political realities of the day, such as, for instance, the (simultaneous) ascension of the new power centers led by representatives of the former ministerial lineages. The authors of the *Zhouxun* must have been well-aware of this. Yet, their creative motivation was, most likely, not confined to the mere attempts to replace an outdated theory but represented a reaction to some specific political events. In the next chapter, I attempt to address the possible circumstances in which the *Zhouxun* was created as well as the goal this book was meant to accomplish, and I start by examining the manuscript's parallels to other texts.

---

[49] Luo Xinhui concludes that two basic models concerning this question can be identified. The earlier accounts, such as the bronze inscriptions from the beginning of the Western Zhou, always see King Wen as the sole recipient of the Mandate, while King Wu is mainly praised for his military conquest of the Shang. In later sources, however, they are both depicted as equally possessing Heaven's blessings to rule over the world (2015, 57–64). Still later, the entire Zhou lineage was declared as the recipient of the Mandate for thirty generations (*Zuozhuan*, Xuan 3).

Chapter 6

Wider Context

The *Zhouxun* contains several parallels to other early Chinese texts. In some cases, these parallels revolve around similar narrative techniques and/or similar vocabulary. In others, however, we are unmistakably dealing with instantiations of the same lengthy narratives. To determine the *Zhouxun*'s position within the early historical and philosophical literature, in the present section, I discuss its parallels to other texts.

Zuozhuan

There are several dimensions along which one can examine the similarities between the *Zuozhuan* and the *Zhouxun*. To begin with, some of the narratives studied here are best understood against the background of the information provided in the former text. Such are the stories about Lord Wen of Jin (ch. 6), Lord Mu of Qin (chs. 7 and 14), Lord Gong of Cao (ch. 8) and Zhao Dun (ch. 9). Some central ideas of the *Zhouxun* also appear to have been formulated under the influence of the *Zuozhuan* (often, in direct opposition to it).[1] The two works show affinity in their systematic use of proverbs, as *yan*, alongside frequent references to the poetic and documentary genres.[2] There are also some parallels in regard to the *shi* quotations. Not only do the two works correspond in quoting the same poetry lines not mentioned in other pre-Qin works,[3] they also use the same combinations of the poetic "signature lines" unatessted elsewhere in the writings of the period.[4] Furthermore, as already pointed out, the formulaic expressions used by Lord Zhaowen to conclude his narratives are very common in the *Zuozhuan*. None of this suggests direct borrowing, but the authors of the *Zhouxun* seem to have been familiar with and influenced by the ideas and techniques of writing history characteristic to that foundational work of Chinese historiography.

---

[1] This concerns primogeniture as well as the ritual. On the latter, see Vermander 2022, 51.
[2] For a list of proverbs in the *Zuozhuan*, see Chu 1970: 7–11. For their analysis, see Chien 2008.
[3] This concerns the lines which correspond to Mao 7 (*Zuozhuan*, Cheng 12; *Zhouxun* 9), Mao 254 (Xi 5 and Zhao 6); *Zhouxun* 4 and 14) and Mao 288 (Xi 22; *Zhouxun* 1). For appearance of these lines in the *Zuozhuan*, see Ho and Chan 2004, 9, 254 and 285.
[4] Chapter 1 quotes the same *shi*-lines (corresponding to Mao 195 and 288) and in the same order as the *Zuozhuan*, Xi 22.7, 395; 355–357.

Lüshi chunqiu

The *Zhouxun* and the *Lüshi chunqiu* share two almost identical narratives.[5] In the *Zhouxun*, they constitute the content of chapters 7 and 9, while in the Qin compendium they can be found in the sections "Ai shi" 愛士 (8.4) and "Baogeng" (15.4) respectively.

In my previous analysis of these two cases, I claim that the two chapters of the *Zhouxun* can be considered the source for the *Lüshi chunqiu* content for several reasons (Fech 2020b). First, the formula "this is what [X] expresses in saying" (*ci* [X] *zhi suo wei ye*), which summarizes both stories, is common in the *Zhouxun*, while in the much more voluminous *Lüshi chunqiu* it can be seen only twice, namely, in the narratives corresponding to the work under investigation here. The same is true of the rhetorical question "how can ..." (*hu ke* (*yi*)). Furthermore, in the *Lüshi chunqiu*, both anecdotes had to be integrated into the larger context by means of brief introductions and concluding generalizations absent from the *Zhouxun*. Finally, and most remarkably, in the "Baogeng" chapter, the narrative following the account with paralles in the *Zhouxun* is dedicated to Lord Zhaowen of Zhou. As a result, the content corresponding to chapter 9 and the story about its alleged author appear together in the *Lüshi chunqiu*. The chances that such an arrangement was coincidental are minimal and, as I argued, it is best explained by assuming that the authors of the "Baogeng" chapter associated the parallel account with Lord Zhaowen as its "author." This was certainly only possible if they were familiar with the latter text (and borrowed from it).

Because the discussed parallel accounts appear in different parts of the *Lüshi chunqiu*, the "Almanacs" (*ji* 紀) and "Examinations" (*lan* 覽), it stands to reason that their authors were following the same editorial principles when dealing with borrowed materials, at least in the case of the *Zhouxun*.[6] This is an important finding in the discussion about the composition of the *Lüshi chunqiu*. In the

---

[5] Han 2015, 278, tentatively determined the *Zhouxun* as predating the *Lüshi chunqiu* based on the two texts' common "Daoist" traits, their general structure and Lü Buwei's 呂不韋 (?–235 BCE) personal connection to the supposed place of origin of the *Zhouxun*. Liao Q. 2018, 75–76, comes to the same conclusion based on a comparison of quotation practices in the two works.

[6] While most scholars agree that the three parts of this work were created successively, the order of their creation is determined differently. As a result, the order of the received text, namely, twelve "Almanacs," eight "Examinations," and six "Discussions" (*lun* 論), has been challenged by several prominent scholars. For instance, Yang Shuda believes that the "Examinations" were produced first, followed by the "Discussions" and finally the "Almanacs" (for a discussion of Yang's arguments, see Lau 1991, 5–6). Unlike Yang, Wang Liqi is convinced of the anteriority of the "Discussions," which are followed by the "Almanacs" and the "Examinations" (2002, 9–12). At the same time, the conventional arrangement of the text has been supported by Ho 2015, 82–85.

following, I show that a comparison between *Zhouxun* and *Hanfeizi* might also shed light on the formation of the latter's system of thought.

The *Hanfeizi*

The *Zhouxun* shows some similarities to the legalist classic *Hanfeizi* in its view of ministers. Even though these similarities are not as clear and extensive as those between the *Zhouxun* and the *Lüshi chunqiu*, they are specific enough to merit an investigation. On the one hand, the two works correspond in their understanding of ministers as a source of mortal danger for the sovereign and propose similar strategies to keep them at bay.[7] On the other, both texts acknowledge ministers' great importance. In what follows, I deal with these correspondences in the order of their mention.

To begin with, the two texts converge on the paramount significance of "rewards and punishments" (*shangfa* 賞罰) and their correct distribution. The ruler is the sole authority responsible for meting out rewards and punishments. The very first sentence of the *Zhouxun* states:

> 2/2 為人君者，賞罰不可以不當，賞罰不當則毋以使民。 2/21
> A ruler's rewards and punishments must not be inappropriate. If his rewards and punishments are inappropriate, he will have no means to employ people.

This passage places the people on the receiving end of "rewards and punishments" and does not specify what constitutes their "appropriateness" or "inappropriateness." However, in the *Hanfeizi*, rewards and punishments are considered "the two handles" of the ruler, indispensable for efficient governance and his personal safety (Goldin 2013b, 5–6). Their effectiveness is rooted in the human propensity to seek pleasure and benefits and to avoid suffering and detriment. The correctness of their distribution is based on the principle of *xingming* 形名 and depends on how exactly a minister is able to live up to his propositions (Goldin 2013b, 9–10).

Furthermore, the two works correspond in proposing secretive behavior and furtiveness as the best way of dealing with subordinates. The first chapter of the *Zhouxun* underscores the pivotal importance for a monarch to be well-informed about his subordinates' sentiments, yet not to express his opinion:

---

[7] For a previous study of the topic, see Han 2015, 268–271.

65 / Chapter Six

11/2 為人君者，不可以不好聽，不好聽則毋從智（知）下之請（情），故必聽而勿聞，【11】智（知）而默前。此䛐（諺）之所謂曰：「不狂不聾，不能為人公」者也。故《書》曰【12】「大智佁（似）狂」，其此之謂乎？13/9

A ruler must not fail to be fond of listening (to others). If he is not fond of listening, he will not know the sentiments of his subordinates. And so, it is imperative (for him) to listen but not be heard; to know but remain silent. This is what a proverb expresses in saying: "If you are not mad and deaf, you cannot become the duke of the people." And so, when a Document says: "Great wisdom resembles madness," does it [not] give expression to this [case]?

Accordingly, the ability to feign ignorance is identified as the main prerequisite for securing political authority. The particular reason for this deceitful behavior is not clarified. Still, the *Zhouxun* falls back on the authority of proverbs and Documents to support its argument.

The following instruction by Lord Zhaowen from the same chapter provides some clarification as to why it is necessary for a ruler to conceal his feelings and thoughts:

15/12 為人君者，喜怒不可還（旋）發之於【15】前。有所唯，未可以還（旋）唯之。有所非，未可以還（旋）非之。穆穆乎！賢主之【16】心，如臨深淵，其誰能極之？故《詩》曰：「戰戰淩淩（兢兢），如臨深淵，如履（履）薄冰。」夫【17】君人者將如臨深淵，而臣人者將如履（履）薄冰。此䛐（諺）之所謂曰：「為【18】主不易，為臣不易」者也。夫為人君而有所唯，則還（旋）唯之，則所唯【19】者，其庸必唯㦯？有所非，則還（旋）非之，則所非者，其庸必非乎？故為【20】人君而是非不當，則為不明。為上而不明，其下將代之。故《詩》曰【21】「敬之敬之，天度定之」，此之謂也。22/12

A ruler must not make an immediate display of joy or anger. If he approves of something, he must not express his approval immediately. If he disapproves of something, he must not express his disapproval immediately. So profound! The heart of a worthy sovereign! As if approaching a deep abyss, who can fathom it? And so, an Ode says, "Be apprehensive, be cautious, as if approaching a deep abyss, as if treading on thin ice." Now, the ruler should be as if approaching a deep abyss, and the minister should be as if treading on thin ice. This is what is expressed in the proverb, "To be a sovereign is not easy; to be a minister is not easy." Now, if a ruler has something he approves of and expresses his approval immediately, is what he approves of truly what should be approved of? If a ruler has something he disapproves of and expresses his disapproval immediately, is what he disapproves of truly what should be disapproved of? And so, a ruler whose [expressions of] approval and disapproval are inappropriate, is not clairvoyant. A superior who is not clairvoyant will be replaced by his subordinates. And so, [when] an Ode says, "Be reverent, be reverent. The Heavenly measure will bring you stability," it gives expression to this.

The *Zhouxun* promotes such behavior out of concern for the objectivity of emotion-based judgements. Therefore, the ruler is advised to refrain from immediate display of emotions and conclusions, and to assess any situation rationally. On the other hand, the *Hanfeizi* discourages a monarch from disclosing what he really thinks and feels, taking it as axiomatic that ministers will take advantage of his revelation to grab hold of sovereign power ("Zhudao" 主道 (Wang X. 2003, 26)). It is at this point that Han Fei usually brings in depictions of the obscure, ineffable Way as a cosmological counterpart to the ruler's proposed surreptitiousness.

Finally, there is a passage that concludes the first month's instruction:

22/13 為人君者，不可以通其群臣之言，通其群臣之【言】，則 [22] 臣相智（知）情，臣相智（知）情則不和，不和則乳（亂）主，乳（亂）主則主危。故《書》曰「周之密之，重之閉之，[23] 福則存矣。」此為人君者所謹慎也。24/13

A ruler must not communicate the words of his minsters to one another. If he communicates the words of his ministers to one another, they will all know one another's true sentiments. If the ministers all know what each other truly feels, they will not be in harmony. If they are not in harmony, they will plunge the sovereign into chaos. If they plunge the sovereign into chaos, the sovereign will be in danger. And so, a Document says: "Be secretive! Be furtive! Take it seriously! Keep it locked up! Then you will be able to preserve your blessings." These are things about which a ruler should be cautious and apprehensive.

Accordingly, when communicating the words of his ministers to one another, a ruler will cause "disharmony" among them. Possibly, this refers to the building of cliques and factions among the subjects, which can become so powerful as to undermine the ruler's position. In the already familiar manner, the *Zhouxun* concludes the argument with a *shu* quote. The justification for particular political practices is thus again provided by invoking the authority of a respected text. The *Hanfeizi* also contains a number of passages that admonish the ruler against allowing ministers to communicate with each other and against revealing their words to one another. Otherwise, it is said, they will be unwilling to speak their mind and the monarch will thereby lose the all-important access to information and eventually forfeit his position.[8]

Their basic similarity notwithstanding, the two texts place the discussion of the ruler-minister relationship into two radically different contexts: authoritative sayings in the *Zhouxun* and cosmological speculations in the *Hanfeizi*.[9] This suggests that the "poker-face" philosophy they espouse might have been first formulated as a kind of practical knowledge without any justification through higher principles.[10] It is not a coincidence that we find some expressions of this philosophy in the manuscript *Xizhe junlao* without any recourse to cosmological speculations (Cook 2017, 227). It was only later when this idea was integrated into larger bodies of text that it became connected to various ideological stances. It thus seems unlikely that Han Fei deduced this tenet from a particular cosmology.[11] Rather, it would appear that Han Fei's strategies for "empowering the ruler vis-à-vis his aides," which are often considered his main "ideological innovation" (Pines 2013b, 72–73), were ultimately not his. His unique contribution was of a different kind, namely, to combine all the different ideas presented above in a single system of thought with which he had hoped to attain his political goals.

As for the appreciation of ministers found in the *Zhouxun* and the *Hanfeizi*, it also serves different ends. In the *Hanfeizi*, it is contrasted with their habitual demonization and, most likely, it was meant to draw the ruler's attention to "a devoted minority within the officialdom" (Pines 2013b, 82), who had superior understanding of governance and to whom the ruler should relegate his power. As such heroic figures, Han Fei regarded the illustrious ministers Yi Yin 伊尹, Guan Zhong 管仲, Wu Qi 吳起 and, ostensibly, also himself. According to Yuri Pines, the use of the *Laozi*-inspired vocabulary and practices of self-concealment, quietude and non-action had the insidious goal of neutralizing the ruler, rendering him completely subdued by the political system that he was supposed to steer (Pines 2013b, 83). Following this logic, Han Fei's references to the Way as the cosmological counterpart of the ruler were also deceptive, emphasizing only those aspects of the Dao-centered cosmology which would compel the ruler to act in accordance with Han Fei's own schemes. In the *Zhouxun*, where there is

---

[8] *Hanfeizi* "Wang zheng" 亡徵 (Wang X. 2003, 110) and "Wai chu shui you shang" 外儲說右上 (ibid., 310).

[9] This, of course, is not the only difference between these two works. For instance, the *Zhouxun* operates neither with the cosmological concept of the Way nor with the legalist terms of "law" (*fa* 法), "power of authority" (*shi* 勢), "techniques" (*shu* 術) or "performance and title" (*xingming* 形名) central to the *Hanfeizi* (Liu Z. 2020, 309–317).

[10] For Han Fei's poker-face philosophy, see Goldin 2013b, 17.

[11] Albert Galvany 2013, 104 proposes that this particular view of ruler-minister relationship was based on "certain cosmological patterns, derived in great measure from expositions in the *Laozi* and similar texts."

neither vilification of the ministers nor association of the ruler with the ineffable Dao, a contrasting treatment of ministers seems to have been caused by different consideration. Possibly, it simply reflects the historical realities of early China where there were enough examples of both states which came to dominance due to able ministerial assistance and states which were destroyed at the hands of treacherous aides. In any case, the setting of the *Zhouxun*, in which a powerholder provides instructions to his designated successor, serves as a much more suitable background for expressing distrust and warnings against ministerial disloyalty than the writings of a person, who himself aspired to become an aide to a ruler.[12]

Possible Quotations of the *Zhouxun*

In light of the possibility that the *Zhouxun* was known to the authors of the *Lüshi chunqiu*, several other passages from the latter deserve our attention. The first appears in section 15.1, "Shenda" 慎大, the opening of the same chapter which contains the above discussed "Baogeng":

賢主愈大愈懼，愈彊愈恐。[…] 故賢主於安思危，於達思窮，於得思喪。《周書》曰：「若臨深淵，若履薄冰」，以言慎事也。[13]
A worthy sovereign, the greater he becomes, the more apprehensive he grows; the stronger he gets, the more fearful he grows. […] And so, a worthy sovereign, when at peace, he contemplates danger, when successful, he contemplates failure, when gaining, he contemplates loss. [When] a Document of Zhou says: "Be as facing a deep abyss, as if treading on thin ice," it discusses [the necessity of] being cautious about undertakings.

The quoted fragment from a Document of Zhou has a counterpart in the famous poem "Xiaomin" (Mao 195). Therefore, it is sometimes used to corroborate the view that, in (some) early works, the genre designations *shu* and *shi* were used interchangeably (Xu T. 2009, 316). However, these two lines are also quoted (as *shi*) in a discussion of a "worthy sovereign" (*xianzhu* 賢主) in the first chapter of the *Zhouxun* (17/18–25). It, thus, seems entirely possible that the authors of the "Shenda" section identified this content as belonging to the documentary type because of its appearance in the *Zhouxun*. In any case, the authors of the Qin compendium appear to not have been dogmatic about genre distinctions, switching between the *shi* and *shu* labels as the situation required (Fech 2020, 195).

---

[12] Yuri Pines 2013b, 82 expresses Han Fei's dilemma as follows: "How should a ruler treat an intellectual who claimed that no intellectual could be trusted?"
[13] Chen Q. 2001, 850; compare the translation in Knoblock and Riegel 2000, 337.

The second example appears in section 19.5, "Shiwei" 適威. There, we find another quotation from a *Zhoushu* with a counterpart in the *Zhouxun*:

《周書》曰：「民善之則畜也，不善則讎也。」有讎而眾，不若無有。[14]

A Document of Zhou says, "As for the people, if you treat them well, they will be your supporters; If you do not treat them well, they will be your enemies." To have multitudes of enemies is worse than having none.

While the provenance of these two *shu*-lines has been debated, having no parallels in the transmitted Document compilations,[15] the *Lüshi chunqiu* names kings Tang and Wu as the two ancient rulers who were able to embody the principle of benevolent government promoted therein. Now, in the last chapter of the *Zhouxun*, King Wen of Zhou instructs his son, the future King Wu, with the following words (187/5–188/4):

天下之民，爾能愛之，斯而畜也。海內之眾，爾弗能利，斯而讎也。
The people of All-under-Heaven! If you are able to care for them, they will yield to you. The masses within the [four] seas! If you are unable to benefit them, they will be your enemy.

This close parallel might suggest the same scenario as above: the authors of the "Shiwei" made use of the *Zhouxun* and indicated their source as a "Document of Zhou." If this is correct, then two of the four *Zhoushu* citations made in the *Lüshi chunqiu* (Xu T. 2009, 324) would go back to the *Zhouxun*.

In the *Huainanzi* there is also a quotation from an unknown *Zhoushu* with a verbatim counterpart in the *Zhouxun*, which goes as follows:

《周書》曰：「掩雉不得，更順其風。」[16]
A Document of Zhou says: "If you try to catch a pheasant and do not get any, adjust [your hunting techniques] to suit their habits."

---

[14] Chen Q. 2001, 1289; compare translation in Knoblock and Riegel 2000, 493.
[15] While some scholars ascribe them to a writing authored by the Duke of Zhou, others view them as a lost fragment of the *Yi Zhoushu* (Xu T. 2009, 329). There are also similar lines in the *Huainanzi* (He N. 1998, 874) and *Shuoyuan* (Xiang 1987, 152).
[16] *Huainanzi* "Lanming xun" 覽冥訓 (He N. 1998, 498; Major 2010, 230).

The parallel passage in the *Zhouxun* reads:

176/21 薝（諺）曰：「挊（掩）雉【176】弗得，銀（更）順其風。」 177/6
A proverb says: "If, when trying to catch pheasants, you fail, change [your approach] to suit their habits."

As can be seen, the two texts determine the literary genre of the relevant content differently: a proverb versus a document. Considering the above instance of a *shi*-fragment quoted in the *Lüshi chunqiu* as a Document of Zhou, we may hypothesize that the authors of the *Huainanzi* were following a similar strategy. Namely, they borrowed this proverb from the *Zhouxun* yet gave it a designation reflecting its supposed literary genre.[17]

Possible Influence on Other Texts

Chapter 5 of the *Zhouxun* provides a very specific account of the events which took place in the aftermath of the annihilation of the state of Wu. Supposedly, the body of King Helü (r. 514–496) was disenterred ten years after his passing. Unmentioned in other texts, even those which otherwise contain detailed descriptions of the Wu-Yue conflict, the report about the sad fate of Helü's remains appears only in the *Lüshi chunqiu*[18] and Liu Xiang's 劉向 (77–6 BCE) memorial to the Han emperor Chengdi (51–7 BCE) as recorded in the former's biography in the *Hanshu*.[19] Since the authors of (some chapters of) the *Lüshi chunqiu* appear to have been familiar with the *Zhouxun* and incorporated parts of it in their works, it is very likely they took this information from there. As for Liu Xiang, he could have drawn from either of the sources or both of them.

---

[17] Note that in the Tsinghua manuscript *Zifan, Ziyu* 子犯子余 (Zifan and Ziyu) a similar saying is attributed to Lord Mu of Qin. Lord Mu uses it as an analogy for his abilities but makes no references to the Zhou lore (Li X. 2017, 92, slip 10, and 97n40).

[18] *Lüshi chunqiu* "Zhihua" 知化 (Chen Q. 2001, 1562; Knoblock and Riegel 2000, 593): 子胥非不先知化也，諫而不聽，故吳為丘墟，禍及闔廬。"It is not that Wu Zixu did not recognize in advance what would happen, but that he remonstrated and the king would not heed him. Hence, the site of the capital of Wu became a wasted mound, and the catastrophe extended even to Fuchai's father, Helu." The *Lüshi chunqiu* commentator Gao You 高誘 was obviously not aware of the disentombment story as he interpreted these words to the effect that, after the demolishment of Wu's ancestral temple, Helü no longer received sacrificial offerings. (Chen Q. 2001, 1565n9) For further discussion, see Han 2015, 292–293.

[19] *Hanshu* "Chu Yuan Wang zhuan" 楚元王傳 (36.1954): 逮至吳王闔閭，違禮厚葬，十有餘年，越人發之。"When it came to Wu king Helü, in disregard of ritual, he was given an elaborate funeral. [But] after some ten years, the Yue opened his grave."

In light of the above analysis, the following section suggests possible reasons for the creation of the *Zhouxun*.

Political Background and Possible Reasons for Creation

The model of power transfer as developed in the *Zhouxun* presents a combination of hereditary and meritocratic principles, but in a very different way when compared to the idea of "Heaven's Mandate" and dynastic cycle. In fact, the text challenges the rules of inheritance which were an integral part of the latter system.[20] Meritocratic discourse is usually understood as having originated within the class of officeholders stemming from lower aristocracy (*shi* 士), who thereby sought to improve their social standing (Pines 2005a, 272). In view of the emphatic stress on the importance of qualified ministerial assistance (albeit mixed with caution), there can be little doubt that the *Zhouxun* was the product of the same fertile intellectual ground. Yet, as it was evidenced in the foregoing sections, this work supports the political aspirations of a very distinct group of people: those members of royal families who traditionally were at a disadvantage in throne succession, such as, for example, younger progeny or sons by concubines.

In my opinion, this peculiar focus on the most junior members of ruling families is best explained with recourse to chapter 11 which narrates events that allegedly took place in the state of Qin only a few decades prior to the encounters between Lord Zhaowen and Prince Gong. Accordingly, Lord Xian of Qin dismissed his (inept) heir apparent Zhong Jingzi in favor of a (unnamed) son by a concubine (*nie* 孽). Surprisingly, by placing this event in the same chapter as the encounter between Yao and Shun, the authors suggested that both sovereigns demonstrate the same principle of respecting the worthy. In other words, from Lord Zhaowen's perspective, Lord Xian of Qin represented the most recent (and, perhaps, most radical) example of following the meritocratic principles introduced by Yao. Now, there is a wealth of historical evidence that the Qin was a "decisively meritocratic regime" (Pines 2013a, 185–187). Yet, the reference to the establishment of sons by concubines in Qin made in the *Zhouxun* may go back to considerations unrelated to worthiness. As is well known, the father of Qin Shi Huangdi 秦始皇帝, King Zhuangxiang of Qin 秦莊襄王 (r. 250–247 BCE), was a son by a concubine, who succeeded in inheriting the throne only with the help of Lü Buwei 呂不韋 (292–235 BCE), the future patron of the *Lüshi*

---

[20] Note that the rule of primogeniture did not only inform the order of succession but also determined the practice of ancestor worship, enfeoffment etc. For the rules of enfeoffment, see Chen X. 1992, 89–93. For the connection of the *zhaomu* 昭穆 order of ancestor worship with patrilinear succession, see Loewe 2016, 37–38.

chunqiu.²¹ And also, the first emperor himself had a mother of low social standing.²² It thus could be argued that this chapter of the *Zhouxun* was *inter alia* created to show that the installation of King Zhuangxiang (and, possibly, Qin Shi Huang's) was consistent with the most extolled practices of antiquity.²³ It is not unlikely, considering that the *Zhouxun* was known to the authors of the *Lüshi chunqiu*. Then, this account would amount to a veiled attempt of flattering both a Qin ruler and his powerful chancellor.

In fact, as I have argued elsewhere, there are reasons to assume the *Zhouxun* was composed to legitimize Qin's overthrow of Zhou, which was completed in 249 BCE by none other than Lü Buwei.²⁴ That the authors chose to do this in the setting of the *Zhouxun* can be explained through several factors. To begin with, Qin identified themselves with Zhou and saw themselves as the latter's rightful successors (Falkenhausen and Shelach 2014, 44). Moreover, Lord Zhaowen was perceived as the last able ruler of the Zhou dynasty and portrayed as the teacher of King Hui of Qin in the *Lüshi chunqiu*. It is possible that some scholars among the latter's authors attributed the rise of Qin (King Hui was the first Qin ruler to be assume the title "king") to Lord Zhaowen and his teachings. Furthermore, the theoretical openness of the *Zhouxun* rendering a ruler's worthiness the main precondition and justification for the conquest of other countries is consistent with Qin ideology. Considering this, it is not unlikely that Lord Zhaowen's instructions were created to provide a theoretical framework and justification for the Qin's conquest of the Zhou.

Philosophical Affiliation

In addition to bearing direct testimony to the philosophical discourse of long-gone times, the *Zhouxun* has another intriguing side to it. Namely, in the bibliographical chapter of the *Hanshu*, "Yiwenzhi" 藝文志, there is a mention of a work with the same title. The *Zhouxun* that was kept in the Han imperial library

---

²¹ *Shiji* "Lü Buwei liezhuan" 呂不韋列傳 (85.2506; Vyatkin 1996, 295–296). Bodde 1986, 42. Note the similarity between King Zhuangxiang's speech to Lü Buwei as recorded in the *Shiji* "Lü Buwei liezhuan" (85.2506) and Lord Zhaowen's address to Zhang Yi in the "Bao geng" chapter of the *Lüshi chunqiu* (Chen Q. 2001, 902).
²² *Shiji* "Qin Shi Huang benji" 秦始皇本紀 (6.223; Nienhauser 1994a, 127).
²³ Depictions of this Qin sovereign as having "spread virtue" (*shi de* 施德) and "extended kindness to the people" (*bu hui yu min* 布惠於民) found in the *Shiji* "Qin benji" (5.219; Nienhasuer 1995, 122) are similar to the ruler's ideal promoted by the *Zhouxun*.
²⁴ *Shiji* 5.219; Adapted from Nienhauser 1994a, 122: 東周君與諸侯謀秦，秦使相國呂不韋誅之，盡入其國。"The Lord of East Zhou plotted with the feudal lords against Qin. Qin had Lü Buwei, the Prime Minister, punish him and annexed his entire territory." For my earlier contributions, see Fech 2018, 174–176, and 2020b, 215–217.

comprised 14 chapters or *pian* 篇 and was listed under the "Daoism" section (*Hanshu* 30.1730). The concomitant comment by Liu Xiang was rather unflattering, stating: "A petty book from among the people, its sayings are vulgar and trivial" (*ren jian xiao shu, qi yan su bo* 人間小書，其言俗薄).[25] So, the question we are facing is whether that "trivial" work of Daoist philosophy was identical to the Peking University manuscript carrying the same name. This question has been answered differently in recent publications and scholars who weighed in on it usually reach their conclusion by comparing the Peking version with some representatives of Daoist philosophy. Scholars who defend the Daoist affiliation of the work, highlight certain aspects of it (distinct ideas,[26] linguistic properties,[27] as well as its overall conceptual soundness[28]) which they deem characteristic of Daoism, while their opponents attempt to do the same to demonstrate the work's basic incongruity with Daoist tenets[29] and textual practices.[30] Regardless of specific arguments from both sides, having two different texts with the same title and similar scope is a highly unlikely coincidence. Therefore, it appears that the *Hanshu* entry and Peking University versions go back to the same source.

However, with no Dao-based cosmology, only sporadic mentions of cultivation practices, a plethora of notions associated with Ru teachings, and frequent quotations of the Odes and Documents, the *Zhouxun* looks like a very unusual representative of Daoism. In my opinion, the only aspect which could justify its categorization as "Daoist" is the idea that "Great wisdom resembles madness" (*dazhi sikuang* 大智似狂) from chapter 1. To begin with, this maxim is formulated as a paradox, very characteristic of central Daoist works, especially, the *Laozi*. Juxtaposed here as antonyms, "wisdom" and "madness" form a paradoxical message which corresponds to one of three main types of paradoxes in the *Laozi* (de Reu 2006, 282). Then, we find here the "celebration of *kuang*" which was a salient feature of another Daoist work, the *Zhuangzi* (McLeod 2021, 23). Even though in the latter, "madmen" were associated with the "wilds, with untamed humanity,

---

[25] Yan Shigu 顏師古 in *Hanshu* 30.1732n9. This entry seems to indicate that the copy of the *Zhouxun* available to Liu Xiang came from a private collection, and that, prior to that, the text was not part of the imperial library. Compare to Liu Xiang's editorial comment to the *Shuoyuan* 說苑 (Xiang 1987, 1).

[26] Yan Buke 2012a, 308 emphasizes the idea of madness.

[27] Yuan Qing 2017, 71–72 maintains that the frequent use of negations demonstrates the "sentiment of fear" (*kongju qingxu* 恐懼情緒) characteristic of the HuangLao branch of Daoism.

[28] Han highlights the correspondence between self-cultivation and politics (2015, 270–271) as well as the pronounced eclecticism of the *Zhouxun* (2015, 275).

[29] Cheng Shaoxuan 2013, 564–566 points out the philosophical discrepancy between the *Zhouxun* and the *Zhuangzi*.

[30] Kusano Tomoko 2018, 44 shows that the text's quotations from the canonical compilations of *Shi* and *Shu* are incompatible with the Daoist rejection of the Confucian canon.

nonhuman animals, the overgrown forest, the various barbarians" (*ibid.*, 92)[31]. Furthermore, the ruler's ability to conceal his thoughts, labelled as "madness" in the *Zhouxun*, is directly associated with the (possession of the) Way in the *Hanfeizi* and *Liutao,* i.e., books which are traditionally affiliated with Daoism and/or the HuangLao doctrine. In both of these works, the adage that "the Way is in what cannot be seen" (*dao zai bu kejian* 道在不可見) refers to the secretive demeanor of a ruler.[32] Therefore, it is not unlikely that either Liu Xiang or his son Liu Xin 劉歆 (46 BCE–23 CE), the author of the *Qi lüe* 七略, on which Ban Gu's 班固 (32–92) "Yiwenzhi" was based (Wolff 1999, 64), or Ban Gu himself, characterized the text as Daoist based on this content.

Certainly, it could also be argued that the *Zhouxun*'s philosophical affiliation in the "Yiwenzhi" simply reflected the original background of its creation as part of the Daoist "school of thought," which was known to the authors of the early bibliographies. Yet, the existence of a unified Daoist school during the pre-imperial times is yet to be demonstrated. This, of course, is not to deny the existence of various teacher-student lineages concerned with specific macrobiotic practices (Roth 2021, 8) or that the Jixia academy was a fertile breeding ground for the syncretic ideas that later came to be known as HuangLao philosophy (Hu 1998, 2). But there are justified doubts that, in the pre-Qin period, these practices or ideas were pursued as expressions of a consolidated "Daoist" worldview. Instead, what we find in these texts is a great variety of (often contradictory) views even with regard to the most characteristics notions, such as *wuwei* or *ziran* (Liu X. 1991). Considering the initially very "loose" school identities, it is small wonder that the *Guanzi* could be given a "Legalist" affiliation in the *Qi lüe*, while appearing under the "Daoist" section in the *Hanshu*'s bibliography (Chen L. 2005, 12). Perhaps the *Zhouxun* entry's positioning in the catalogue between texts associated with "Laozi," on the one hand, and the "Yellow Emperor," on the other,—the two main groups in the Daoist section (Seidel 1978, 31)—, could also be interpreted as reflecting the author's aporia when determining the exact affiliation of the work.

Therefore, the Daoist affiliation of the *Zhouxun* in the *Hanshu* is unlikely to signal that it was originally conceived to express a Daoist view of history, but it is rather indicative of the need to categorize traditional knowledge based on the political realities of the Han dynasty. Under these circumstances, it seems advisable to avoid extrapolating the characteristics of this text onto the early stages in

---

[31] By associating madness with the powerholder, the *Zhouxun* is also different from the numerous stories in which famous officials, such as Jizi, Wu Zixu, Fan Li and Jiran, feigned madness "either to achieve exemption from obligations and responsibilities or to protect themselves in times of political upheaval" (Schwermann 2007, 549).

[32] *Hanfeizi* "Zhu dao" (Wang X. 2003, 28) and *Liutao* "Wu tao" 武韜 (Cao and An 2012, 52).

Chapter Six

the development of Daoist philosophy. The existence of an early branch of Daoism, which approved of the Odes and Documents, seems thus unlikely.

Part Two

Translation

1

First Month

The first meeting between Lord Zhaowen of Zhou and Prince Gong reportedly took place on the first day (*gengdan* 更旦) of the first month (*zhengyue* 正月) of an unspecified year, at an unspecified time of the day. Except for the last chapter, all other meetings also take place on the first day of each month. No other details of the event are provided. We learn neither the exact location of the meeting, nor the number of people present, nor their respective positions.

Focus falls squarely on Lord Zhaowen's instructions, while Prince Gong remains silent throughout the text. As for the mode of instruction, the royal protagonist reads the text out loud, which was evidently prepared prior to the meeting. At the same time, with the author's and the scribe's identity unclear, the reader is led to believe that the originator of the ideas presented was Lord Zhaowen himself. At the end of the instruction, Prince Gong is given the manuscript of the speech, presumably to privately familiarize himself with its content.

Unlike other chapters, this month's instruction contains no historical examples. Lord Zhaowen begins each instruction with the formula "a ruler (...) must not" (*wei ren jun zhe... bu ke(yi)* 為人君者 ...不可(以)), emphasizing the admonishing character of his speech as directed at a person occupying the highest position in a state. Ten instructions (except number 10) use chain argument, while seven conclude with one or several quotations from different sources:

Table 10: Quoted Sources in Chapter 1

1	2	3	4	5	6	7	8	9	10	11
		Pengzu			*yan*	*shi* (Mao 26)	*yan*; *shu*	*shu*	*shi* (Mao 195); *yan*; *shi* (Mao 288)	*shu*

These quotations show that, in addition to the formal structure, the argument was validated through references to traditional lore.

In the recovered version, the chapter comprises twenty-five bamboo slips (1–25), while one additional slip (between 8/9) appears to be missing. Measuring twenty-six slips, it was the second longest textual unit in the manuscript. In view of the lacuna, it is possible that the total number of admonitions presented in

78 / Translation

this chapter was twelve, reflecting the overall number of months in a regular calendar year (Han 2015, 251–252).

Translation

1/1 • 維歲正月更旦之日，龔（共）大子朝，周昭文公自身貳之，用茲念也。【1】曰：2/1

• It was on the first day of the first month of the year, when Crown Prince Gong came to court. Lord Zhaowen of Zhou personally enjoined him with these (following) reminders. He said:

2/2 為人君者，賞罰不可以不當，賞罰不當則毋以使民。2/21

A ruler's rewards and punishments must not be inappropriate. If his rewards and punishments are inappropriate, he will have no means to employ the people.

2/22 為人君【2】者，決獄不可以不正，不正則善人怠善，而姦人勸姦。故國德君正曰【3】「聖」，官正曰「敬」，此治民之道也。4/11

A ruler's court decisions must not be unjust. If they are unjust, good people will neglect goodness and evil people will be encouraged to evil. And so, in a virtuous state, a just ruler is called "sagely," and just officials are called "respectful." This is the way to rule the people.

4/12 為人君者，不可以輕言，輕言則多失，多失則【4】多悔。故彭祖曰「戒之戒之，言不可追」，此之謂庠？5/18

A ruler must not treat words lightly. If he treats words lightly, he will incur many losses. If he incurs many losses, he will have many regrets. And so, [when] the *Pengzu* says: "Beware, beware! Words cannot be taken back!," does it [not] give expression to this?

5/19 為人君者，不可以言【5】不智，言不智則自鄩（窮）也。處上立（位）而數自鄩（窮）也，其何以正下？6/23

A ruler's words must not be unwise. If his words are unwise, he will bring trouble unto himself. If he is in the top position and frequently brings trouble unto himself, how can he correct his subordinates?

6/24 為人君者，【6】不可以盡請（情）於其臣，盡請（情）於其臣，將何以君人？7/18

A ruler must not fully disclose his true feelings to his ministers. If he fully discloses his true feelings to his ministers, how can he rule others?

7/19 為人君者，不可以大毅（愨），毅（愨）則大【7】信人，大信人則可皇（誆），可皇（誆）則可以奪。䜴（諺）曰：「踵之恃而踵是失。」以䜴（諺）正之，則守國【8】……不達，不達則氣不治，氣不治則放（妨）於䜱（壽）。9/15

A ruler must not be too guileless. If he is guileless, he will trust others too much. If he trusts others too much, he can be deceived. If he can be deceived, he can be robbed (of his position). A proverb says: "Heels provide support, and heels lead astray." Correct [the ruler] with this proverb, then protecting the state…
… not successful. If he is not successful, his vital energy will be disordered. If his vital energy is disordered, this will impede his longevity.

9/16 為人君者，不可以大酒，大酒則大芒（荒），主大【9】芒（荒）而臣不芒（荒）者，國非其國已。故《詩》曰「耿耿不寐，如有隱憂」，此之謂【10】也。11/1

A ruler must not overindulge in wine. If he overindulges in wine, he will become greatly confused. If the sovereign is greatly confused and the ministers are not confused, then the state is not his state. And so, [when] an Ode says: "Disturbed am I, and sleepless, as if suffering from a hidden sorrow," it gives expression to this.

11/2 為人君者，不可以不好聽，不好聽則毋從智（知）下之請（情），故必聽而勿聞，【11】智（知）而默前。此䜴（諺）之所謂曰：「不狂不聾，不能為人公」者也。故《書》曰【12】「大智怡（似）狂」，其此之謂乎？ 13/9

A ruler must not fail to be fond of listening (to others). If he is not fond of listening, he will not know the sentiments of his subordinates. And so, it is imperative (for him) to listen but not be heard; to know but remain silent. This is what a proverb expresses in saying: "If you are not mad and deaf, you cannot become the duke of the people." And so, when a Document says: "Great wisdom resembles madness," does it [not] give expression to this?

13/10 為人君者，不可以信讒，信讒則苛民。苛民則正（政）乳（亂）。正（政）乳（亂）【13】則民移，民移則國空虛，國空虛而城不守。主欲毋危，其得已乎？故《書》曰「失之【14】於本，不可反（返）於末」，此之謂乎？ 15/11

A ruler must not believe slander. If he believes slander, he will be harsh to the people. If he is harsh to the people, his rule will be chaotic. If his rule is chaotic, the people will move away. If the people move away, the capital will be empty and weak. If the capital is empty and weak and its walls unprotected, then, though the sovereign wishes to avoid peril, can he achieve it? And so, [when] a

Document says: "What is lost at the roots, cannot be recovered at the branches," does it [not] give expression to this?

15/12 為人君者，喜怒不可還（旋）發之於【15】前。有所唯，未可以還（旋）唯之。有所非，未可以還（旋）非之。穆穆乎！賢主之【16】心，如臨深淵，其誰能極之？故《詩》曰：「戰戰淩淩（兢兢），如臨深淵，如履（履）薄冰。」夫【17】君人者將如臨深淵，而臣人者將如履（履）薄冰。此庸（諺）之所謂曰：「為【18】主不易，為臣不易」者也。夫為人君而有所唯，則還（旋）唯之，則所唯【19】者，其庸必唯庫？有所非，則還（旋）非之，則所非者，其庸必非乎？故為【20】人君而是非不當，則為不明。為上而不明，其下將代之。故《詩》曰【21】「敬之敬之，天度定之」，此之謂也。

22/12
A ruler must not make an immediate display of joy or anger. If he approves of something, he must not express his approval immediately. If he disapproves of something, he must not express his disapproval immediately. So profound! The heart of a worthy sovereign! Like approaching a deep abyss who can fathom it? And so, an Ode says, "Be apprehensive, be cautious, as if facing a deep abyss, as if treading on thin ice." Now, the ruler should proceed as if facing a deep abyss, and the minister should proceed as if treading on thin ice. This is what is expressed in the proverb, "To be a sovereign is not easy; to be a minister is not easy." Now, if a ruler has something he approves of and expresses his approval immediately, is what he approves of truly what should be approved of? If a ruler has something he disapproves of and expresses his disapproval immediately, is what he disapproves of truly what should be disapproved of? And so, a ruler whose [expressions of] approval and disapproval are inappropriate, is not clairvoyant. A superior who is not clairvoyant will be replaced by his subordinates. And so, [when] an Ode says, "Be reverent, be reverent. The Heavenly measure will bring you stability," it gives expression to this.

22/13 為人君者，不可以通其群臣之言，通其群臣之【言】，則【22】臣相智（知）情，臣相智（知）情則不和，不和則乳（亂）主，乳（亂）主則主危。故《書》曰「周之密之，重之閉之，【23】福則存矣。」此為人君者所謹慎也。24/13

A ruler must not communicate the words of his various minsters to one another. If he communicates the words of his ministers to one another, they will all know one another's true sentiments. If the ministers all know what each other truly feels, they will not be in harmony. If they are not in harmony, they will plunge the sovereign into chaos. If they plunge the sovereign into chaos, the sovereign will be in danger. And so, a Document says: "Be secretive! Be furtive! Take it seriously! Keep it locked up! Then you will be able to preserve your blessings." These are things about which a ruler should be cautious and apprehensive.

24/14 已學（教）大子用茲念，欺〈斯〉乃受（授）之 【24】書，而曰自身屬（囑）之曰：女（汝）勉毋忘歲正月更旦之馴（訓）。【25】

Having instructed the crown prince with these reminders, [Lord Zhaowen] gave him the text [of his speech] and personally cautioned him, saying: "Strive not to forget the instructions from the first day of the first month of the year."[1]

Comments

Thematically, this chapter stands out in that Lord Zhaowen does not emphasize here the value of moral virtues. Instead, attention is at first given to more practical governing matters such as (1) the correct distribution of "rewards and punishments" and (2) making just court decisions. The scope of legal cases the ruler should be involved in is not specified. At the same time, that "officials" (*guan* 官) are mentioned (the only time in the entire text) shows that the text did not demand the ruler to personally resolve all legal cases.[2]

Subsequently, after a brief discussion of the importance of the correct use of language (3 and 4), the focus shifts to the relation between the ruler and his subordinates, who are recognized as a potential threat to the ruler. To keep the subordinates at bay the monarch is advised to: 5) not fully disclose his sentiments to his ministers; 6) not be guileless; 7) not overindulge in wine; 8) be fond of listening; 9) not believe slander; 10) not display his emotions; and finally, 11) not communicate the words of his minsters to one another.

These points emphasize the correctness of the ruler's judgements and, consequently, his intellectual abilities or "wisdom" (*zhi* 智). Precise judgment allows a powerholder to make correct decisions in regard to administrative matters and to strike the right tone in his relationship with subordinates. Consequently, sovereign wisdom encompasses both correct decision-making and correct behavior.

As mentioned above, seven of the admonitions presented here make use of either the Odes, the Documents, the proverbs or the *Pengzu*. Among these sources, the *Pengzu* stands out for being introduced by its title. This special treatment might be explained by the popularity of the eponymous protagonist—an official from the Shang dynasty whose longevity became proverbial[3]—or/and by the attention the *Zhouxun* pays in several chapters to the issue of longevity. In any case, the *Pengzu* is introduced in the text through a formula usually reserved only for the *shu* sources. It could be thus argued that chapter 1 explicates the

---

[1] Lord Zhaowen's instructions are often ambiguous in regard to the speaker's identity. Hence, I refrain from using quotation marks for his speech, except for the concluding cautions.
[2] Some Western Han accounts which suggested that "dispute settlement either by common consent or by jurisdiction" (Khayutina 2015, 263) was part of Zhou royal obligations were late speculations reflecting the political realities of the time of their composition (*ibid.*, 273).
[3] See, for instance, *Zhuangzi* "Xiaoyao you" 逍遙遊 (Guo Q. 1990, 11; Watson 2013, 2).

quotation of materials belonging to three different genres: the Documents, Odes and proverbs. The appearance of these sources demonstrates that, in addition to using the power of logical persuasion, chapter 1 also falls back on "traditional" lore to make a point.

The situation around the *shu*-material (the most frequently quoted genre in this chapter as well as the entire manuscript) presents itself as follows. The lines attributed to the *Pengzu*: "Beware, beware! Words cannot be taken back!" (戒之戒之，言不可追) can be found verbatim in the Shuihudi 睡虎地 manuscript *Weili zhidao* 為吏之道, but, there, they are not ascribed to any person or genre.[4] Variations of the saying, "What is lost at the roots, cannot be recovered at the branches" (失之於本，不可返於末), appear in several early works, but are likewise not attributed to any specific tradition.[5]

On the other hand, the line, "Great wisdom resembles madness" (大智似狂), is sometimes associated with *shu*-lore in other works.[6] The same is true for the sequence, "Be secretive! Be furtive! Take it seriously! Keep it locked up! Then you will be able to preserve your blessings" (周之密之，重之閉之，福則存矣).[7] But even these supported cases have no parallels in the transmitted anthologies of Documents. It would thus appear that this attribution primarily served the purpose of invoking a sense of authority.

The quotations involving proverbs present a similarly complex and, at times, confusing picture. Some of them, such as, "Heels provide support, and heels lead astray" (踵之恃而踵是失), have no counterparts in other writings of the period. Others are characterized in a similar way as in the *Zhouxun*. For instance, "To be a sovereign is not easy; to be a minister is not easy" (為主不易，為臣不易), is called a "saying of the people" (*ren zhi yan* 人之言) by none other than Confucius.[8]

---

[4] Shuihudi Qin mu zhujian zhengli xiaozu 1990, 173. For a brief discussion, see Hulsewé 1978, 182–185. Note that the text with the same title *Pengzu* belonging to the Shanghai Museum collection (Li L. 2003) does not contain these lines.

[5] See the Guodian manuscript *Cheng zhi wen zhi* 成之聞之 and the *Heguanzi* 鶡冠子. Han 2015, 280–281.

[6] A similar adage, as part of a longer saying, is attributed to the semi-legendary foundational minister of the Zhou dynasty, Taigong, in a quotation of the *Zhoushu* in the encyclopedia *Taiping yulan* 太平御覽 (Han 2015, 280).

[7] The first two lines appear verbatim, identified as *shu*, in the edict of the Han emperor Wendi (r. 180–157 BCE) as recorded in the *Hanshu* biography of the eminent official Chao Cuo 晁錯 (200–154 BCE). (*Hanshu* "Yuan Ang, Chao Cuo zhuan" 爰盎晁錯傳 (49.2290))

[8] But in the *Lunyu* "Zi Lu" 子路 (Cheng Shude 1990, 918) the exact wording of the saying is: "To be a ruler is difficult, to be a minister is not easy" (*wei jun nan, wei chen bu yi* 為君難，為臣不易).

Yet others are attributed to different genres. A close variant of the adage, "If you are not mad and deaf, you cannot become the duke of the people" (不狂不聾，不能為人公), is called a proverb in the *Shenzi* 慎子[9], while the *Taiping yulan* quotes a similar saying from the *Zhoushu* (Han 2015, 280). What distinguishes the *Zhouxun* from all these cases is that by quoting proverbs using the same frames as documents and poetry, the text treats them as representatives of a distinct genre and elevates their status.

All quoted poetry lines in this chapter have parallels in the *Shijing*. The lines, "Disturbed am I, and sleepless, as if suffering from a hidden sorrow" (耿耿不寐，如有隱憂), corresponds to the first stanza of the poem "Bozhou" (Mao 26), part of the "Guofeng" section.[10] The next passage, "Be apprehensive, be cautious, as if facing a deep abyss, as if treading on thin ice" (戰戰淩淩，如臨深淵，如履薄冰), matches the last lines of the poem "Xiaomin" (Mao 195), which is part of the "Xiaoya" section.[11]

Finally, the lines, "Be reverent, be reverent. The Heavenly measure will bring you stability" (敬之敬之，天度定之), corresponds to the opening of the poem "Jingzhi" (Mao 288), one of the "Zhousong" 周頌 odes in the arrangement of the transmitted *Shijing*. However, the last three characters of the line *tiandu dingzhi* 天度定之 differ from their counterparts in *tianwei xiansi* 天維顯思 (Heaven is so bright) in the transmitted "Jingzhi" graphically, phonetically, and semantically.[12] The transmitted reading is also supported by the Tsinghua manuscript *Zhougong zhi qinwu* 周公之琴舞.[13] In view of this, it appears possible that the quoted ode was intentionally modified to emphasize the role of Heaven in consolidating power.

Two instructions employ several marked quotations. First, in instruction 8 (11/2–13/9), the admonition concludes by citing a proverb and a Document in this order:

---

[9] Harris 2016, 128–129: 諺云：不聰不明，不能為王；不瞽不聾，不能為公。"If one's hearing is not keen and one's eyesight not clear, one cannot be a king. If one is not blind and deaf, then one cannot be public minded."

[10] As for the reason for its introduction in a passage dealing with alcohol abuse, it has been noted that in Mao 26 the trope of wine drinking (*jiu* 酒) appears immediately after these two lines (Kusano 2019, 192). Apparently, the *Zhouxun* authors were aware of this as they chose a passage from a canonical work to conclude this admonition.

[11] This sequence evidently constituted the "signature lines" of the poem appearing in texts as different as the *Zuozhuan*, *Lunyu*, *Xiaojing*, *Huainanzi*, *Wenzi* etc. (Ho and Chan 2004, 152–154).

[12] The characters *jing* 敬 and *ding* 定 in the *Zhouxun* version belong to the group *geng* 耕, whereas, in the received text, the rhyme is built between character *zhi* 之 and *si* 思: both belonging to the group *zhi* 之 (Cheng and Jiang 1999, 593).

[13] For transcription, see Li X. 2012, 132–143. For discussion on the basic features of the text and its relationship to the received version, see Li S. 2012b and Shaughnessy 2015.

84 / Translation

A ruler must not fail to be fond of listening (to others). If he is not fond of listening, he will not know the sentiments of his subordinates. And so, it is imperative (for him) to listen but not be heard; to know but remain silent. This is what a proverb expresses in saying: "If you are not mad and deaf, you cannot become the duke of the people." And so, when a Document says: "Great wisdom resembles madness," does it [not] give expression to this?

The document-line seems to have a higher status, functioning as a conclusion to the entire passage. The proverb, by introducing the tropes of madness and deafness, plays an important role as a bridge between the opening part of the passage and its conclusion.[14] As a result, a wise ruler, who is completely aware of his subordinates' sentiments (by way of listening) and, at the same time, is able to conceal this fact (feigning deafness), comes to be likened to a "madman."

The next example from instruction 10 (15/12–22/12) is the most complex piece of argumentative writing in the *Zhouxun*, featuring two quotations of the Odes (corresponding to Mao 195 and 288)[15] and one proverb. In addition, this passage is the only piece from chapter 1 which is not composed using the literary form of anadiplosis. The structure of the passage can be represented in the following way. The left and right strands are associated with the juxtaposed elements (the ruler's approval versus disapproval; the ruler versus the minister), while the middle part can be related to both:[16]

A ruler must not
make an immediate
display of joy or an-
ger.
(15/12–16/1)

---

[14] Note that madness does not feature in the proverb quoted in the *Shenzi*, where the emphasis falls squarely on visual and auditory perception (see footnote 9). At the same time, sensory perception plays no role in the discussion of the great wisdom (as madness) attributed to Taigong's *Zhoushu*: "Great wisdom resembles madness. Neither insane nor mad, your name will not become well-known. Neither mad nor insane, you will not be able to accomplish undertakings" (大知似狂。不癲不狂，其名不彰；不狂不癲，不能成事) (Han 2015, 280). Thus, it seems that also here the authors of the *Zhouxun* modified the sources available to them to create a "proverb" which would link auditory perception and the trope of madness.

[15] The only other passage which quotes the same lines from Mao 195 and 288 (in the same order), is to be found in the *Zuozhuan*, Xi 22.7, 395; 355–357.

[16] Rudolf Wagner (2000, 62–69) coined the designation "interlocking parallel style" to refer to this organizational pattern.

First Month / 85

If he approves of something, he must not express his approval immediately. (16/2–10)		If he disapproves of something, he must not express his disapproval immediately. (16/11–19)
	So profound! The heart of a worthy sovereign! As if approaching a deep abyss, who can fathom it? (16/20–17/10)	
	And so, an Ode says, "Be apprehensive, be cautious, (17/11–17)	
as if approaching a deep abyss, (17/18–21)		as if treading on thin ice." (17/22–25)
	Now, (17/26)	
the ruler should be as if approaching a deep abyss, (18/1–8)		and the minister should be as if treading on thin ice. (18/9–17)
	This is what is expressed in the proverb (18/18–23)	
"To be a sovereign is not easy; (18/24–19/3)		to be a minister is not easy." (19/4–9)
	Now, if a ruler (19/10–14)	
has something he approves of and expresses his approval immediately, is what he approves of truly what should be approved of? (19/15–20/6)		has something he disapproves of and expresses his disapproval immediately, is what he disapproves of truly what should be disapproved of? (20/7–20/22)

And so,
a ruler whose [expressions of] approval
and disapproval are
inappropriate, is not
clairvoyant.
(20/23–21/11)
A superior who is not
clairvoyant will be replaced by his subordinates.
(21/12–21)

And so, [when] an
Ode says,
"Be reverent, be reverent. The Heavenly
measure will bring
you stability,"
it gives expression to
this.
(21/22–22/12)

In addition to the strict organizational pattern, the passage is noteworthy in that the phrase "as if approaching a deep abyss" appears both in Lord Zhaowen's "own" speech (17/2–5) and the subsequent quotation from "Xiaomin" (17/18–21). It thus seems that the speech preceding the quotation was constructed with the latter in mind and in a way that would set the stage for its appearance. This practice of incorporating poetry lines can also be attested in many other early works, including the *Zuozhuan* and the excavated manuscript *Wuxing* 五行.[17]

What is more, the interpretation of "Xiaomin" that we find here is highly unusual, insofar as the subject of the sentence "as if approaching a deep abyss" is the ruler and the subject of the sentence "as if walking on thin ice" is the minister. Consequently, the first line: "Be apprehensive, be cautious!," expresses the anxious state of mind of both parties. The proverb "to be a sovereign is not easy; to be a minister is not easy," reaffirms this idiosyncratic reading. Stated more radically, the fragment of an Ode is interpreted to fit the message of the proverb. Subsequently, the last poem "Jingzhi" is also interpreted in light of the antagonistic ruler-minister relationship.

---

[17] For an example in the former, see the *Zuozhuan*, Cheng 12.4, 858; 798. For the *Wuxing*, see Goldin 2005, 33–34; Wang Bo 2011, 475–484.

Context

Some of the instructions presented in this chapter appear similar to ideas promulgated by the "legalist" thinker Han Fei. Unlike Han Fei, however, the *Zhouxun* does not demonize ministers as their actions are understood to be completely reactive to the behavior of the ruler. If the latter manages to position himself correctly, subordinates will not pose any threat to his position. Another difference consists in the fact that in Han Fei's work the warnings against ministers are pronounced in the context of cosmological speculations, while "Lord Zhaowen" refers to the lore associated with authoritative (later: canonical) scriptures and collective human wisdom expressed in proverbs. Without suggesting a direct link between the two works, their affinity seems to be speaking to the common and ubiquitous character of these ideas.

2

Second Month

The instruction attributed to the second month provides a prototypical structure to most other chapters of the *Zhouxun*. This structure is such that Lord Zhaowen first presents an historical account, then extracts a moral lesson from it and, finally, makes a personal appeal to Prince Gong in light of the information provided. The historical accounts always begin with the word "in the past," synopses are usually marked with either "and so" or (when capping a story with an authoritative source) "this is what X refers to," while most personal admonitions of Prince Gong start either with the formula "now, you" or with "now, I." In most cases, there is clear thematic affinity among the three constitutive parts of the chapters.

    The present chapter stands out in that it presents two accounts and does so in reversed chronological order. Only chapter 11 has the same peculiar arrangement of content. Here, Lord Zhaowen presents, in the order of mentioning, accounts involving the two earliest dynastic founders in Chinese history, King Tang of Shang (ca. 1570–1045 BCE)[1] and Yu of the preceding Xia (ca. 2070–1600 BCE)[2]. Both rulers are portrayed as instructing their alleged successors, Tai Jia and Qi respectively, about the necessity of moral cultivation lest they be dismissed. As problematic as such parallels are historically, they establish the normativity of certain political practices. Purportedly, the transition of power in China has been ever since regulated by a combination of hereditary and meritocratic principles. For only the most able sons were chosen to ascend the throne. In this account, fathers were personally involved in the education of their offspring and the establishment of their successors. Lord Zhaowen's instruction of Prince Gong is informed by the same principles.

    The chapter consists of sixteen bamboo slips (26–41), while one slip (between 32/33) appears to be missing. The top of slip 29 is broken off and so there is a lacuna comprising four graphs. Graph 32/22 was rendered illegible because of erasure. Thematically, I divide the chapter into the first (27/2–32/7) and the second historical precedent (32/8–33/15), Lord Zhaowen's interpretation

---

[1] Keightley 1999, 232.
[2] For this dating and the dubious historicity of the Xia dynasty, see Major and Cook 2017, 60–61.

thereof (33/16–34/8) and, finally, his direct appeal to Prince Gong (34/9–38/23), closing with a quotation from a Document of Zhou (39/11–39/19).

Translation

26/1 • 維歲二月更旦之日，龏（共）大子朝，周昭文公自身貳之，用茲念也。
【26】曰： 27/1

• It was on the first day of the second month of the year, when Crown Prince Gong came to court. Lord Zhaowen of Zhou personally enjoined him with these (following) reminders. He said:

27/2 昔殷武湯身敬（儆）太甲曰：「朕（朕）子九人，唯爾為嗣，劃（豈）獨（獨）女（汝）宜？它斯【27】可置。女（汝）不好善，其庸智（知）不代？為能孝弟（悌），辟（譬）之若天，誰敢弗戴？爾【28】口口口，口兼（義）奠（尊）仁，而隊（遂）為民天；女（汝）弗能勉，而自令為地。唯毋為【29】地，人將履（履）之。唯毋為天，其誰敢視之？ 30/14

In the past, Tang, the "Militant"[3], of Yin, personally admonished Tai Jia, saying, "I have nine sons. Although you are my heir, is it really only you who is suitable? [Any of] my other sons could be established. You are not fond of goodness, so how do you know that you will not be replaced? If you can be filial and brotherly, you will be like Heaven. Who would dare not to support you? If you [X][X][X][X] righteousness, and honor humaneness, you will then become like Heaven to the people. If you are unable to put effort [into this], you will make yourself like the earth. If you are like the earth, the people will tread on you. If you are like Heaven, who would dare to look at you?"

30/15 夫天之與地相去遠矣，而【30】為人君與為人臣之相遠也，有（又）遠於天之去地也。承國主者，其【31】胡可以毋務好善？[4] 32/7

Now, heaven and earth are far away from each other, but the distance between ruler and minister is even farther than that between heaven and earth. How can a successor to the ruler not strive to be fond of goodness?

32/8 昔禹貳啟曰：「勉務好唯，而戒毋作非，口國失【32】……弗好務，將或代之。諸置嗣者，莫立不治。」 33/15

In the past, Yu enjoined Qi, saying, "Make effort to be fond of doing right and be careful to do no wrong, [X] state will be lost... not fond of exerting yourself,

---

[3] Tang is given this moniker in the *Shiji* "Yin benji" (3.95).
[4] In the published version, this is part of Tang's instruction.

someone will replace you. When it comes to installing an heir, nobody establishes a chaotic person."

33/16 自昔及今，從古以來，劼（豈）【33】有不賢而可任國哉？34/8
From the past to the present, from the ancient times on, could an unworthy person ever be entrusted with the state?

34/9 今女（汝）不能蒽（聰）明元聖，其何以獨（獨）得奉祭祀？[5] 【34】若吾不寬而無惠於民也。唯（雖）然，爾能令而百姓毋弗（我）思也，則而【35】立（位）可以幸於不危矣。爾為不能意眾百姓而使之，皆欲吾復生【36】也，則成周之民非而民已。爾有鄩（鄏）邑，而成周之人不為女（汝）民，其【37】何以守國？有土有國而無德於民，其安得為君？已得為君，自令【38】不得，愚孰大焉？故《周書》曰：「皇天降殃，愚實為始」，其此之謂乎？ 39/23

Now, you [appear] unable to be clairaudient, clairvoyant, exemplary, and sagacious, how can you alone obtain [the position of] offering worship and sacrifice? [Only] if I am unkind and not lenient to the people [then I shall establish you]. Even so, if you can make the "hundred surnames" not think about me, then, with luck, your position will not be imperiled. [But] if you cannot assess the [intentions of the] masses and "hundred surnames" but [still] employ them, they will all wish that I live again, and then the people of Chengzhou will not be your people. You have the City of Ru, but if the people of Chengzhou are not your people, how will you preserve the state? If you have the territory, if you have the capital but lack the [virtue-inspired] gratitude of the people, how can you obtain the position of ruler? If, having already obtained the position of ruler, you cause yourself to lose it, what could be more foolish than this? And so, [when] a Document of Zhou says: "When august Heaven sends down disaster, it surely begins with foolishness," does it [not] give expression to this?

39/24 已【39】學（教）泰（太）子用茲念，斯乃受（授）之書，而自身屬（囑）之曰：女（汝）勉毋忘歲二月【40】更旦之馴（訓）。【41】
Having instructed the crown prince with these reminders, [Lord Zhaowen] gave him the text [of his speech] and personally cautioned him, saying: "Strive not to forget the instructions from the first day of the second month of the year."

---

[5] According to the editors, the content of slip 34 still represents Yu's speech.

Comments

Given the complexity of the chapter, I analyze each section separately.

1. Tang's Instruction of Tai Jia (27/2–32/7)

The main notion of this passage is "goodness" (*shan* 善), which, in turn, appears to be constituted by a combination of filial piety, brotherly love, righteousness, and humaneness. Through their cultivation, a successor to the throne will naturally win the support of the population, making himself comparable to the Heaven. Neglecting them, on the other hand, will render him like the earth, and the people will treat him with contempt. The latter will lead to forfeiting one's claims to power.

This passage begins with a long sequence of twenty (mostly) tetrasyllabic rhyming lines (27/2–30/14):

1	昔殷武湯		In the past, Tang, the "Militant," of Yin,
2	身儆太甲曰：		personally admonished Tai Jia, saying,
3	朕子九人，		"I have nine sons.
4	唯爾為嗣，	之	Although you are my heir,
5	豈獨汝宜？	歌	Is it really only you who is suitable?
6	它斯｜可置。	職	[Any of] my other sons could be established.
7	汝不好善，		You are not fond of goodness,
8	其庸知不代？	職	so how do you know that you will not be replaced?
9	為能孝悌，	脂	If you can be filial and brotherly,
10	辟譬之若天，		you will be like Heaven.
11	誰敢弗戴？	之	Who would dare not to support you?
12	爾｜□□□，		If you [X][X][X]
13	口義尊仁，	真	[X] righteousness, and honor humaneness,
14	而遂為民天；	真	you will then become like Heaven to the people.
15	汝弗能勉，	元	If you are unable to put effort [into this],
16	而自令為地。	歌	you will make yourself like the earth.
17	唯母為｜地，		If you are like the earth,
18	人將履之。	脂	the people will tread on you.
19	唯母為天，		If you are like Heaven,
20	其誰敢視之？	脂	who would dare to look at you?"

The rhyme pattern between most lines is irregular, including the combination of the rhyme groups *ge* 歌/ *zhi* 職, *zhi* 職 / *zhi* 之 as well as *zhen* 真 / *yuan* 元. These are common combinations for the late pre-imperial period texts appearing *inter alia* in the *Lüshi chunqiu* (Zhang S. 2008, 403–408).

Semantically, the heaven/earth dichotomy involves the opposing scenarios of either elevating (lines 12–14 and 17–18) or denigrating oneself (lines 15–16 and 19–20) in the eyes of one's subordinates, depending on one's dedication to moral cultivation. The two strands of argument represent two options available to a powerholder or his successor.

Following this, the text introduces a general rule (30/15–32/7) by means of particle *fu* 夫 (Wagner 2015, 63), which builds on the heaven/earth and ruler/subject dichotomies and which could be reasonably attributed to either Tang or Lord Zhaowen. In any case, a different meter indicates a change in the speech's status.

1	夫天之與地相去遠矣，	元	Now, heaven and earth are far away from each other,
2	而|為人君與為人臣	真	but the distance between ruler and minister
3	又遠與天之去地也。		is even farther than that between heaven and earth.
4	承國主者，		How can a successor to the ruler
5	其|胡可以毋務好善？	元	not strive to be fond of goodness?

By presenting social hierarchy as even more pronounced than the natural example of heaven and earth, the *Zhouxun* makes the usurpation of power through subordinates appear as a real aberration of natural order. The appearance of the rhetorical question suggests that by cultivating "goodness" a ruler follows the natural order and consolidates his position of power.

2. Yu's Instruction of Qi (32/8–33/15)

The treatment of Yu and Qi is even more schematic and populated by stereotypical preaching formulas to the effect that one should strive to do "right" (*wei* 唯) and avoid doing "wrong" (*fei* 非). One's actions are assessed in terms of their likely outcome of gaining or losing political authority, as well as the right to succeed the ruler.

Just as it was the case with Tang, Yu's admonitions of Qi are also highly stylized, consisting mainly of rhyming tetrasyllabic lines:

1	昔禹貳啟曰：		In the past, Yu enjoined Qi, saying,
2	「勉務好唯，	微	"Make effort to be fond of doing right
3	而戒毋作非，	微	and be careful to do no wrong,
4	口國失|		[X] state will be lost…
5	……弗好務，	幽	… not be fond of making an effort,
6	將或代之。	職	someone will replace you.
7	諸置嗣者，	之	When it comes to installing an heir,
8	莫立不治。」	之	nobody establishes an unruly person."

Because there is a lacuna in the extant passage, we can estimate that, initially, it contained at least twenty-four more characters (one slip), corresponding to six tetrasyllabic lines, making the total number of lines 14.

3. Lord Zhaowen's Summary (33/16–34/8)

According to the editors, the next passage still belongs to Yu's speech. Indeed, in terms of meter and rhyme, these four lines closely correspond to the above-mentioned content:

1	自昔及今，		From the past to the present,
2	從古以來，	職	from the ancient times on,
3	豈|有不賢		could an unworthy person ever
4	而可任國哉？	職	be entrusted with the state?

Yet, I maintain that this passage could present Lord Zhaowen's speech, constituting an attempt to draw lessons from historical precedents. The references to past and present, indeed, appear to support this view. Judged from Lord Zhaowen's position, Yu and Qi represented the furthest possible point in history where the establishment of worthy sons had already been practiced. This renders the temporal gap between the past and the present remarkable, demonstrating how long-standing this tradition was. In Yu's case, however, contrasting past with present would have been far less persuasive, as he knew the pioneers of meritocratic succession (unnamed here) personally. Through its formal affinity to Yu's speech, this short paragraph serves as a bridge between the already presented content and what will follow below.

4. Lord Zhaowen's Address to Prince Gong (34/9–39/23)

Lord Zhaowen continues his instructions with a direct address to Prince Gong. The already impressive catalogue of virtues that Tang and Yu demanded from their successors is further extended here to include clairaudience, clairvoyance, exemplarity, and sagacity. These terms refer rather to acuity of sense perception than moral excellence. The connection between sensual virtuosity and moral values is addressed in various early works of Chinese philosophy, perhaps most systematically, in the excavated manuscript *Wuxing*.⁶ But this complex issue is not elaborated upon here.

Particularly interesting is the following passage in which Lord Zhaowen presents two scenarios of how things will play out for Prince Gong if he inherits the throne without possessing the necessary moral attributes:

1	雖然，		Even so,
2	爾能令而百姓毋我思也，	職	if you can make the "hundred surnames" not think about me,
3	則而|位可以幸於不危矣。	歌	then, with luck, your position will not be imperiled.
4	爾為不能意眾百姓而使之，	之	[But] if you cannot assess the [intentions of the] masses and "hundred surnames" but [still] employ them,
5	皆欲吾復生|也，	耕	they will all wish that I live again,
6	則成周之民非而民已。	真	and then the people of Chengzhou will not be your people.

The first scenario entails the maintenance of power (lines 2–3) and the second its loss (lines 4–6). However, even the first development is far from ideal as it guarantees only the bare survival of the powerholder. What follows from this is the necessity of molding one's character in the way proposed by the text.

The rhyme in this section is constituted exclusively by the characters occupying the penultimate positions in the respective lines and belonging to different rhyme groups: *zhi* 職/ *ge* 歌/ *zhi* 之 and *geng* 耕/*zhen* 真. Again, these combinations were common in the texts of the period. Meter is likewise inconsistent, fluctuating between six and eleven characters in each line.

In the concluding part of his address, Lord Zhaowen introduces yet another pivotal term by admonishing Prince Gong that a throne contender who is lacking in *de* 德 (here: virtue-inspired gratitude of the people)⁷ will forfeit his position. That such foolish behavior leads to a certain demise is restated in the concluding quotation from the Document of Zhou:

---

⁶ For the transcription of the Guodian version, Jingmen shi bowuguan 1998, 147–154; For the transcription of the Mawangdui version, see Guojia wenwuju gu wenxian yanjiushi 1980, 17–28. For the translation of both the Guodian and the Mawangdui version, see Csikszentmihalyi 2004, 277–371; For some other notable treatments, see Cook 2012, 465–520; Meyer 2012, 283–352.

⁷ For such interpretation of *de*, see Nivison 1996, 32.

1	爾有鄏邑，		You have the City of Ru,
2	而成周之人不為汝民，		but if the people of Chengzhou are not your people,
3	其|何以守國|？	職	how will you preserve the state?
4	有土有國而無德於民，		If you have the territory, if you have the capital but lack the [virtue-inspired] gratitude of the people,
5	其安得為君？		How can you obtain the position of ruler?
6	已得為君，		If, having already obtained the position of ruler,
7	自令|不|得|，	職	you cause yourself to lose it,
8	愚孰大焉？	職	what could be more foolish than this?
9	故《周書》曰：		And so, [when] a Document of Zhou says:
10	「皇天降殆，	之	"When august Heaven sends down disaster,
11	愚實為始」，	之	it surely begins with foolishness,"
12	其此之謂乎？		does it [not] give expression to this?

While the quotation from a Document of Zhou has no exact counterparts in the transmitted sources, this is the only case in the *Zhouxun* when the supposed affiliation of a Document is revealed. Considering that this chapter introduces a historical dimension to the *Zhouxun*, it could be argued that this attribution was meant to give voice to the Zhou tradition to complement depictions of the two preceding dynasties. In this way, the first three hereditary dynasties can all supply a ruler with important guidelines for governing practices. At the same time, by mentioning a Document of Zhou in the last sentence of the present chapter, Lord Zhaowen was possibly hinting at the the topic of the subsequent instruction: the reasons for the successful establishment of the Zhou dynasty.

Curiously, Lord Zhaowen refers to Prince Gong as residing in the City of Ru and, at the same time, as a contender to the throne in Chengzhou, Lord Zhaowen's own domain. As discussed in the first part of this book, beginning with 367 BCE, the domain of Zhou was divided into two polities with their respective ruling families dwelling in the capitals in the City of Ru and Cheng Zhou. Under these circumstances, the plot of the *Zhouxun* is simply ahistorical. But, regardless of the historicity of this narrative, the task confronting Prince Gong was daunting indeed: to win the allegiance of the population inhabiting a territory which was not one's own (if not outright foreign). Intriguingly, this dilemma was not unlike the problems rulers faced when attempting to establish their rule over the population in a newly conquered territory.

The ideal contender to the throne as depicted here is required to embody a vast array of moral and intellectual virtues of the highest order. At the same time, the questions of feasibility and practicality of such expectations did not seem to concern the authors. Neither did they show ways to achieve these lofty ideals. Rather, they seem to have attempted to provide a comprehensive list of values to make the text relevant in the context of contemporaneous political and philosophical discourse.

Context

Both accounts presented in chapter 2 deviate from other early records in significant ways. As for the exchange between Cheng Tang and Tai Jia, by depicting them as father and son, the *Zhouxun* contradicts numerous sources where Tai Jia features as Tang's grandson and becomes sovereign only after several other rulers had occupied the Shang throne following Tang's death.[8] On the other hand, the portrayal of Tai Jia as being "not fond of goodness" (*bu haoshan* 不好善) and incurring King Tang's criticism should be distinguished from his occasional depictions as a prominent example of a "depraved son" (*jianzi* 姦子) (of Tang) who was unable to turn to "goodness."[9] We can assume that, in the *Zhouxun*, Tai Jia was able to reform himself, firstly, because it follows from Lord Zhaowen' conclusion that it was never "permissible to entrust an unworthy person with the state," and, secondly, it is implied by the manuscript's logic of the "survival of the worthy" which stipulates that no political entity will ever endure without able leadership.

Tang's educational role in regard to Tai Jia constitutes another unique feature of this account. In most other writings, this role is played by the wise minister Yi Yin 伊尹, who, having installed Tai Jia[10], did not refrain from sending the latter into exile for self-reformation after detecting signs of moral decay.[11] In fact, the "ancient script" *Shangshu*, which despite its evidently late composition

---

[8] See *Mengzi* "Wan Zhang shang" (Jiao 1987, 647; Lau 2003, 209) and *Shiji* "Yin benji" 殷本紀 (3.98. Nienhauser 1994a, 45).

[9] *Guoyu* "Chuyu shang" 楚語上 (Xu Y. 2002, 484; Taskin 1987, 245).

[10] *Shiji* "Yin benji" (3.98; Nienhauser 1994a, 45). On the interplay between the right of virtue and the right of heredity in the interactions between Yi Yin and Tai Jia as well as different variations of their story, see Allan 2016, 95–100.

[11] *Zuozhuan*, Xiang 21.5, 1060–1061; 1087: 伊尹放大甲而相之，卒無怨色。"Yi Yin exiled Taijia but later Yi Yin continued as Taijia's minister, and to the end Taijia showed no resentment." See also *Shiji* "Yin benji" 殷本紀 (3.98) and *Guoyu* "Jinyu si" 晉語四 (Xu Y. 2002, 347; Taskin 1987, 177). However, according to the *Guben zhushu jinian* 古本竹書紀年 (Fang and Wang 1981, 23–25) Tai Jia killed Yi Yin to prevent him from usurping power.

date still contains genuinely old material[12], features several edifying speeches ascribed to Yi Yin directed at Tai Jia and reminiscent of the *Zhouxun* in their tone and general setting.[13] In this way, we see that the *Zhouxun* presents a picture of King Tang that contains some elements associated with Yi Yin. The latter's complete absence from the manuscript also appears unique in view of the wealth of excavated manuscripts where he appears as the wise aide on the side of Cheng Tang.[14] Evidently, in the present chapter, ministerial wisdom is incorporated in the figure of the wise father-ruler.

Another characteristic feature of the *Zhouxun* is its complete silence on the fact that Tang became the ruler of All-under-Heaven by overthrowing his superior and the last ruler of the preceding Xia dynasty, Jie.[15] Nor does the manuscript mention the involvement of higher powers in this process, such as Heaven or the Lord on High (*Shangdi* 上帝).[16] However, Tang's warnings against the subversion of the naturally given ruler/subordinate hierarchy could be read as summarizing his previous experience of dealing with a ruler who undermined his position by being unkind.[17]

The appearance of Yu and Qi as ruler and successor in the second account is also dubious from the perspective of most early historical sources. There, Qi is said to have risen to rule the realm only three years after Yu's death.[18] Considering this, instruction of the kind depicted in the *Zhouxun* could not have taken

---

[12] Nylan 2001, 132, and Shaughnessy 1993, 386.

[13] See chapters "Yin xun" 伊訓, "Tai Jia" 太甲 and "Xian you yi de" 咸有一德 (Lau and Chen 1995, 15–18; Legge 1879, 92–103).

[14] See the Mawangdui manuscript *Jiu zhu* 九主 (For transcription and brief analysis, see Ling X. 1974, 21–44; Yates 1997, 181–191). Moreover, there are numerous Tsinghua manuscripts, which feature Yi Yin in the same capacity. They are: *Yinzhi* 尹至 (Transcription in Li X. 2010, 127–131. For a description, see Liu G. 2016, 92, 112–114), *Yingao* 尹誥 (Transcription in Li X. 2010, 132–134; Liu G. 2016, 92, 116–119), *Chi jiu zhi ji Tang zhi wu* 赤鳩之集湯之屋 (Transcription in Li X. 2012, 166–170. Sun F. 2021), *Tang zai Chimen* 湯在啻門 (Transcription in Li X. 2011, 141–148. For English translation and analysis, see Meyer 2018, 139–166) and *Tang chu yu Tang qiu* 湯處於湯丘 (Transcription in Li X. 2011, 134–140. For content analysis, see Guo L. 2018, 293–295).

[15] *Guoyu* "Luyu shang" 魯語上 (Xu Y. 2002, 172; Taskin 1987, 92). *Shiji* 2.88; Nienhauser 1994a, 38. On Tang's role as Jie's minister in the Shangbo manuscript *Rongchengshi* 容成氏, see Allan 2015, 213.

[16] An example can be found in the "Tang shi" 湯誓 chapter of the *Shangshu* (Gu and Liu 2005, 878–899; Karlgren 1950b, 20).

[17] According to the *Shangshu dazhuan* 尚書大傳 "Tang shi" 湯誓 (Lau 1994, 4.2/11/24–27), Tang accepted the throne only after having received several requests from the *zhuhou* 諸侯. His initial refusal was "meant to demonstrate that he too does not wish to be a despot, but has the best interests of the realm at heart" (Vankeerberghen 2007, 93).

[18] See *Mengzi* "Wan Zhang shang" 萬章上 (Jiao 1987, 647; Lau 2003, 207) and *Shiji* 2.83–84; Nienhauser 1994a, 36.

place. Moreover, the manuscript is silent about another delicate topic associated with Yu and Qi, namely, that Yu abdicated the throne in favor of his worthy minister Yi (*Shiji* 2.83). Narratives of how Qi was eventually able to become sovereign, thus establishing the first dynasty in China, differ radically. While some sources glorify Qi's abilities, others vilify him.[19] Possibly, this incongruous treatment of Qi can be taken to suggest his transformation in the manner of Tai Jia, from an inept to a worthy contender to the throne.[20] In any case, Yi's complete absence from the scene parallels the silent treatment of Yi Yin. Therefore, it becomes evident that, at least at this point in the book, the authors did not intend to demonstrate how crucial the worthy aides were. Instead, they attempted to attribute the political successes of the early dynasties and their long duration solely to the educational zeal of their founders, directed at their sons.

Interestingly, the succession of rulers that the manuscript presents in chapter 2, Yu–Qi for Xia and Tang–Tai Jia for Shang, corresponds to the *Shangshu*, where Qi and Tai Jia feature as the next generation of kings after Yu and Tang.[21] This might suggest that the historical vision of the *Zhouxun*, at least in regard to the earliest periods of Chinese history, was informed by *shu* documents.

Finally, in addition to the reasons listed above, the fact that the historical account of the *Zhouxun* opens with the Shang dynasty could be explained by considering Tai Jia's popular portrayal as a prodigal, who, after some initial problems, was able to reform himself. As such, he could be setting the tone in a book which is centered around educational issues (that is, Prince Gong's transformation).

---

[19] According to the *Mengzi* "Wan Zhang shang" (Jiao J. 1987, 647; Lau 2003, 207) and *Shiji* 2.83–84; Nienhauser 1994a, 36, Yi voluntarily left the empire to Qi. As opposed to this, in the account of the *Guben zhushu jinian* (Fang and Wang 1981, 2) Qi killed Yi, whereas the *Zhanguo ce* (Fan X. 2006, 1675) and the *Rongchengshi* (Allan 2015, 249) report that Qi attacked (*gong* 攻) Yi and took the rule from him.
[20] On the different representations of Qi and his relation to Yi, see Allan 2016, 74–76.
[21] For Qi, see the "Gan shi" 甘誓-chapter of the *Shangshu* (Gu and Liu 2005, 854–877; Karlgren 1950b, 18). For the statistics on early quotations from the *shu* documents associated with Tai Jia, see Xu T. 2009, 377.

3

Third Month

Lord Zhaowen's third instruction invokes one of the most significant events in the entire course of Chinese history, namely, the establishment of the Zhou dynasty through King Wen (r. 1099–1050 BCE) and his son, King Wu (r. 1049/45–1043 BCE).[1] This momentous event, as reported in the *Zhouxun*, was only possible because King Wen implemented correct principles of power transfer by establishing his son Fa 發, the future King Wu, as successor.

In other words, the decision to install Fa demonstrates that King Wen valued "worthiness" (allegedly embodied by Fa) over the conventional criteria regulating power transfer as personified by his three other sons who remain unnamed here. The latter are characterized either by nobility (*gui* 貴), seniority (*zhang* 長), or the father's emotional attachment (*ai* 愛), none of which is connected to their characters.[2] Another interesting point is that, in his decision to elevate Fa, King Wen is said to have followed the advice of one of his most able ministers, Hong Yao.[3] This is very different from the complete oblivion of worthy aides in the previous chapter and the explicit warnings against ministers in chapter 1. Yet, at this juncture, the manuscript only hints at the significance of wise counsel, fully developing this theme only in later chapters.

The chapter is written on twelve bamboo slips (42–53), and one slip is judged to be missing. The position of the verso line on slip 47 seems at odds with the relevant marks placed on the adjacent slips, though its content fits seamlessly into the discussion (*Beida Mss.* 110).

Unlike the previous chapter, here we find an historical anecdote with a storyline surrounding the Zhou dynasty's ascension to supremacy (43/1–49/5). Together with Lord Zhaowen's summary of this anecdote (50/6–51/11) and concluding rhetorical question (51/12–52/3), the chapter consists of three main

---

[1] For a brief depiction of the events surrounding the Zhou's ascension to power, see *Shiji* "Zhou benji" (4.116–130; Nienhauser 1994a, 57–64) and Shaughnessy 1999, 309–311. On the Zhou's conquest of Shang, see Li F. 2013, 117–123.
[2] On the important traditional criteria employed in the selection of an heir apparent, see *Gongyang zhuan* "Yin gong yuan nian."
[3] For more on Hong Yao, see *Shangshu* "Jun shi" 君奭 (Gu and Liu 2005, 1553–1607; Karlgren 1950b, 59–60); *Shiji* "Yin benji" (3.106; Nienhauser 1994a, 50).

parts. As above, I indicate these different parts by organizing them into separate paragraphs.

Translation

42/1 • 維歲三月更旦之日,龏(共)大子朝,周昭文公自身貳之,用茲念也。【42】曰:43/1

• It was on the first day of the third month of the year, when Crown Prince Gong came to court. Lord Zhaowen of Zhou personally enjoined him with these (following) reminders. He said:

43/2 昔周文王問於閎夭曰:「余有子四人,惑(或)貴惑(或)愛,惑(或)長惑(或)賢,吾【43】將誰置?」夭對(對)曰:「置貴而不賢,是猷(猶)獨(獨)令岐山之二女為府史也。【44】剴(豈)能自守?置愛而不賢,是猶獨令三月之嬰兒處中野,而美之【45】以夏后之璜也,剴(豈)能無亡?置長而不賢,是猶獨令昆吾之九鼎【46】……患於不利?」文王曰:「善。」乃自禮發以為大子。及文王毫(薨),大子發立,【47】節(即)有天下,環(旋)正海內。其同生三人,節(即)扁(偏)封之,其地之廣夾(狹)既大【48】於岐周。後世聞之,莫不稱譽文王之聖也,皆以文王為善立嗣,【49】而智(知)所屬任。50/5

In the past, King Wen of Zhou asked Hong Yao, saying, "I have four sons: one is of noble birth, one is my favorite, one is the first born, one is worthy; whom should I install [as successor]?" [Hong] Yao replied: "To install the noble and not the worthy, would be like appointing the two women from Mount Qi as scribes in charge of the archives.[4] Could they really maintain this position? To install the favorite and not the worthy, would be like placing a three-month old toddler in an open field and decorating him with the [precious] jade half disc of

---

[4] The identity of "the two women from Mount Qi" (*Qishan zhi er nü* 岐山之二女) is not clear. The possible candidates include two daughters of Emperor Yao, who married them to Shun (see, among others, *Mengzi* "Wan Zhang shang" (Jiao 1987, 615)), or two daughters of the head of the Minshan 岷山 lineage, Yan 琰, and Wan 琬, whom the last Xia emperor Jie abducted from their home. The last event is mentioned in the *Guben Zhushu jinian* (Fang and Wang 1981, 16) as well as the newly found *Rongchengshi* (Allan 2015, 250) and, most likely, also *Yinzhi* 尹至 (Liu G. 2016, 117). In the latter case, Qishan would be a scribal error for Minshan. However, the former scenario seems more likely as the "nobility" of two daughters of Yao is specifically addressed in the story about Shun's ascension to the throne in the *Shiji* "Wu di benji" 五帝本紀 (1.33; Nienhauser 1994a, 12).

the Xiahou clan.[5] Could he really avoid perishing? To install the first born and not the worthy would be like letting the nine tripods of Kunwu[6]… worry about the disadvantages?" King Wen said: "Excellent!" Thereupon, he personally performed the ritual enacting Fa as the crown prince. When King Wen expired, crown prince Fa was enthroned. As soon as he came into possession of All-under-Heaven, he immediately put the territory within the [four] seas into order. [Fa] enfeoffed his three brothers with territories even larger than [the heartland of] Zhou around Mount Qi [that he possessed].[7] When later generations heard about this, there were none who did not praise the sagacity of King Wen. Everyone believed that King Wen excelled at establishing his heir and knew whom to entrust with the responsibility [of the state].

50/6 故屬子國而能守之，則追譽其親。予而失之，則非【50】徒亡國而已，有（又）將傷其先人。51/11
And so, if a son is entrusted with a state and is able to preserve it, then he will reflect fame back upon his parents. But if, when given [a state], he loses it, then he not only ruins the state, he also harms his predecessors.

51/12 承國主者，其胡可毋務遂孝而謹【51】慎其身？52/3
How can a successor to the ruler not endeavor to be filially pious and cautious about himself?

52/4 已學（教）大子用茲念，斯乃受（授）之書，而自身屬（囑）之曰：女（汝）勉毋【52】忘歲三月更旦之馴（訓）。【53】
Having instructed the crown prince with these reminders, [Lord Zhaowen] gave him the text [of his speech] and personally cautioned him, saying: "Strive not to forget the instructions from the first day of the third month of the year."

---

[5] The jade half disc of the Xia ruling line 夏后之璜 was granted to the Lord of Lu. See *Zuozhuan*, Ding 4.1, 1536; 1748 and 1748n45). The authors of the *Huainanzi*, "Jingshen xun" 精神訓 (He N. 1998, 520), called it the epitome of a precious thing (*bao zhi zhi* 寶之至).
[6] The nine tripods cast at Kunwu mountain was the ubiquitous symbol of sovereign power in early China. For a story about their creation and how they were "lost" (*shi* 失) by vanishing dynasties, see *Mozi* "Geng Zhu" 耕柱 (Sun Y. 2001, 423–424; Johnston 2010, 641–643). Many images presented here are connected to the Xia dynasty.
[7] On the symbolic importance of Mount Qi for the Zhou dynasty, see Khayutina 2008, 25.

Comments

This chapter highlights the pivotal importance of Lord Zhaowen's summaries and subsequent rhetorical questions for the interpretation of historical narratives. In the story, King Wu is reported to stand out solely through his worthiness. However, the synopsis interprets his abilities and achievements in light of his service to the ancestors. Finally, the concluding rhetorical question implies that through his successes King Wu made his late father even more famed and celebrated among the people, thus demonstrating his "filial piety" (*xiao* 孝). As such, King Wu's filial piety was predicated on him greatly expanding the initial scope of the Zhou territory and becoming a sovereign over the All-under-Heaven. Additionally, King Wu's concern about his family members also shows itself in how selflessly he divided the conquered territories among his (less able) brothers, making them rulers over the great areas.

Turning to the linguistic characteristics of the chapter, we find here fewer tetrasyllabic lines and rhymes. Particularly interesting is the construction of the last two units (Lord Zhaowen's summary of events and the rhetorical question) (50/6–52/3). Their interrelatedness is suggested through the common end-rhyme *zhen* 真 (characters *qin* 親, *ren* 人 and *shen* 身). Moreover, the two sentences in the summary part are antithetical, depicting two opposing scenarios. Therefore, the relation between the three sentences can be represented as:

(1) 故
And so,

(2) 屬子國而能守之，
則追譽其親。
If a son is entrusted with a state and is able to preserve it, then he will reflect fame back upon his parents.

(3) 予而失之，
則非│徒亡國而已，
又將傷其先│人。
But if, when given [a state], he loses it, then he not only ruins the state, he also harms his predecessors.

(4) 承國主者，
其胡可毋務遂孝而謹│慎其身│？
How can a successor to the ruler
not endeavor to be filially pious and cautious about himself?

By adding the concluding rhetorical question, the authors effectively turned the two strands into concrete illustrations of what constitutes filial piety and what does not.

Context

By presenting King Wu's rise as the head of the Zhou lineage and, eventually, the conqueror of All-under-Heaven as resulting solely from his father's wise decision on the issue of succession, the authors of the *Zhouxun* created a narrative that greatly deviates from other historical writings describing the same events. First, elsewhere, King Wu is reported to have a lot more brothers.[8] Evidently, four was very convenient for an account where worthiness was juxtaposed with the (other three) frequently considered criteria for successor selection. Moreover, in the presentation of the *Zhouxun*, Fa was neither the first born, nor the favorite, nor the most exalted (in terms of his maternal lineage) offspring of King Wen and, therefore, a very improbable candidate to become the new leader of the Zhou. This claim likewise contains several problematic points.

To begin with, we can identify two basic positions regarding Fa's status among King Wen's sons. First, the chapter of the *Shiji* dedicated to the history of the ruling house of Zhou proper, "Basic Annals of the Zhou" 周本記, does not suggest King Wen had any sons born prior to Fa (*Shiji* 4.118; Nienhauser 1994a, 59). The *Zuozhuan*, too, speaks of the future King Wu as having only younger brothers.[9] On the other hand, however, another *Shiji*-chapter, "Hereditary House Guan and Cai," reports that, initially, King Wen had another designated successor, his eldest son Yikao the Elder 伯邑考, who was demoted in favor of Fa.[10] Even though Yikao the Elder is said to have predeceased Fa's enthronement (having fallen victim to the cruel punishment of being cooked alive at the order of the last Shang ruler, the infamous tyrant Zhou[11]), his demotion was a popular topic in the late Warring States and early imperial periods as attested in several books of the time.[12] Accent falls on the incongruity of King

---

[8] *Shiji* "Guan Cai shijia" 管蔡世家 (35.1563; Nienhauser 2006, 191, 191n3) writes about nine brothers of King Wu. According to the *Zuozhuan*, Ding 4.1, 1541; 1751, King Wu had eight younger brothers by the same mother.
[9] *Zuozhuan*, Ding 4.1, 1541; 1751.
[10] *Shiji* 35.1563 and 35.1570; Nienhauser 2006, 191–192 and 205. We can possibly detect here Sima Qian's unwillingness to complicate his main account of the Zhou history with details that could potentially obscure the direct link between the exalted dynastic founders, Kings Wen and Wu.
[11] See Liang Yusheng's note on Bo Yikao in Wang and Wang 1988, 352. Fragments of the *Liutao* 六韜 excavated in Dingzhou also mention this gruesome incident, referring to King Wen's son as Yiqiao the Elder, 伯邑巧 (Hebei sheng wenwu yanjiusuo Dingzhou Hanmu zhujian zhengli xiaozu 2001, 80, slips 2264 and 2263).
[12] *Liji* "Tan Gong shang" 檀弓上 (Yang T. 2004, 53; Legge 1885, 120); *Huainanzi* "Fanlun xun" 氾論訓 (He N. 1998, 917; Queen, Major and Puett 2010, 492).

Wen's decision with the traditional ritual system, for which he is sometimes praised.[13]

The *Zhouxun* appears to be in line with the latter version of early Zhou history, both in stressing that Fa was not King Wen's eldest offspring and that King Wen operated outside the norms of the traditional ritual system when "personally" (*zi* 自) establishing Fa as his successor. However, in contrast to the *Zhouxun*, these sources sometimes name Dan 旦, the future Duke of Zhou 周公, as another one of King Wen's worthy sons (*Shiji* 35.1563; Nienhauser 2006, 193). The *Zhouxun* is also unique in suggesting that Fa was of a less noble maternal lineage than his other siblings. Most available records depict him as the (second born) son of King Wen's principal wife.[14] As such, he was the most natural successor to his father's position (after Bo Yikao's death).

Closely connected with the issue of how many brothers he had is the account of how many of his brothers King Wu enfeoffed after ascending the throne. The above-mentioned chapters of the *Shiji*, understandably, name a significantly higher number of fiefs that King Wu bestowed on his brothers.[15] Moreover, the idyllic picture around the positive outcomes of King Wu's actions found in the *Zhouxun* leaves unmentioned the fact that, soon after his death, two of his brothers rebelled against the Zhou court, and peace was reached only after three years of combat (*Shiji* 4.132; Nienhauser 1994a, 64). King Wu's decision to return to the west after his conquest of the Shang in the east, is named among the reasons for the outbreak of the civil war (Li F. 2006, 65).

Most significantly, the notion of the Heaven's Mandate, the main ideological invention of Zhou aristocracy to justify their overturn of the preceding Shang (Allan 2015, 13–14), is absent from this account. Likewise absent are various constitutive elements of this theory such as the brutal tyranny of the last Shang ruler, Zhou (*Shiji* 3.105–109; Nienhauser 1994a, 49–52), the centrality of "virtue" as the main prerequisite for wielding political power, the importance of heeding advice from wise ministers[16] etc. While putting aside this complex ideological background as well as the interplay between its different components, the *Zhouxun* instead makes a strong case for worthiness, by claiming that it will prove effective under any circumstances and in any situation.

---

[13] *Huainanzi ibid.*
[14] There is also a view that Bo Yikao's mother was not King Wen's principal wife. Shaughnessy 1999, 309n38.
[15] *Shiji* 35.1564; Nienhauser 2006, 193. For a chart of the branch lineages established under the Western Zhou kings, including King Wu, see Khayutina 2021, 74.
[16] On the connection between possession of Heaven's mandate and able ministers, see *Shangshu* "Jun shi" 君奭 (Gu and Liu 2005, 1560; Karlgren 1950b, 59–60).

4

Fourth Month

The introductory passage from this chapter is missing. However, the remaining parts reveal that this content belonged to chapter four. Lord Zhaowen's instruction is dedicated to the events that took place in the state of Chu around five hundred years after the establishment of the Zhou dynasty, covered in the previous chapter. The shift is significant not only in terms of time, as Chu was traditionally viewed as the "cultural Other of the Zhou world" (Pines 2020, 123).[1] Even though recent archeological discoveries have mitigated this view, "the Northern Bias" in regard to Chu remains very influential in academic circles even today (Cook and Blakeley 1999, 1–2).

The account discusses a critical moment in the history of this state when it was invaded by the army of the neighboring state of Wu, perhaps the most influential power in interstate affairs around the turn of the 6th and 5th centuries BCE. Pressed by Wu's assault, Chu's sovereign, King Zhao of Chu (r. 515–489), was forced to abandon his capital and flee for his life, but was able to recover lost territories in the following year.[2]

The moral of the story is summarized by Lord Zhaowen to the effect that it was King Zhao's humane attitude in the face of Wu's aggression that inspired a staunch spirit of resistance among the inhabitants of the Ying, which allowed Chu to eventually turn the tide in his favor and offset the initial successes of the adversary King Helü of Wu (r. 514–496). This is the first historical account of the *Zhouxun* which does not explicitly deal with the problem of succession. Yet the lessons drawn from it are still relevant to someone who is about to assume political power.

This is one of the shortest accounts in the manuscript. Except for the missing opening slip, the rest of the chapter is complete and includes eleven slips (54–64). Thematically, it consists of the narrative (54/1–61/4), Lord Zhaowen's assessment of the reported events, which, this time, contains a *shi* line (61/5–62/13) and finally, a rhetorical question directed at Prince Gong (62/14–23).

---

[1] For a concise discussion on Chu's identity and relation to Zhou, see *ibid.*, 122–147.
[2] *Shiji* "Shi'er zhuhou biao" 十二諸侯年表 (14.665). For a detailed description of the events of this campaign, see *Shiji* "Wu Taibo shijia" 吳太伯世家 (31.1466; Nienhauser 2006, 17–18). And *Shiji* "Chu shijia" 楚世家 (40.1715; Nienhauser 2006, 413–415). For a summary of events, see Blakeley 1999, 17.

Translation

【・維歲四月更旦之日,龏(共)大子朝,周昭文公自身貳之,用茲念也。曰:】
[・It was on the first day of the fourth month of the year, when Crown Prince Gong came to court. Lord Zhaowen of Zhou personally enjoined him with these (following) reminders. He said:]

54/1 昔吳攻郢,昭王陲(垂)泣以辭(辭)其民曰:「與人之兄處而殺其弟,吾【54】弗忍也。與人之父居而殄其子,吾何以國為?為它人臣與為吾臣,【55】剴(豈)有以異?楚吳其何澤(擇)?皆勉侍矣。吾將去女(汝),往適遠方。」乃與其【56】奴宵出。夜半,郢人求君弗得,師若失親,莫不瀾泣。於是乃挂幼【57】扶老,抱負赤子,以從昭王。謂昭王曰:「以眾則楚不如吳,以勇則【58】吳不如楚。民請還,為致勇之寇。」乃反(返),至于干(邗)王之所,令吳闔廬【59】一夜未嘗不三徙臥。闔廬無聊,不倆(倆)楚得,恐失其身,乃復歸郢,【60】若其始也。61/4

In the past, when [the state of] Wu attacked [the capital of Chu] Ying, King Zhao was shedding tears as he bid farewell to his people, saying: "Dwelling with people's older brothers, while killing their younger brothers, is something that I cannot bear to do. Residing with people's fathers, while exterminating their sons, how could I do this for the sake of [retaining control over] the state? Is there really a difference between being someone else's subject and being my subject? What is there to choose between Chu and Wu? In both cases, it is all about exerting oneself to serve [the ruler]! I am going to leave you behind and go to a faraway place." Thereupon, he headed out with his servants at night. In the middle of the night, the people of Ying looked for their ruler but could not find him. The troops felt as if they had lost their father, there were none who did not weep profusely. Thereupon, they carried their young and supported their old, carrying newborns on their backs, [in order] to follow after King Zhao. They said to him: "In terms of [troop] numbers, Chu is inferior to Wu. But in terms of courage, Wu is inferior to Chu. [Your] people ask you to come back, and employ their courage against those bandits." Thereupon he returned and reached the positions of the King of Han[3]. He made Helü of Wu move his sleeping place three times a night. Helü was at the end of his tether. He could not subdue Chu and feared

---

[3] King Helü is referred to both as Helü of Wu and King of Han. Based on a record that Han was fortified by Wu in 486 BCE found in *Zuozhuan*, Ai 9.5, 1652; 1887, Han 2015, 292 conjectures that, for strategic reasons, Wu could not have moved their capital to Han prior to that year. Therefore, the *Zhouxun* is anachronistic when saying that King Helü was based in Han already in 506 BCE. This inconsistency would not be very surprising since the manuscript is ripe with problematic accounts.

he would perish. Thereupon, [King Zhao] again returned to Ying, restoring the status quo.

61/5 昭王有失郢之行，而無德於民，其乏祀必矣，剴（豈）有（又）尚【61】得為君？此《詩》所謂「壞（懷）德維甯（寧）」者也。62/13
King Zhao lost [his capital] Ying and, had he not had the virtue-inspired gratitude of his people, he certainly would have lost the sacrificial altar. How else could he manage to retain his rule? This is what an Ode expresses in saying: "Cherishing virtue secures peace."

62/14 人君其胡可以毋務壞（懷）德？62/23
How can a ruler neglect cherishing virtue?

已【62】學（教）大子用茲念，斯乃受（授）之書，而自身屬（囑）之曰：女（汝）勉毋忘歲四月【63】更旦之馴（訓）。【64】
Having instructed the crown prince with these reminders, [Lord Zhaowen] gave him the text [of his speech] and personally cautioned him, saying: "Strive not to forget the instructions from the first day of the fourth month of the year."

Comments

As follows from his summary of the narrated events and the concluding rhetorical question, Lord Zhaowen interprets King Zhao's flight from Ying and his eventual triumph over King Helü as exemplifying the importance of "virtue." This notion includes two aspects: kindness shown to subordinates (here: the inhabitants of the capital) and the latter's ensuing enthusiastic support. A similar idea was expressed in the personal appeal to Prince Gong in chapter 2, and we will encounter it again on several occasions.

Among the previous cases, this chapter stands out through a less rigid structure. Tetrasyllabic lines appear sporadically, but the rhyme pattern is not clear. Most rhymes appear in direct speech, such as in the Ying inhabitants' plea to King Zhao (58/11–59/12):

1	以眾則楚不如吳，	魚	In terms of [troop] numbers, Chu is inferior to Wu.
2	以勇則|吳不如楚。	魚	But in terms of courage, Wu is inferior to Chu.
3	民請還，		[Your] people ask you to come back,
4	為致勇之寇。	侯	and employ their courage against those bandits.

Lord Zhaowen's interpretation of this anecdote in a certain light is remarkable. While the term "virtue" is completely absent from the narrative itself, the narrator renders it the central issue of the story just by introducing the notion in his summary of events. Moreover, the importance of virtue is further emphasized both in a quotation from an Ode which corresponds to the poem "Ban" (Mao 254)[4] in the *Shijing* and in the concluding rhetorical question. This serves as demonstration that without his virtuous conduct, King Zhao's subordinates would not have been animated to such vigorous resistance and, therefore, he would not have been able to retain his rule.

Context

While Wu's occupation of Chu did indeed take place (see above), the *Zhouxun*, yet again, presents an interpretation of events that is at odds with most other sources. Firstly, King Zhao's popularity and high esteem among Chu people seem dubious against the background of the *Zuozhuan*, *Guoyu* and *Shiji*, where this sovereign is reported to have closely escaped assassination by his subordinates on his flight from Ying.[5] Moreover, in the *Zhuangzi* and *Han Shi waizhuan*, the rationales of those inhabitants of the Chu capital who did follow their leader into exile are revealed as having to do rather with their instinct of self-preservation than loyalty to their ruler.[6] As for King Zhao's eventual reconquering of the capital Ying, it is usually attributed to the internal conflict among the Wu aristocracy.[7] At the same time, military help from the states of Qin and Yue was also a significant factor for Wu's eventual withdrawal (Blakeley 1999, 17). Nor does the *Zhouxun* mention that King Zhao had to move his capital to Ruo 鄀 in the wake of another invasion by Wu in 594.[8]

---

[4] This was also a very well-received poem appearing in several transmitted and some excavated works. For instances, see Goldin 2005, 147 and Kern 2003, 35. However, only the *Zuozhuan* quotes the line appearing in chapter four, as follows from Ho and Chan 2004, 242

[5] *Zuozhuan*, Ding 4.3, 1546–1548; 1757–1759, *Guoyu* "Chuyu xia" 楚語下 (Xu Y. 2002, 524; Taskin 1987, 266–267), *Shiji* 31.1466; Nienhauser 2006, 18, and 40.1715–16; Nienhauser 2006, 414. See also, Milburn 2010, 13.

[6] *Zhuangzi* "Rang Wang" 讓王 (Guo Q. 1990, 974) and *Han Shi waizhuan* (Xu W. 1980, 272–274). For English translation, see Watson 2013, 243–24, and Hightower 1952, 254–256. For the relationship between King Zhao's "miserable flight" from Ying and the inscription on the bells of Marquis Yu of Zeng, see Pines 2020, 85–88.

[7] *Shiji* 31.1467; Nienhauser 2006, 18. The excavated manuscript *Xinian* 繫年 also attributes the withdrawal of Wu troops from Chu to the rebellion against King Helü. See Milburn 2016b, 76 and Pines 2020, 203.

[8] Milburn 2010, 13. The excavated text *Chuju* 楚居 (For transcription, see Li X. 2010, 181–82) even reports that King Zhao never returned to Ying after reclaiming the lost parts of his state (Li S. 2012a, 212).

The only other source providing a similar interpretation of these events is the *Xinshu* 新書 by Jia Yi 賈誼 (201–169 BCE). There, too, Wu troops are said to withdraw because of the determined resistance of Ying inhabitants, which was inspired by their gratitude for King Zhao's kindness.[9] But the two accounts are by no means identical. In the *Xinshu*, King Zhao is reported to have shown compassion to his subordinates in an event that took place prior to Helü's invasion, whereas the *Zhouxun* interprets King Zhao's very flight as a manifestation of his unwillingness to sacrifice his subordinates' lives to oppose Wu. Moreover, and most surprisingly, the *Zhouxun* is unique in making King Zhao explain the rationale for fleeing with the words: "Dwelling with people's older brothers, while killing their younger brothers, is something that I cannot bear to do. Residing with people's fathers, while exterminating their sons, how could I do this for the sake of [retaining control over] the state?"

The same statement was commonly attributed to one of the most prominent early representatives of the Zhou lineage, Grand King of Zhou 周太王, also known as the Grand King, Father Dan 大王亶父, or Ancient Duke, Father Dan 古公亶父[10]. Facing incessant incursions from Di tribes (*di ren* 狄人), the Grand King utters these words to manifest his unwillingness to jeopardize the most precious possession of a political leader: his people's lives. Moved by his exemplary attitude, the people followed him to the foot of Mount Qi 岐山, the area that was destined to become the heartland of the Zhou.[11] Given the foundational significance of this event for the Zhou's "humanistic" self-understanding[12] as well as the Grand King's eminence in the ritual system of the Zhou[13], the attribution of these words to King Zhao of Chu, the head of a polity which was a longtime rival of the Zhou[14], is truly remarkable. Especially when we consider that through this story, Lord Zhaowen, a descendant of the Grand King, was effectively undermining his ancestor's fame and, by extension, the legitimacy of his own rule. Regardless of whether this attribution was made to curry favor with the mighty southern state of Chu or signal departure from conventional Zhou claims to power, the passage under consideration unequivocally demonstrates

---

[9] *Xinshu* "Yu cheng" 諭誠 (Yan and Zhong 2000, 279).
[10] *Shiji* 4.113–114; *Lüshi chunqiu* "Shenwei" 審為 (Chen Q. 2001, 1463–1464); *Zhuangzi* "Rang Wang" 讓王 (Guo Q. 1990, 967) etc.
[11] On the preeminence of Mount Qi over other residences from the early Zhou period, see Khayutina 2008, 25–65.
[12] According to the *Shiji*, auspicious signs announcing the future rise of the Zhou commenced with the Grand King. *Shiji* 4.119; Nienhauser 1994a, 59.
[13] On the central role of the Grand King in the Zhou's ancestral temple system, see Li F. 2013, 144–145.
[14] The first military conflict between these two states took place as early as 960 BCE. Blakeley 1999, 10.

the malleable character of early Chinese anecdotes, where the same actions and words are often attributed to different characters.

5

Fifth Month

In his fifth instruction, Lord Zhaowen moves the discussion to the South-Eastern periphery of the Zhou world by recounting events that took place in the state of Yue only a few decades after the Chu-Wu confrontation described in the previous chapter. Yue's "otherness" in relation to the cultural values of the Central States was emphasized even more unabashedly in writings from the Warring States period than that of Chu.[1]

However, despite its otherness, this state has produced a number of individuals who were admired and emulated also in the Huaxia 華夏 states and who came to occupy an important place in the shared historical and philosophical knowledge of China. The main protagonist of this anecdote, King Goujian of Yue (r. 496–465 BCE), certainly belongs among such individuals.[2] The Yue ruler is depicted here in the last moments of his life, giving final instructions to his heir apparent, who remains unnamed.[3]

The subject of the instruction are King Goujian's mortal enemies, father and son, King Helü and King Fuchai 夫差 (r. 495–473 BCE), whom he defeated after a grueling twenty-year confrontation during some periods of which Yue found itself on the brink of extinction.[4] While King Fuchai, under whose reign Wu was annihilated, understandably features as the epitome of an inept ruler, his father, whose military successes against Chu marked Wu's rapid ascendence to one of the most powerful states of the time, receives an ambivalent appraisal. This ambivalence is a reminder that rulers are judged not solely by their lifetime

---

[1] While most writings of the period treated Yue as barbarians, some authors presented a rather nuanced view of the subject. Thus, we can say with Erica Brindley that "Yue people were not invariably viewed as uncivilized barbarians of low worth" (2003, 24). For thematic correspondences between the Zhou tradition and bronze inscriptions from Yue, see Cook 2011, 332–333.
[2] On Goujian's popularity in Chinese antiquity, see Cohen 2009, 1–35.
[3] For a discussion of the succession of Yue kings since Goujian, see Henry 2007, 11–14.
[4] For a brief early mention of this conflict, see *Zuozhuan*, Ding 14.5, 1595; 1817). For detailed depictions, see the "Wuyu" 吳語 chapter and the two "Yueyu" 越語 chapters of the *Guoyu* (Xu Y. 2002, 536–566, 567–591). For Russian translations of "Wuyu" and "Yueyu," see Taskin 1987, 273–290 and 291–304. For German translation of the "Yueyu" chapters, see Meisterernst 2002, 509–542. See also *Shiji* 31.1468–1475; Nienhauser 2006, 19–24. Long accounts of the conflict are also provided in later works such as the *Yuejue shu* (Li B. 2013) and *Wu Yue chunqiu* (Zhou 1997). For their respective dates of composition, see Schuessler and Loewe 1993, 490–491 and Lagerwey 1993, 474–475.

achievements, but also, perhaps to a greater degree, by their decisions regarding the future trajectory of their states, of which the establishment of an heir apparent is the most important one.

This chapter is comprised of eleven bamboo slips (65–75), and one slip appears to be missing (*Beida Mss.* 111). As it stands, the passage is very uncharacteristic of the *Zhouxun*, consisting only of the narrative centered around King Goujian's admonitions (66/2–74/24), while Lord Zhaowen makes no address to Prince Gong.

Translation

65/1 • 維歲五月更旦之日，龔（共）大子朝，周昭文公自身貳之，用茲念也。
【65】曰： 66/1
• It was on the first day of the fifth month of the year, when Crown Prince Gong came to court. Lord Zhaowen of Zhou personally enjoined him with these (following) reminders. He said:

66/2 昔越王句賤（踐）有疾，乃召其嗣，而與之言曰：「吾所屬（囑）女（汝）無它，其【66】要既盡於不善而勿為。務若闔廬之自令柏（伯）也，而勉毋效其置【67】夫賎（差）也。余告女（汝）於三江之閒，其歌謠之詩，而女（汝）謹聽之，曰：『越之【68】城旦發幕於干（邗），吳既為孟（虛），其執衛〈衛〉闔廬？唯（雖）已弇（掩）貍（埋）之，寇出其骸，【69】莫守其墳，人發其丘，扣以為墼（墼），剴（豈）或禁之？見其若是也，其誰能【70】毋怵惕？』而勉監（鑒）於茲。徒步之人，布衣之士，猷（猶）有羞辱（辱），惡大詢聰（恥），【71】皇（況）在千乘人君之大子？闔廬入地乃十予餘年，而木既出矣。今【72】我去女（汝），往臧（藏）骰（髮）齒。余恐而輕國而不好文理，不愛民而乏絕吾【73】祀，持（特）令我殍（卒）而若闔廬不孕（孝）而已。余恐其若此，吾故不能毋出【74】

In the past, when King Goujian of Yue became ill, he summoned his heir and spoke to him: "What I caution you with is simply this: do not undo yourself at the hands of a bad [heir]. So, make effort to be like Helü in making yourself a hegemon, but be sure not to emulate his installing of [his unworthy son] Fuchai. I will tell you the verses of a folk song from the area between the Three Rivers.[5]

---

[5] While the "Three Rivers" often designate the Wu-Yue area in early texts, the exact meaning of the term is ambiguous. Among alternatives are Min River 岷江, Song River 松江 and Zhe River 浙江 (Xu Y. 2002, 568–569); Song River 松江, Qiantang River 錢塘江 and Puyang River 濮陽江 as suggested by Wei Zhao 韋昭 (204–273), and Song River 松江, Lou River 婁

Listen carefully to what they say: "Yue's earth pounder convicts dismantle graves in Han [to build the walls], Wu is nothing but a wasteland now. Who will defend Helü? Although he has already been buried, the bandits disentombed his remains, and there was no one to protect his grave. People dismantle his burial mound, turning it into a gorge, and was there anyone to put a stop to this? Seeing this happening, who could not be frightened and alarmed?" Make effort to reflect on this. Ordinary people and plain-clothed men of service, still retain a sense of shame, loathing a great disgrace. How much more so the crown prince of a ruler with a thousand chariots? Helü was buried just over ten years ago, but his coffin has already been disentombed. Now, I am about to leave you, going to hide away my remains (lit.: hair and teeth). I am afraid that you will treat the state lightly and not appreciate the elevated patterns, that you will not care for the people and will cut off my sacrifices, so that, after my death, I, like Helü, will not be treated piously (not receive offerings). I am afraid that this will happen and I, thus, cannot but be taken out [from my grave].

【□□□□□□。已學（教）大子用茲念，斯乃受（授）之書，而自身屬（囑）之曰：】75/1 女（汝）勉毋忘歲五月更旦之馴（訓）。【75】
[Having instructed the crown prince with these reminders, [Lord Zhaowen] gave him the text [of his speech] and personally cautioned him, saying:] "Strive not to forget the instructions from the first day of the fifth month of the year."

Comments

Stylistically, King Goujian's speech belongs to the genre of "deathbed admonitions," of which there are many instances among the early Chinese writings. The Yue ruler uses a song popular in the area "between the Three Rivers" as evidence that King Fuchai, whose "lack of goodness" led to Wu's annihilation and disentombment of his father's coffin, was condemned even by people of the lower strata of society, that is, "ordinary people" and "plain-clothed men of service."[6] The crown prince of a great state[7] is naturally obliged to adhere to a much stricter moral code than commoners and should attempt to avoid such a shameful situation at all costs. To this end, King Goujian emphasizes the necessity of "being fond of the elevated patterns" and "caring for the people." Hence, King Fuchai,

---

江 and Dong River 東江, as suggested by Gu Yi 顧夷 (Wu Y. 1993, 213n54). For relevant discussions, see Liu T. 012015, 65–66; He J. 2021, 135n105.

[6] On the function of songs as the "voice of the people," see Lü 2016, 88–89. For analysis of the role of songs in early historical writings, see Kern 2005a, 69–71.

[7] Interestingly, Goujian ranks Yue as having only "thousand chariots," which makes it comparable to Lord Zhaowen's own "small" state.

in addition to lacking goodness, is implicitly accused of also failing to fulfill these two criteria.

King Goujian's account of learning about the ill fate of Helü's remains from a tune sung by the common people appears to imply that he was not personally responsible for this event. At the same time, the men dismantling the tomb to construct walls are identified in the song as Yue (earth pounder) convicts. This can be taken to suggest a state-run operation (Han 2015, 292–293). In my opinion, however, the Yue's official involvement in this matter is not hinted at here. Firstly, this exceptionally humiliating measure would make King Goujian, the epitome of a good ruler, appear in a bad light. Secondly, the people opening the grave are also called "bandits" in the subsequent lines. Thirdly, in a similar passage dedicated to Goujian in the last chapter of the *Zhouxun*, the Yue ruler is said to discover the scene by chance. Therefore, by giving grave diggers the "Yue" identity, the text appears to simply point to Wu's annexation and annihilation through Yue.

Turning to the text's rhetorical features, we see that the chapter is largely composed by long rhymed passages, which predominantly consist of tetrasyllabic lines with the end-rhyme *zhi* 之 (69/16–74/13). However, at times, rhyme and meter show deviations from this pattern. For instance, King Goujian opens his instruction with a sequence of longer sentences with the end-rhyme *ge* 歌 (66/18–68/3). The song, on the other hand, employs in its opening part the rhymes *yuan* 元 and *yu* 魚 (68/23–69/15). Another feature of the passage is that personal names (Helü and Fuchai) as well as proper names (Han 邗) are integrated into the rhyme patterns creating a rhyming historical account and, thus, deviating from the impersonal abstract platitudes which are usually conveyed by tetrasyllabic rhymes (Schaberg 2015, 103).

Opening (66/2–16)

1	昔越王句踐有疾，	質	In the past, when King Goujian of Yue became ill,
2	乃召其嗣，	之	he summoned his heir
3	而與之言曰：		and spoke to him:

Admonition (66/17–67/3)

4	「吾所囑汝無它，	歌	"What I caution you with is simply this:
5	其要既盡於不善而勿為。	歌	do not undo yourself at the hands of a bad [heir].
6	而勉毋效其置夫差也。	歌	but be sure not to emulate his installing of Fuchai.

Fifth Month / 115

Bridge (67/8–22)

7	余告汝於三江之閒，		I will tell you the verses of a folk song
8	其歌謠之詩，	之	from the area between the three rivers.
9	而汝謹聽之，曰：	之	Listen carefully to what they say:

Song (67/23–71/3)

10	「越之城旦	元	"Yue's earth pounder convicts
11	發冢於邗，	元	dismantle graves in Han [to build the walls],
12	吳既為虛，	魚	Wu is nothing but a wasteland now.
13	其孰衛闔廬？	魚	Who will defend Helü?
14	雖已掩埋之，	之	Although he has already been buried,
15	寇出其骸，		the bandits disentombed his remains,
16	莫守其墳，		and there was no one to protect his grave.
17	人發其丘，	之	People dismantle his burial mound,
18	扣以為壑，		turning it into a gorge,
19	豈或禁之？	之	and was there anyone to put a stop to this?
20	見其若是也，	支	Seeing this happening,
21	其誰能毋怵惕？」	錫	who could not be frightened and alarmed?"

Advice (71/4–72/9)

22	而勉鑒於茲。	之	Make effort to reflect on this.
23	徒步之人，		Ordinary people
24	布衣之士，	之	and plain-clothed men of service,
25	猶有羞辱，		still retain a sense of shame,
26	惡大詢恥，		loathing a great disgrace.
27	況在千乘人君之大子？	之	How much more so the crown prince of a ruler with a thousand chariots?

Additional Information (72/10–73/7)

28	闔廬入地乃十于餘年，		Helü was buried just over ten years ago,
29	而木既出矣。		but his coffin has already been disentombed.

Concern (73/8–74/24)

30	今|我去汝，	之 Now, I am about to leave you,
31	往藏髮齒。	之 going to hide away my remains.
32	余恐而輕國而不好文理，	之 I am afraid that you will treat the state lightly and not appreciate the elevated patterns,
33	不愛民而乏絕吾|祀，	之 that you will not care for the people and will cut off my sacrifices,
34	特令我卒而若闔廬不孝而已。	that, after I have died, you will not treat me with filial piety, as was the case with Helü.
35	余恐其若此，	支 I am afraid that this will happen,
36	吾故不能毋出	and I, thus, cannot but be taken out [from my grave].

The complexity of the account might explain Lord Zhaowen's absence from this chapter (or his at best marginal presence), for we find here an admonition directed at the heir apparent, a precedent (song), a reflection on it and an expression of concern. Most of these elements are usually connected to Lord Zhaowen, whose appearance is thus rendered unnecessary.

Context

As was the case in most previous chapters, we encounter the problem of anachronism here as well. Namely, at the moment of King Goujian's final speech (465 BCE), King Helü, who passed away in 496 BCE, must have been dead for more than thirty (and not just ten) years. Therefore, Goujian's account implies that King Helü's disentombment took place well during the rule of King Fuchai, who ascended the throne following his father's death. The historically highly problematic dating was, most likely, created to emphasize the rapidity of Wu's decline.

But had the event itself ever taken place? Doubts are justified, given that none of the numerous texts providing minute descriptions of various aspects of the Wu-Yue conflict report about the sad fate of Helü's remains. We find references to this incident only in the *Lüshi chunqiu*[8] and Liu Xiang's biography in the *Hanshu* (36.1954). But since the authors of the *Lüshi chunqiu* as well as Liu Xiang were evidently familiar with the *Zhouxun* and incorporated parts of it in their works, it is very likely that they took this information from there.

Several points seem to support the view that this account indeed originated in the *Zhouxun*. Some of these points simply follow from the logic of the story,

---

[8] *Lüshi chunqiu* "Zhihua" 知化 (Chen Q. 2001, 1562; Knoblock and Riegel 2000, 593).

while others take into account the broader historical context. As for the former, it is logical to assume that the image of Helü's open tomb would represent the greatest fear for a man such as King Goujian who himself was about to embark on the journey to the netherworld. As for the historical context, the story is reminiscent of the events that took place during Helü's invasion of Ying, mentioned in chapter 4.

Accordingly, Helü's minister Wu Zixu 伍子胥 (?–484 BCE), avenging his father's and brother's deaths, who fell victim to slander while serving at the court of King Ping of Chu (?–516 BCE), opened the tomb of this king and whipped his corpse.[9] The exceptionally humiliating treatment of the Chu monarch's remains is mirrored in the reference to King Helü in the *Zhouxun*.[10] Therefore, we cannot exclude the possibility that his shameful fate, as reported in the latter, was an expression of the author's idea of historical retribution.[11] At the same time, we can see this motive as expressing Goujian's revenge for the (in some accounts: self-inflicted) humiliation which he experienced during his captivity in Wu.[12]

In the common perception, King Fuchai's ineptness was largely caused by his decision not to annihilate the state of Yue when he had the chance to do so. At the same time, in making this decision, he is usually portrayed as following the advice of the corrupt Prime Minister Pi 太宰嚭 and rejecting the loyal Wu Zixu's vigorous admonitions.[13] In so doing, he is contrasted to King Goujian, who is said "to have gone to considerable troubles to recruit good advisors" (Milburn 2010, 22).

In fact, in most narratives centered around the Wu-Yue conflict, the importance of ministers is such that monarchs appear reduced to "the position of a figure-head at best, and at worst a puppet, controlled by the intelligence of others" (Milburn 2010, 10). In this chapter of the *Zhouxun*, however, the importance of ministerial counsel does not play any role at all. Instead, the theme of "caring for the people" features prominently. On this point, Fuchai and Goujian are again represented as diametrically opposed to each other. While the

---

[9] *Shiji* 31.1466. According to another version of the story found in *Zuozhuan*, *Guoyu* and other *Shiji* chapters, Wu Zixu only whipped King Ping's tomb, not his corpse. However, there are no reasons to regard the "corpse" version as inauthentic or of a later date. For a discussion of the topic, see Nienhauser 1994b, 54n45.

[10] That Wu Zixu's extraordinary actions were perceived as transgressing the Way of Heaven follows from his criticism by Chu minister Shen Baoxu 申包胥. See *Shiji* "Wu Zixu liezhuan" 伍子胥列傳 (66.2177; Nienhauser 1994b, 55).

[11] Interestingly, King Helü's first invasion of Chu, which culminated in the sacking of Ying, was often perceived in the ancient sources as having been "orchestrated by Wu Zixu in revenge for his father's death" (Milburn 2010, 13).

[12] The ability to bear humiliation can be seen as one of the central motives in the Goujian story (Cohen 2009, 31–33).

[13] Cohen 2009, 30; Milburn 2010, 14. According to *Shiji* 31.1475; Nienhauser 2006, 24, in his last words, Fuchai expressed regret for not having followed Wu Zixu's advice.

former is routinely accused of subjecting his population to severe treatment[14], Goujian is presented as a kind and compassionate monarch in a number of received texts as well as some excavated texts, such as the Tsinghua manuscript, *Yue Gong qi shi* 越公其事.[15]

The answer to the question whether King Goujian succeeded in educating his unnamed heir (thus becoming a truly great ruler) cannot be answered definitively when considering only the transmitted sources, which, while proving the existence of Yue until 333 BCE[16], are very quiet on the time after its annihilation of Wu (Brindley 2015, 89–91). This paucity is sometimes taken as emphasizing Goujian's unique position in the history of the state of Yue (Milburn 2010, 23). However, some newly emerged historical accounts, such as the *Xinian*, provide compelling evidence that the state of Yue remained a very powerful political player in the interstate affairs of the Chinese world until the very end of the fifth century BCE.[17] Therefore, the above question would have received an unreservedly positive answer from a Zhanguo reader.

---

[14] *Guoyu* "Yueyu xia" (Xu Y. 2002, 580).

[15] For transcription, see Li X. 2017, 112–151. On the differences between the account of this manuscript and the transmitted sources discussing the Wu-Yue conflict, see Li S. 2017, 79. For the summary of King Goujian's "five policies" (*wuzheng* 五政) with which he won popular support, see Tsai 2020, 65–66. On the possible "Huang-Lao" affiliation of the "five policies," see Yuan Q. 2020, 185–191.

[16] *Shiji* "Yue wang Goujian shijia" 越王句踐世家 (41.1751).

[17] On the alliance between the states of Jin and Yue and their joint military campaigns against the state of Qi in the years 441, 430 and 404 BCE, see Pines 2020, 113–116, 223, 231–233.

6

Sixth Month

In the sixth chapter, the discussion moves about one hundred fifty years back in time from the Wu-Yue conflict. Here, Lord Zhaowen provides an account of the events around the establishment of the Ducal Son Chong'er 重耳 as the ruler of the mighty state of Jin. Having received the posthumous title Lord Wen of Jin (r. 636–628 BCE), Chong'er belongs among the most charismatic rulers of the Chunqiu era. His military successes and rapidly growing political influence elevated him to the position of "hegemon,"[1] whose mission was "to serve the function of guardian of the Zhou feudal system" (Hsu 1999, 555).

However, at the outset of his political career, there was little to suggest that Chong'er would once become a dominating figure in the interstate political events of the Zhou world. To begin with, he was not the heir apparent of his father, Lord Xian of Jin (r. 676–651 BCE).[2] Furthermore, he had to flee from Jin in the wake of the major succession crisis that broke out following the machinations of his father's consort, Li Ji 驪姬, who attempted to eliminate other claimants to the Jin throne in order to clear the way to power for her son, Xiqi 奚齊.[3]

In the end, after nineteen years spent in exile and after several other individuals succeeded Lord Xian, Chong'er was able, with vital support from the state of Qin, to establish himself at the ruler of Jin. While anecdotes about Chong'er, especially his long journey in exile, constitute the mainstay of early Chinese historical literature[4], the *Zhouxun* does not mention any of the complex political details surrounding his eventual ascent to power. Instead, the grandeur of his character is firmly emphasized as the very factor which secured him the people's unwavering support and, eventually, made his political rise possible.

With a scope of sixteen bamboo slips (76–91), the present chapter belongs among the longest in the *Zhouxun*. In addition, it has no lacunae and could be

---

[1] For the specific events leading up to the assumption of this title, see Pines 2020, 83.
[2] The original successor to Lord Xian was Chong'er's older half-brother Shensheng 申生. See *Zuozhuan*, Zhuang 28.2, 239; 213.
[3] As a result of Li Ji's schemes Shensheng was forced to commit suicide, while Chong'er and his younger half-brother Yiwu 夷吾 had to save their lives by leaving Jin. See Xi 4.6, 299; 269–271.
[4] For extensive records of his wanderings, see *Zuozhuan*, Xi 5.2, 305; 274 and Xi 23.6, 404–411; 365–371. For analysis of the literary characteristics of Chong'er stories, see Khayutina 2006, 20–47.

reconstructed in its entire original length. Thematically, it is constituted by the account of the individuals who came to rule over the state of Jin in the wake of Lord Xian's death in the time from roughly 656 BCE to 607 BCE (77/2–83/16), a succinct summary of these events using a Document (83/17–84/11), as well as Lord Zhaowen's long personal plea to Prince Gong (84/12–90/6).

Translation

76/1 • 維歲六月更旦之日，龏（共）大子朝，周昭文公自身貳之，用茲念也。
【76】曰：77/1

• It was on the first day of the sixth month of the year, when Crown Prince Gong came to court. Lord Zhaowen of Zhou personally enjoined him with these (following) reminders. He said:

77/2 昔晉獻公有子四人，皆易為嗣。（奚）齊先立，而不能自治，淺智【77】而愚，眾弗述（遂）置。紳（卓）子繼之，不宵（肖）以疑，其下既不樹（附），民莫之戴。二子【78】已發（廢），夷吾乃代，棄德反施，無仁而善倍（背），虜以入秦，身大蓐（辱）聭（恥），歸【79】而從嚻（虁）。圉子立（蒞）事，德仁無行，布惠弗丞，群臣莫臣，弗肎（肯）為使，失【80】立（位）亡國，其身環（旋）代。茲四主者，非不已嘗君百姓，有嗣不智不慧，【81】故皆云（殞）極（殛）。四主無後，重耳乃置，李〈孝〉弟（悌）茲（慈）仁，眾莫弗喜，述（遂）長有晉。【82】子孫繼嗣，非徒不廢，有（又）柏（伯）於世，大盈（逞）其志。83/16

In the past, Lord Xian of Jin had four sons, each of them in turn replaced the other as heir. Xiqi was established first, but he was not able to regulate himself. Being of shallow wisdom, he was foolish, and the masses did not support his installation. Zhuozi succeeded him, but raised doubts due to his unworthiness. His subordinates did not cling to him [completely], none among the people supported him. After these two sons were abandoned, they were replaced by Yiwu. He discarded virtue and was opposed to conferring it upon others. Lacking humaneness, he was skillful at betrayal. He entered Qin as a prisoner, experiencing a great disgrace and shame. Soon after returning [to Jin], he passed away. When Yuzi was put in charge of affairs, neither virtue nor humaneness was carried out. He did not extend kindness frequently, and none of the ministers ministered to him, unwilling to be in his service. [And so,] he lost his position and put the state to ruin, and was replaced immediately. As for these four rulers, it is not that they did not already rule over the "hundred surnames," but rather that, as successors, they were unwise and imprudent, and so, they all vanished. These four rulers had no descendants, and so Chong'er was installed. He was filial, brotherly, compassionate and humane, are there was no one among the masses who did not like him. So, he succeeded in ruling Jin for a long time, and his sons and grandsons inherited his position. Not only was he not discarded, he became a hegemon of his age, freely exercising his will.

83/17 此《書》之所謂曰：「主擇【83】臣，臣亦擇主」者也，既箸（書）於志。84/11

This is what a Document expresses in saying: "A ruler chooses his minister; but a minister chooses his ruler as well." It is already manifest in the records.

84/12 今女（汝）能茲（慈）孝，尊仁貴信，余唯（雖）未爾立，【84】而身自令，余唯（雖）已終，至于季年，眾之立女（汝）也，若日之必出，猶將【85】戴天。爾遠信仁而不能茲（慈）孝，惡學曾（憎）善而不聽教道（導），余唯（雖）身置【86】女（汝），人將代女（汝），民莫而骨〈肯〉好。夫有士〈土〉之主，將民之與處，而民不爾【87】好，其孰在而所？莫居而去，國既空虛，爾欲守國，其將誰與居？非【88】我與而言，告女（汝）其然，它人其孰敢既出茲言？烏（嗚）乎（呼）！戒哉！尚勉承【89】教，而謹慎勿曼（慢）。90/6

Now, if you are able to be compassionate and filial, to honor humaneness and value trustworthiness, then, even though I haven't established you [as heir], you will ensconce yourself. So, when I am near my end, reaching my final years, the masses will establish you as certainly as the sun will rise, [treating you] as Heaven above them. But if you distance yourself from trustworthiness and humaneness and are not able to be compassionate and filial; If you despise learning, loathe goodness and do not heed teachings and counsels; then, even if I personally install you, others will replace you, and none among the people will like you. Now, the ruler of a territory dwells there with his people. If your people dislike you, who will remain there with you? With no one residing there and everybody leaving, the state will become empty and void. Even if you wished to preserve the state, who would reside there with you? If not for me talking to you, telling you the way things are, would other people dare to utter these words? Ah well! Be cautious! Devote yourself to receiving instructions and pay attention to not getting sluggish!

90/7 已學（教）大子用茲念，斯乃受（授）之書，而自身屬（囑）之曰：【90】女（汝）勉毋忘歲六月更旦之馴（訓）。【91】

Having instructed the crown prince with these reminders, [Lord Zhaowen] gave him the text [of his speech] and personally cautioned him, saying: "Strive not to forget the instructions from the first day of the sixth month of the year."

Comments

In the first part, a historical period of several decades is covered in just a few stanzas. Accordingly, Lord Xian of Jin had four sons who consecutively became his successors and whose names were Xiqi, Zhuozi, Yiwu, and Yuzi. However, due to their moral or intellectual shortcomings, none of them succeeded in winning his subordinates' lasting support (referred to variously as the "people," the "masses," the "subjects" and the "hundred surnames." Xiqi is accused of being "foolish," Zhuozi of being "unworthy," Yiwu exemplifies a whole range of failures such as "discarding virtue," "being inhumane," "excelling at betrayal," and, finally, Yuzi is found to be lacking virtue, humaneness and kindness. While the reign of Lord Xian's four sons ended in disgrace, Chong'er's installation to the Jin throne saw it occupied by one who was "filial, brotherly, kind, and humane." Astonishingly, this narrative implies that Chong'er was not Lord Xian's son. Furthermore, by saying that he became a ruler because his predecessors on the throne "had no progeny" the text even suggests that he did not belong to the direct line of succession. The reader is thus left wondering as to his exact relation to the ruling family of Jin. In any case, it was Lord Wen's moral excellence that is said to have inspired the people's enthusiastic support, facilitating his long rule over Jin and the smooth succession of power to his descendants.

Lord Zhaowen summarizes the historical narrative part with a *shu* line: "A ruler chooses his minister; but a minister chooses his ruler as well." This is to say, the given period of Jin history can be fully explained by recurring to the wisdom contained in the documentary tradition. While absent from the *Shangshu* or *Yi Zhoushu*, a close modification of these two lines is found in many early works, among which the *Yanzi chunqiu* and *Da Dai Liji* 大戴禮記 appear to be the earliest. However, none of these texts associate the content in question with *shu* lore (Han 2015, 281).

The passage at hand provides yet another intriguing example of a historical account couched in rhyme, as it consists almost entirely of rhymed tetrasyllables (groups: *zhi* 之 and *zhi* 職).

Opening (77/2–12)

1	昔晉獻公有子四人，		In the past, Lord Xian of Jin had four sons,
2	皆易為嗣。	之	each of them in turn replaced the other as heir.

Xiqi (77/13–78/6)

3	奚齊先立，		Xiqi was established first,
4	而不能自治，	之	but he was not able to regulate himself.
5	淺智|而愚，		Being of shallow wisdom, he was foolish,

6	眾弗述遂置。	職	and the masses did not support his installation.

Zhuozi (78/7–22)

7	桌子繼之，		Zhuozi succeeded him,
8	不肖以疑，	之	but raised doubts due to his unworthiness.
9	其下既不附，		His subordinates did not cling to him
10	民莫之戴。	之	none among the people supported him.

Yiwu (78/23–80/3)

11	二子|已廢，		After these two sons were abandoned,
12	夷吾乃代，	職	they were replaced by Yiwu.
13	棄德反施，		He discarded virtue and was opposed to conferring it upon others.
14	無仁而善背，	之	Lacking humaneness, he was skillful at betrayal.
15	虜以入秦，		He entered Qin as a prisoner,
16	身大辱恥，	之	experiencing a great disgrace and shame.
17	歸|而從斃。		Soon after returning [to Jin], he passed away.

Yuzi (80/4–81/7)

18	圉子蒞事，	之	When Yuzi was put in charge of the affairs,
19	德仁無行，		neither virtue nor humaneness was carried out.
20	布惠弗亟，	職	He did not extend kindness frequently,
21	群臣莫臣，		and none of the ministers ministered to him,
22	弗肯為使，	之	unwilling to be in his service.
23	失|位亡國，	職	[And so] he lost his position and put the state to ruin,
24	其身旋代。	職	and was replaced immediately.

Summary (81/8–82/4)

25	茲四主者，		As for these four rulers,
26	非不已嘗君百姓，		it is not that they did not already rule over the "hundred surnames,"
27	有嗣不智不慧，|	質	but rather that, as successors, they were unwise and imprudent,
28	故皆殞殄。	職	and so, they all vanished.

Chong'er (82/5–83/16)

29	四主無後，		These four rulers had no progeny,
30	重耳乃置，	職	and so, Chong'er was installed.
31	孝悌慈仁，		He was filial, brotherly, compassionate and humane,
32	眾莫弗喜，	之	are there was no one among the masses who did not like him.
33	遂長有晉。|		So, he succeeded in ruling Jin for a long time,
34	子孫繼嗣，	之	and his sons and grandsons inherited his position.
35	非徒不廢，	月祭	Not only was he not discarded,
36	又伯於世，	月祭	he became a hegemon of his age,
37	大逞其志。	之	freely exercising his will.

Synopsis (83/17–84/11)

38	此書之所謂曰：		This is what a Document expresses in saying:
39	「主擇|臣，		"A ruler chooses his minister;
40	臣亦擇主」者也，		but a minister chooses his ruler as well."
41	既書於志。	之	It is already manifest in the records.

In addition to the regular meter and rhyme, the passage also shows a systematic pattern in regard to the length of the respective units dedicated to each ruler. The accounts about Xiqi and Zhuozi are told in stanzas comprising four lines, the stories about Yiwu and Yuzi measure seven lines each, and finally, Chong'er, is dealt with in a passage of nine lines. The scope of the respective passages does not correspond to the duration of these individuals' reigns. In fact, the cumulative time that Xiqi, Zhuozi and Yuzi occupied (at times, only nominally) the Jin throne did not exceed one year.[5]

Lord Zhaowen's appeal to Prince Gong is closely related to the first two parts. The East Zhou ruler reiterates that moral excellence (presumably embodied by Chong'er) is the only way to win subordinates' unwavering support (and, in this way, to enforce one's installation). Close parallels to the historical part might also be revealing as to the relation between Lord Zhaowen and Prince Gong. Namely, because according to the former's account Chong'er was able to claim the throne while not being Lord Xian's son, it would not be too farfetched to assume that Prince Gong was not among the most immediate candidates to Lord Zhaowen's throne, i.e., not his eldest son.

---

[5] *Shiji* "Shi'er zhuhou nianbiao" 十二諸侯年表 (14.585–586, 593).

Similar to the preceding parts, the personal plea to Prince Gong is constructed by means of rhymed passages. However, it comprises four thematic units, each one characterized by a specific rhyme group. Moreover, the first two units are thematically juxtaposed, providing two different scenarios for Prince Gong's consideration: a positive one, which depicts the consequences of developing the virtues exemplified by Chong'er; and a negative one, where such virtues are dismissed. This structure renders Lord Zhaowen's exemplifications more convincing by demonstrating to Prince Gong that there are no alternatives to following humaneness, kindness etc.

After making clear to Prince Gong the consequences of his actions, Lord Zhaowen reiterates the importance of the people and, in the concluding unit, admonishes him to act according to the received instructions:

Positive Ramifications (84/12–86/2)

1	今汝能慈孝，		Now, if you are able to be compassionate and filial,
2	尊仁貴信，	真	to honor humaneness and value trustworthiness,
3	余雖未爾立，		then, even though I haven't established you [as heir],
4	而身自令，	耕	you will ensconce yourself.
5	余雖已終，		So when I am near my end,
6	至于季年，	真	reaching my final years,
7	眾之立汝也，		the masses will establish you
8	若日之必出，		as certainly as the sun will rise,
9	猶將｜戴天。	真	[treating you] as Heaven above them.

Negative Ramifications (86/3–87/10)

10	爾遠信仁		But if you distance yourself from trustworthiness and humaneness
11	而不能慈孝，	宵	and are not able to be compassionate and filial;
12	惡學憎善		If you despise learning, loathe goodness
13	而不聽教導，	幽	and do not heed teachings and counsels;
14	余雖身置｜汝，		then, even if I personally install you,
15	人將代汝，		others will replace you,
16	民莫而肯好。	幽	and none among the people will like you.

Importance of the People (87/11–88/23)

17	夫有土之主，	侯	Now, the ruler of a territory
18	將民之與處，	魚	dwells there with his people.

19	而民不爾好，		If your people dislike you,
20	其孰在而所？	魚	who will remain there with you?
21	莫居而去，	魚	With no one residing there and everybody leaving,
22	國既空虛，	魚	the state will become empty and void.
23	爾欲守國，		Even if you wished to preserve the state,
24	其將誰與居？	魚	who would reside there with you?

Final Admonition (88/24–90/6)

25	非我與而言，	元	If not for me talking to you,
26	告汝其然，	元	telling you the way things are,
27	它人其孰敢		would other people dare
28	既出茲言？	元	to utter these words?
29	嗚呼！戒哉！		Ah well! Be cautious!
30	尚勉承教，		Devote yourself to receiving instructions
31	而謹慎勿慢。	元	and pay attention to not getting sluggish!

As can be seen, each unit is marked by a specific rhyme. The next unit characterized by the end-rhyme *yu* 魚 speaks of the ruler's popularity as shown in the people's willingness to dwell with him in the same place. Accordingly, an unpopular ruler will not be assassinated but left alone in his state. In the passage marked by the rhyme *yuan* 元, Lord Zhaowen cautions his heir as to the singularity of the communicated information by claiming that no subordinate would dare to say these words.

Context

When compared to other accounts dedicated to this period of Jin history, the present chapter makes some highly dubious claims. Regarding the number of Lord Xian's progeny, both the *Zuozhuan* and the *Shiji* determine it as nine.[6] Additionally, Lord Xian's third son (as reported here), Yuzi, was, in reality, born to Yiwu.[7] Furthermore, the claim that the four rulers had no (other) progeny is questionable in light of reports that Yiwu had several sons apart from Yuzi.[8]

---

[6] *Zuozhuan*, Xi 24.1, 418; 379. *Shiji* "Jin shijia" 晉世家 (39.1662; Nienhauser 2006, 334).
[7] *Zuozhuan*, Xi 23.4, 402; 363.
[8] *Shiji* 39.1655; Nienhauser 2006, 320.

In general, the *Zhouxun* presents Xiqi, Zhuozi, Yiwu, and Yuzi as vanishing due to their alleged moral shortcomings and the resulting animosity from their subordinates. This is debatable for several reasons. Xiqi and Zhuozi, Lord Xian's sons by Li Ji and her younger sister, were murdered, even prior to their ascension to the Jin throne, by Chong'er's supporters, under the pretext of their questionable legitimacy.[9] While the first was installed by Lord Xian himself, the second was established by the loyal minister Xun Xi 荀息, who later sacrificed his life to defend his protégé.[10] Therefore, Xiqi and Zhuozi's portrayal as morally corrupt and lacking any ministerial support is problematic. In fact, the otherwise very close depictions of the same events in the *Lüshi chunqiu* and the excavated manuscript *Xinian* contain no moral evaluation of these two individuals.[11]

The picture changes, however, when we take a look at Yiwu, also known as Lord Hui of Jin 晉惠公 (r. 650–637 BCE), and his son Yuzi, who ruled over Jin for a brief period in 637 BCE and received the posthumous title of Lord Huai of Jin 晉懷公. They are indeed often presented together as "having no close associates" (*wu qin* 無親) and being "abandoned" (*qi* 棄) by the people both outside and inside of Jin (*wai nei* 外內).[12] The animosity that they experienced in foreign affairs has in both cases to do with the state of Qin. The traditional depiction of events is such that, while Lord Hui was installed by Lord Mu of Qin 秦穆/繆公 (r. 659–621 BCE)[13], he went back on his promises to reward the Qin's support[14] and, moreover, did not reciprocate the Qin's aid during a famine.[15]

This understandably antagonized his benefactor, Lord Mu, who launched an attack on Jin and captured Lord Hui during the battle of the Plains of Han 韓原 (645 BCE).[16] Yuzi was sent to Qin as a hostage to replace his father, yet managed to escape and return to Jin when Lord Hui became ill, to be installed as the next ruler of Jin.[17] Yuzi's flight from Qin marks the decisive turn in Chong'er's fortune, because Lord Mu of Qin is reported to have summoned and elevated

---

[9] *Zuozhuan*, Xi 9.4, 328–329; 295–297. In the eyes of Jin's minister Li Ke 里克, Chong'er was a more legitimate successor to Lord Xian than the two sons by concubines. On the dilemma of Jin ministers in this conflict, see Pines 2020, 52–54
[10] *Zuozhuan*, Xi 9.4, 329; 297.
[11] *Lüshi chunqiu* "Yuan luan" 原亂 (Chen Q. 2001, 1587–1588; Knoblock and Riegel 2000, 602–603). See also a parallel passage in the *Xinian* "Di liu zhang" 第六章 (Li X. 2011, 150; Milburn 2016, 78–79 and Pines 2020, 173–175).
[12] *Zuozhuan*, Xi 23.6, 409; 378, and *Shiji* 39.1662; Nienhauser 2006, 334.
[13] *Zuozhuan*, Xi 9.6, 330; 297.
[14] *Shiji* 39.1650; Nienhauser 2006, 315.
[15] *Zuozhuan*, Xi 14.4, 348; 313; *Shiji* 39.1653; Nienhauser 2006, 318.
[16] *Zuozhuan*, Xi 5.4, 356; 321; *Shiji* 39.1653–54; Nienhauser 2006, 318–319.
[17] *Shiji* 39.1655–56; Nienhauser 2006, 320–321.

him to punish Yuzi's betrayal.[18] The latter's subsequent murder is attributed either to Qin[19], or the population of Jin[20] or to a (morally questionable) personal order by Chong'er[21].

By almost completely leaving out details related to foreign relations, the *Zhouxun* presents a very incomplete account which can be interpreted accurately only by a reader familiar with the unfolding of historical events and their broader political context. For instance, Lord Hui's "discarding of virtue" (*qi de* 棄德) and being "skillful at betrayal" (*shan bei* 善背) should be seen in light of his connection to Lord Mu of Qin, and would be incorrect if interpreted as referring to his interstate politics. Likewise, the (wrong) claim that the "four sons" had no progeny appears less incomprehensible when viewed against the background of the *Zuozhuan*. There, in the wake of Lord Huai's killing of Hu Tu 狐突, Diviner Yan 卜偃 pronounces his verdict to the effect that a ruler who lacks "bright virtue" (*ming de* 明德) and yet engages in "slaughter" (*lu* 戮) of the people, is bound to have no progeny.[22] In this case, the prediction about Lord Huai's future might have been presented in chapter 6 as a historical fact concerning all Jin rulers who were lacking qualification.

When it comes to Lord Wen, he is generally portrayed as appreciating the value of the worthy *shi* from a young age[23] and, eventually, coming to enjoy great support from the worthy men of Jin even before his seizure of power, which is in accord with the *Zhouxun*.[24] At the same time, however, it is commonplace that Chong'er, like his younger brother Yiwu, was installed by Lord Mu of Qin.[25] The *Zhouxun* is missing this crucial information and presents these events as concerning the internal affairs of the state of Jin only. As for his character traits, Chong'er is associated with a number of moral virtues in the *Zuozhuan* and *Shiji*, some of which are also mentioned in this chapter[26], yet the *Zhouxun* presents by far the

---

[18] *Guoyu* "Jinyu si" 晉語四 (Xu Y. 2002, 333; Taskin 1987, 170).
[19] *Shiji* 39.1656; Nienhauser 2006, 321.
[20] *Guoyu* "Jinyu san" 晉語三 (Xu Y. 2002, 317; Taskin 1987, 161). *Xinian* "Di liu zhang" 第六章 (Li X. 2011, 150; Milburn 2016, 79 and Pines 2020, 175).
[21] *Zuozhuan*, Xi 24.1, 414; 373 and 373n11.
[22] *Zuozhuan*, Xi 23.4, 403; 363.
[23] *Shiji* 39.1656; Nienhauser 2006, 321.
[24] *Shiji* 39.1660; Nienhauser 2006, 331.
[25] Li and Chang 1988, 41–42. Not all the political parties in Jin were satisfied with this decision, and Chong'er closely escaped an assassination attempt carried out by the former ruler's supporters (*Zuozhuan*, Xi 24.1, 414; 375).
[26] He is characterized as "ambitious but temperate, cultured, and possessed of ritual propriety" (*guang er jian wen er you li* 廣而儉，文而有禮) in *Zuozhuan*, Xi 23.6, 409; 301. In the *Shiji*, 39.1663; Nienhauser 2006, 335, he shows the highest appreciation to the people who "guided me with benevolence and righteousness and admonished me with virtue and kindness" (*dao wo yi ren yi, fang wo yi de hui* 導我以仁義，防我以德惠).

most "complete" account in this regard. At the same time, Lord Wen's extensive administrative reforms that are dealt with in some details in some transmitted and excavated texts, are not mentioned here.²⁷ This underscores the idealistic character of the manuscript under consideration. The same disinterest toward historical details becomes apparent in the claim that Lord Wen and his progeny secured rule over Jin for a long time. For the next major succession crisis occurred in Jin already following the death of Lord Wen's son, Lord Xiang 晉襄公 (r. 627–621 BCE) (Durrant, Li, and Schaberg 2016, 459). The emergent weak leader (and Lord Wen's grandson) Lord Ling 晉靈公 (r. 620–607 BCE) was finally assassinated by the members of the powerful ministerial lineage of Zhao,²⁸ which, if we follow the logic of the *Zhouxun*, demonstrated his utter ineptness.

The peculiarities of the historical account presented in the *Zhouxun* can be thus explained as stemming from its presupposition that only morality guarantees the unswerving support of the population and, as such, presents the single most important precondition for establishing stable political rule. The consequences of this radical claim are far-reaching, as the ruling monarch's choice and approval of a candidate appear not to play a decisive role in the process of power transfer. This, at least, is the point that Lord Zhaowen makes in his admonition of Prince Gong. Mencius, for instance, still believes that a legitimate successor, in addition to possessing virtue, should be recommended by the sovereign to Heaven.²⁹ We thus see yet again that in the philosophical system of the *Zhouxun*, Heaven no longer plays as a decisive role.

---

²⁷ *Lüshi chunqiu* "Yuan luan" (Chen Q. 2001, 1587; Knoblock and Riegel 2000, 603), *Shiji* 39.1662; Nienhauser 2006, 333. For a summary, see Li and Chang 1988, 42–43. The excavated manuscript *Jin Wen Gong ru yu Jin* 晉文公入于晉 (Li X. 2017, 101) mentions Lord Wen as promoting several governing activities, bringing to conclusion unresolved courtyard cases, reducing and writing off debts, introducing sacrifice rituals, fixing irrigation facilities, encouraging peasants to engage in farm works, strengthening the military and others. Through these measures, he is reported to have firmly established his authority among the other regional lords by the ninth year of his rule. Among others achievements, the *Jin Wen Gong ru yu Jin* also mentions Duke Wen's conquest of the state of Cao 曹. See also Ma 2017, 90.
²⁸ *Zuozhuan*, Xuan 2.3, 662; 597.
²⁹ *Mengzi* "Wan Zhang shang" (Jiao 1987, 647; Lau 2003, 209).

7

Seventh Month

In the seventh chapter, Lord Zhaowen shifts the discussion to events that took place in the state of Qin some years prior to Lord Wen's establishment. We thus find ourselves in the Western area of the Zhou world, in the state that will eventually succeed Zhou in establishing a new unified rule over China. The main protagonist of the events recorded here is Lord Mu of Qin (r. 659–621 BCE), who was mentioned in the previous account. Lord Mu was an extraordinary man in many regards. Among his talents was his ability to employ worthy men[1] as well as his great devotion to his people (*Shiji* 5.194; Nienhauser 1994a, 101). He was the first Qin monarch to be mentioned in the *Chunqiu* 春秋 and it was under his rule that Qin became a major political player for the first time. In addition to directly influencing domestic affairs in the neighboring Jin through establishing Lord Hui and Lord Wen, he greatly expanded the size of his state through successful military campaigns.[2] These accomplishments earned him the title of hegemon, at least in regard to the Rong 戎, whom he soundly defeated in 623 BCE.[3]

The main reason why later historiographers were rather reserved in their praise of Lord Qin was that he allegedly had a great number of men, including some notable worthies, interred by his side, in accordance with the Qin's funerary custom of burying people alive alongside the deceased.[4] By "taking away the good men (of the domain)" (*duo zhi shan ren* 奪之善人),[5] goes the verdict of the noble man (*junzi* 君子) in the *Zuozhuan*, Lord Mu had "discarded his people in death" (*si er qi min* 死而棄民) and ultimately weakened his state. Therefore, the "noble man" made the famous prediction (which came to be proven wrong) that

---

[1] *Zuozhuan*, Wen 3.4, 530; 479.
[2] His descendent Lord Xiao of Qin 秦孝公 (361–338 BCE) glorified Lord Mu in the following way. *Shiji* 5.202; Adapted from Nienhauser 1994a, 108: 東平晉亂，以河為界，西霸戎翟，廣地千里，天子致伯。"[Lord Mu] pacified the chaos in Jin to the east so as to make the Yellow River serve as the border, while he ruled as Hegemon over the Rong and Di in the west, thus expanding our territory to one-thousand *li* [on a side]; he founded the [royal] enterprise for later generations and made [our state] exceedingly glorious, by causing the Son of Heaven to confer upon him the status of Hegemon."
[3] *Shiji* 5.194–195; Nienhauser 1994a, 101–102. See also Pines et al. 2014, 14.
[4] *Shiji* 5.194–195; Nienhauser 1994a, 101–102.
[5] *Zuozhuan*, Wen 6.3, 547; 491.

Qin will never again march eastwards (*bu fu dong zheng* 不復東征).⁶ While being silent on the Qin custom of human sacrifice at this juncture, the *Zhouxun* addresses it in chapter 11.

The story narrated by Lord Zhaowen in this chapter contains events that took place a while apart from each other.⁷ In the beginning, Lord Mu is shown as extending magnanimous treatment to some people from the countryside (*ye ren* 野人) who killed and ate his steed.⁸ One year later, the group of men associated with these "rustics" is reported to have come to Lord Mu's rescue during the battle of the Plains of Han (645 BCE), just when he was about to get killed by officers of the Jin army. With their help Qin claimed a decisive victory over Jin, capturing Lord Hui of Jin, one of the ill-fated protagonists from the preceding chapter. Hence, the victory that had a great significance for establishing Qin as a major power on the interstate arena of the time could ultimately be attributed to Lord Mu's kind treatment of the low-born people of his state (Lin J. 1981, 30–32).

As it stands, the chapter includes eight bamboo slips (92–99), with two slips now missing (*Beida Mss.* 112). As such, it represents the shortest textual unit in the *Zhouxun*. The content of Lord Zhaowen's speech can again be divided into a historical narrative about Lord Mu's activities prior to and during the battle at Hanyuan (93/2–97/4), a moral lesson following from these events by means of a Document citation (97/5–98/3), and a rhetorical question addressing Prince Gong (98/4–98/15). Because the story is almost identical to an account in the *Lüshi chunqiu* 8.5, I use the relevant parts of the latter (text in curly brackets) to reconstruct the original reading of chapter 7.

Translation

92/1 • 維歲七月更旦之日，龏（共）大子朝，周昭文公自身貳之，用茲念也。
【92】曰：93/1

• It was on the first day of the seventh month of the year, when Crown Prince Gong came to court. Lord Zhaowen of Zhou personally enjoined him with these (following) reminders. He said:

93/2 昔秦穆公乘馬而車為敗，右服失而野人得之，穆公自往求 【93】

---

⁶ *Zuozhuan*, Wen 6.3, 549; 493). On how this prediction could be used to date *Zuozhuan*, see Pines 2002, 224.
⁷ The parallel account of the *Lüshi chunqiu* speaks of one year, while *Shuoyuan* reports about three years. For a discussion, see Henry 2021, 298n96.
⁸ On the difference between the inhabitants of the cities (*guoren* 國人) and *yeren*, see Tong 2019, 170–171.

{之，見埜人方將食之於歧山之陽。繆公歎曰：「食駿馬之肉而不還飲酒，余恐其傷女也！」於是徧飲而去。處一年，為韓原之戰，晉人}⁹

94/1 已環穆公之車矣，晉梁（梁）囚（由）靡已扣穆公之左驂矣，晉惠公之右【94】路石奮杸擊穆公之左袂，其甲隫者已六札矣。野人嘗食馬肉【95】於岐〈岐〉山之陽者三百于餘人，畢為穆公奮於車下，述（遂）大尅（克）晉，虜【96】惠公以歸。97/4

In the past, when Lord Mu of Qin rode in a chariot, it had a mishap. The right horse got loose and was caught by some men from the countryside. When Lord Mu went himself to find… {it, he saw that the men from the countryside were about to dine on it on the southern slope of Mount Qi. The lord exclaimed, "The meat of a noble steed, if eaten without pairing with wine, I am afraid it will hurt you." So, passing around some wine, he left. A year later was the battle of the Plains of Han. The army of Jin}[10] … had already surrounded Lord Mu's chariot and Liang Youmi of Jin[11] had already grabbed ahold of Lord Mu's left horse. [Sitting] to the right of Lord Hui of Jin, Lu Shi seized a spear and attacked Lord Mu's left arm, striking off six layers of his armor.

[At this time,] more than three hundred men [from the families of those][12] who had eaten the meat of [Lord Mu's] horse at the southern slope of Mount Qi, all started fighting for Lord Mu at the side of his chariot. As a result, the lord won a great victory over Jin, capturing Lord Hui and returning (with him).

97/5 此《書》之所謂曰「君君子則正以行德，賤人則寬以盡其【97】力」者也。98/3

This is what a Document expresses in saying: "When ruling gentlemen, be upright to elicit their virtue. [When ruling] men of low rank, be lenient to exhaust their strength."

---

[9] The missing part is reconstructed based on the parallel in the *Lüshi chunqiu* (Chen Q. 2001, 464). It contains 29 graphs which corresponds to the content of two bamboo slips of the *Zhouxun*, where the average number of graphs per slip is 24.

[10] Compare translation in Knoblock and Riegel 2000, 202–203.

[11] Liang Youmi 梁由靡 was a Jin officer who appears in the depiction of this battle in the *Zuozhuan*, Xi 15.4, 356; 321, as the chariot driver for Han Jian 韓簡. The latter belonged to the third generation of ministerial Han lineage in the state of Jin, which later came to establish the state of Han. (*Shiji* "Han shijia" 韓世家 (45.1865n3: "Suoyin" 索隱 commentary) The Plains of Han was an allotment bestowed upon the Han lineage by Jin rulers. (*Shiji* 45.1865n1: "Suoyin") In contrast to the *Zuozhuan*, in this account, Liang Youmi is portrayed in the company of Lord Hui of Jin and the otherwise unknown Lu Shi 路石.

[12] Commenting on this passage, Chen Q. 2001, 468n14 notes that the text should be interpreted as saying that the men who had eaten the animal gathered a 300-men-strong force out of the members of their families, and not that those same three hundred men actually ate one horse.

98/4 人君其胡可以毋務惠於庶人？98/15
How can a ruler not strive to be kind towards commoners?[13]

98/16 已學（教）大子用茲念，斯乃 [98] 受（授）之書，而自身屬（囑）之曰女（汝）勉毋忘歲七月更旦之馴（訓）。[99]
Having instructed the crown prince with these reminders, [Lord Zhaowen] gave him the text [of his speech] and personally cautioned him, saying: "Strive not to forget the instructions from the first day of the seventh month of the year."

Comments

According to the conventional interpretation of the story, the three hundred men who rescued Lord Mu at the battlefield were the same "rustics" who benefitted from this Qin ruler's generosity and lenience one year before the military operation.[14] This would be plausible only if we assume that by the time of Qin's invasion against Jin these men were already conscripted into the Qin army. For, otherwise, their miraculous appearance amidst the fierce battle of two mobile army formations[15] and at the place that was deep in Jin territory[16], far away from their native Mount Qi, would be inexplicable. Moreover, as "rustics" they would be too ill-equipped to fight some of the best officers of the Jin army.[17] Another way to resolve these incongruencies is to assume that Lord Mu's rescuers were Qin soldiers who were related to the "rustics" and knew of Lord Mu's previous generosity towards their kin. This interpretation is congruous with the sentence structure and has, on top of that, the advantage of not having to account for how Lord Mu's wine (and steed) could have been sufficient to more than three hundred men. It also renders kind treatment of subordinates even more imperative for powerholders, by showing how greatly they could benefit, even from indirect recipients of their kindness.[18]

---

[13] On the meaning of the term *shuren* 庶人 in early China, see Loewe 2010, 300–301 and Tong 2019, 117.
[14] Zhang S. 1986, 227; Wilhelm 1971, 101; Knoblock and Riegel 2000, 203. See also Nienhauser 2006, 319n166.
[15] On the importance of chariots for warfare operations during the Chunqiu period, see Sawyer 1993, 9.
[16] *Zuozhuan*, Xi 15.4, 356; 318.
[17] According to some scholars, this defeat might have inspired Jin to "reorganize its military to include people of the *ye* regions" (Hsu 1999, 573).
[18] This interpretation is also supported by a similar story about Zhao Jianzi, which appears in the *Lüshi chunqiu* immediately after Lord Mu's account. Although Zhao Jianzi is said there to have been kind to one person only, in a critical moment he received help from no less than 1400 men. For discussion, see Chen Q. 2001, 465.

Uncharacteristically, there are almost no rhymes in the present narrative. The only rhyme is formed by the graphs *de* 德 (97/18) and *li* 力 (98/1) (both belonging to group *zhi* 職) in the quotation of a Document. In there, the opening character *jun* 君 (to rule) evidently refers to both subsequent lines. In this way, the quoted content can be divided into three parts whose relationship can be depicted as follows:

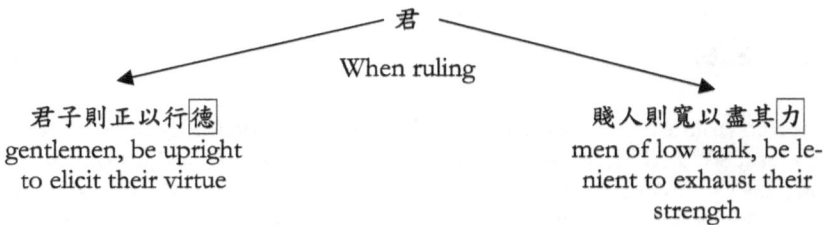

The common end-rhyme makes clear that the two contrasting argumentative strands (gentlemen versus men of low rank) belong to the same textual unit. This *shu*-line cannot be found in any extant compilations of Documents.

Although the summary and rhetorical question are very brief, they are essential for understanding Lord Zhaowen's interpretation of the story, capturing its moral. Accordingly, to secure the enthusiastic support of the low strata of society, a sovereign needs to treat them with leniency and kindness. As we can see, in this example, these two virtues are treated almost synonymously.

Context

This narrative about Lord Mu of Qin getting vital help from the rustics whom he previously treated magnanimously was very popular during the Warring States and early imperial periods.[19] However, these works interpret the story as exemplifying either the importance of "gratitude inspiring kindness" (*dé*)[20] or

---

[19] *Huainanzi* "Fanlun xun" (He N. 1998, 13.975); *Han Shi waizhuan* "Juan shi" 卷十 (Xu W. 1980, 10.351–352); *Shiji* "Qin benji" 秦本紀 (5.188–89); *Shuoyuan* "Fu en" 復恩 (Xiang 1987, 6.125).

[20] The *Huainanzi* (He N. 1998, 13.975) interprets it as "an example of earning [people's] gratitude with little effort" (*ci yong yue er wei de zhe ye* 此用約而為德者也). The *Shiji* "Qin benji" speaks of repaying "kindness in the horse eating incident" (*bao shi ma zhi de* 報食馬之德) (5.189; Nienhauser 1994a, 97). The *Shuoyuan* (Xiang 1987, 6.125) sees it as a case of "how blessings return to the one who spreads kindness" (*ci de chu er fu fan ye* 此德出而福反也).

"humanness" and "care for the people" (*ai ren*).²¹ This is slightly different from the *Zhouxun*, which interprets the narrative in terms of leniency and kindness.

In some cases, not only appraisal of the events, but the events themselves are narrated in a substantially different way when compared to the *Zhouxun*. To give one early example, in the account of the *Zuozhuan*, Lord Mu was rescued from imminent detainment by the interference of a worthy Jin official, Qing Zheng 慶鄭, who disagreed with his sovereign's (Lord Hui) actions.²² This deviation shows, yet again, the malleable character of early Chinese anecdotes and their openness to carrying different meanings.

The account of the *Shiji* is especially noteworthy because it attempts to incorporate all the available accounts into one logically sound narrative. Sima Qian appears to have been aware of the incongruency around the question of how three hundred "rustics" could have suddenly appeared on a distant battlefield in a foreign state and attempted to resolve it. Accordingly, their gratitude for Lord Mu's kindness was so great that, when hearing about his plans to punish Lord Hui of Jin, they requested to follow the Qin army. When seeing Lord Mu's predicament, they charged forward to give their lives to repay his kindness (*Shiji* 5.189; Nienhauser 1994a, 97). Yet, a scenario containing so many coincidences does not seem very plausible.

---

²¹ *Han Shi waizhuan* "Juan shi" 卷十 (Xu W. 1980, 10.352).
²² *Zuozhuan*, Xi 15, 356; 321.

8

Eighth Month

During Prince Gong's audience on the first day of the eighth month, Lord Zhaowen presents yet another story featuring Lord Wen of Jin (r. 638–628 BCE). This time, the instruction is based on the events that unfolded following the Jin punitive expedition against the domain of Cao 曹 in 632 BCE.[1] The (here unmentioned) reason for this invasion was the great disrespect shown by Lord Gong of Cao 曹共公 (?–618 BCE) to Chong'er, when the latter happened to pass through this domain during his long years of wandering. Namely, upon learning about Chong'er having anomalous "fused ribs," Lord Gong stooped so low as to secretly watch his guest take a bath.[2] In some versions of the account, there is also a significant detail that, in demonstrating disrespect toward Chong'er, Lord Gong ignored the advice of his worthy minister Xi Fuji 僖負羈, who, recognizing the great abilities of the Ducal son from Jin, demanded he be treated courteously.[3]

Lord Gong's (called here just: "ruler of Cao") haughty disregard of the wise counsel constitutes the starting point in the storyline of this chapter. It manifests itself in his alleged disdain for a saying which, written in a text, was stored away in a "metal box" (*jingui* 金匱) on the premises of the Cao's royal ancestral temple, only to be discovered by Lord Wen's entourage when dismantling their enemies' place of ritual worship.[4] Recognizing the disdain for worthy ministers as the main reason for Cao's demise, Lord Wen is said to have actively sought out his subordinates' wise counsel. This story demonstrates Lord Wen's trust in his ministers' judgment, and, moreover, that successful government relies on common general principles valid for all polities and under all circumstances.

Apart from chapter six, this is the only complete large unit of the text. It includes eleven bamboo slips (100–110), all of which are intact. Its content can be divided into two familiar parts: historical narrative (101/2–109/6) and a brief plea to Prince Gong (109/7–21).

---

[1] *Zuozhuan*, Xi 28.3, 453; 411.
[2] *Zuozhuan*, Xi 23.6, 407; 367.
[3] *Guoyu* "Jinyu si" (Xu Y. 2002, 328); Sima Qian identifies Lord Gong's ignorance of Xi Fuji's advice as manifestation of his lack of virtue. *Shiji* 35.1574; Nienhauser 2006, 212.
[4] On the trope of "metal-bound coffer" (*jinteng zhi gui* 金縢之匱) in early Chinese texts (both excavated and transmitted), see Meyer 2014, Huang 2018 and Krijgsman 2019.

Translation

100/1 • 維歲八月更旦之日，龏（共）大子朝，周昭文公自身貳之，用茲念也。【100】曰：101/1

• It was on the first day of the eight month of the year, when Crown Prince Gong came to court. Lord Zhaowen of Zhou personally enjoined him with these (following) reminders. He said:

101/2 昔晉文君伐蠿（曹），剋（克）之，而夷其宗廟。穿地三仞而得金匱焉，其【101】中有書曰：「非駿勿駕，非爵（雀）勿䍙（羅）。」文君問於咎犯曰：「是何謂也？」咎【102】犯對（對）曰：「非駿勿駕，毋使肖（小）人也；非雀勿䍙（羅），毋大不仁也。」文君曰：【103】「是善言也，而蠿（曹）君貴之，何故以亡？」咎犯對（對）曰：「賢君之貴善言也，令【104】工庸（誦）之於廟，令史䌛（籀）之於朝，日聞於耳。今蠿（曹）君之貴善言也，入【105】之於地而已，深狸（埋）而弗視，不亡絫（奚）侍（待）？」文君曰：「善哉！」於是始坐，未【106】嘗不先聽道君之治，與乳（亂）主之過。每聞道君之治，未嘗不曰其【107】誰能及此。每聞乳（亂）主之過，未嘗不自謂幾其若此。人之求多聞【108】見也，以監（鑒）戒也。
109/6

In the past, Lord Wen of Jin attacked Cao. When he conquered it, he leveled their ancestral temple. After digging down into the earth three *ren* deep, [his people] discovered a metal box, inside of which was a text, saying: "Do not ride it, unless it is a noble steed; do not catch it, unless it is a peacock." Lord Wen asked Jiufan: "What does it mean?" Jiufan replied: "'Do not ride it, unless it is a noble steed,' means do not employ petty people; 'do not catch it, unless it is a peacock,' means do not magnify the inhumane."

Lord Wen said: "These are excellent words, and the Lord of Cao valued them. Why then did he perish?" Jiufan replied: "When a worthy ruler [truly] values excellent words, he orders his music master to chant them in the ancestral temple, and orders his scribes to recite them at court, in order to hear them every day. Now, the way the Lord of Cao valued excellent words, was just to put them into the earth, to bury them deeply and to not look at them. What can such a ruler expect but to perish?"

Lord Wen said: "Excellent!" Therefore, when opening a gathering, he always first listened to [the stories about] the [good] order of rulers [in possession] of the Way and the mistakes of disordered rulers. Whenever he heard about the [good] order of rulers [in possession] of the Way, he always exclaimed: "Who can reach these [heights]?" Whenever he heard about the mistakes of disordered rulers, he always said about himself: "I come very close to committing these [same mistakes]." He sought to augment his knowledge from others, in order to understand what he should be careful about.

109/7 今我語女（汝），而爾弗能行，余恐而有代也。109/21
Now, I am instructing you but you [seem] unable to carry out [my instructions]. I am afraid that you will be replaced.

109/22 已學（教）大【109】子用茲念，斯乃受（授）之書，而自身屬（囑）之曰：女（汝）勉毋忘歲八月更旦之馴（訓）。【110】
Having instructed the crown prince with these reminders, [Lord Zhaowen] gave him the text [of his speech] and personally cautioned him, saying: "Strive not to forget the instructions from the first day of the eighth month of the year."

Comments

To emphasize the benighted state of mind of Cao's ruler(s) the writing containing the wise saying on the way of governance has reportedly been concealed twice. The script was first placed in a metal box, which was interred in the ground to the impressive depth of three *ren* 仞, which is equivalent to 5.54 meters.[5] The meaning of the saying *feijun wujia, feique wuluo* 非駿勿駕，非爵勿羅, especially its latter part, has been the subject of considerable debate. While most scholars agree on reading *feijun wujia* to the effect of "Do not ride it, unless it is a noble steed," the second part contains graphs 爵 and 羅, which are open to different interpretations. I would like to mention three different takes on their meaning at this juncture.

According to one early view, *jue* 爵 should be taken in its original meaning as "rank," further as "reward," and 羅 as *ji* 羈 in the verbal meaning of to "request" or to "task." As a result, the sentence promoted the idea that a ruler should not employ people without rewarding them (Yan B. 2012b, 311). Another early view that found a larger number of supporters interpreted *jue* 爵 as a phonetic loan for *que* 雀 (sparrow) and 羅 as *luo* 羅 (to catch) resulting in the sentence "do not catch/eradicate it, unless it is a (harmful) sparrow" (Chen J. 2012; Lin Z. 2015, 200; Hou 2018). In this case, the images of the two sentences: "noble steed" and "harmful sparrow" respectively, were opposed to each other.[6] Finally, the third view rejects the alleged opposition between the two parts of the saying by

---

[5] One *ren* measured eight *chi* 尺 (Wang Li 2000, 17), while one *chi* during the Spring and Autumn period was equivalent to 23.1 centimeters (*ibid.*, 1807).
[6] Lin Qingyuan 2019, 76–77 conjectures that 爵 stands for a harmful rodent 貜 (rat) and, therefore, can be counted into this group too.

claiming that they expressed similar a meaning. Accordingly, *que* 雀 was not a harmful sparrow, but a bird that could be compared to a humane person (*ren ren* 仁人), just like 騸 signified not the eradication of the harmful, but the employment of the humane (Zhang H. 2017, 52–53).

In my translation, "peacock," I partly follow the third interpretation, because the two lines "Do not employ petty people" (*wu shi xiao ren* 毋使小人) and "Do not magnify the inhumane" (*wu da buren* 毋大不仁) both seem to warn the ruler not to employ unworthy people in his service. This warning is best understood in the context of Lord Gong's alleged policies and decisions in regard to employing officials, which will be dealt with in the next section.

Significantly, the meaning of the saying is explained to Lord Wen by his wise retainer and maternal uncle, Jiufan 咎犯 or 舅犯, also known as Zifan 子犯 or Hu Yan 狐偃.[7] Lord Wen follows Jiufan's interpretation showing, unlike his hapless counterpart from Cao, great respect for the worthy follower's opinion. As a result, Lord Wen is shown to have actively sought out his subordinates' wise counsel. The narrative partly conflicts with Lord Wen's depictions as heeding the advice of his retainers from an early age. In any case, in the concluding admonition of Prince Gong, Lord Zhaowen expects his heir apparent to emulate Lord Wen by heeding his own advice. The implied parallel between heeding the advice of one's subjects (Lord Wen) and following the admonitions of one's sovereign (Prince Gong) appears rather forced. However, in both cases the advisors have kin ties to their advisees. Could this be the reason for singling out Jiufan among other worthy retainers?

The composition of the chapter shows a certain degree of sophistication in its frequent use of rhyme and a number of parallel units. It may be represented as follows:

1. Opening (101/1–102/4)

1	昔晉文君伐曹，	幽	In the past, Lord Wen of Jin attacked Cao.
2	克之，		When he conquered it,
3	而夷其宗廟。	宵	he leveled their ancestral temple.
4	穿地三仞而得金匱焉，		After digging down into the earth three *ren* deep, [his people] discovered a metal box,

---

[7] On the relation between Lord Wen and Zifan as well as the latter's great role in the political life in the state of Jin as recorded in the *Zuozhuan*, see Fang C. 2001, 131–135. Zifan also appears in the Tsinghua manuscript *Zifan, Ziyu* as answering, together with another illustrious retainer of Lord Wen, Ziyu, inquiries from Lord Mu of Qin about the moral qualities of the Ducal son (For transcription, see Li X. 2017, 91–99). By praising his superior, Zifan is shown as instrumental for Lord Mu's installation of Chong'er as the next Jin ruler (Chen Y. 2017, 80). On Jiufan in comparison to other famous "founding ministers" of the pre-imperial era, see Allan 1972–73, 93–95.

5	其|中有書曰：		inside of which was a text, saying:

2. Inscribed Maxim (102/5–12)

6	非駿勿駕，	歌	"Do not ride it, unless it is a noble steed;
7	非雀勿羅。	歌	do not catch it, unless it is a peacock."

3. Jiufan's Explanation of the Maxim (102/13–106/19)

8	文君問於咎犯曰		Lord Wen asked Jiufan:
9	是何謂也？	物	"What does it mean?"
10	咎|犯對曰：	物	Jiufan replied:
11	非駿勿駕，	歌	"'Do not ride it, unless it is a noble steed,'
12	毋使小人也；	真	means do not employ petty people;
13	非雀勿羅，	歌	'do not catch it, unless it is a peacock,'
14	毋大不仁也。	真	means do not magnify the inhumane."
15	文君曰：		Lord Wen said:
16	是善言也，	元	"These are excellent words,
17	而曹君貴之，		and the Lord of Cao valued them.
18	何故以亡？	陽	Why then did he perish?"
19	咎犯對曰：		Jiufan replied:
20	賢君之貴善言也		"When a worthy ruler [truly] values excellent words,
21	令|工誦之於廟，	宵	he orders his music master to chant them in the ancestral temple,
22	令史籀之於朝，	宵	and orders his scribes to recite them at court,
23	日聞於耳。		In order to hear them every day.
24	今曹君之貴善言也，		Now, the way the Lord of Cao valued excellent words,
25	入|之於地而已，	歌	was just to put them into the earth,
26	深埋而弗視，	脂	to bury them deeply and to not look at them.
27	不亡奚待？	之	What can such a ruler expect but to perish?"
28	文君曰：善哉！		Lord Wen said: "Excellent!"

4. Adoption of a New Practice (106/20–109/6)

29	於是始坐，	歌	Therefore, when opening a gathering,
30	未｜嘗不先聽道君之治，		he always first listened to [the stories about] the [good] order of rulers [in possession] of the Way
31	與亂主之過。	歌	and the mistakes of disordered rulers.
32	每聞道君之治，	之	Whenever he heard about the [good] order of rulers [in possession] of the Way,
33	未嘗不曰		he always exclaimed:
34	其｜誰能及此。	支	"Who can reach these [heights]?"
35	每聞亂主之過，	歌	Whenever he heard about the mistakes of disordered rulers,
36	未嘗不自謂		he always said about himself:
37	幾其若此。	支	"I come very close to committing these [same mistakes]."
38	人之求多聞｜見，		He sought to augment his knowledge from others,
39	以鑒戒也。	之	in order to understand what to be careful about.

5. Lord Zhaowen's Admonition (109/10–21)

40	今我語汝，	魚	Now, I am instructing you
41	而爾弗能行，		but you [seem] unable to carry out [my instructions],
42	余恐而有代也。	職	I am afraid that you will be replaced."

This chapter is constructed by alternating single (lines 1–5, 8–9 etc.) and parallel units (lines 6–7, 11–12 and 13–14, 30–31 etc.).

Context

In the *Zhouxun*, both the Cao's ruler and his polity are portrayed as having perished as a result of the Jin's attack. This is different from the *Zuozhuan* and the *Shiji*, where Lord Wen eventually restored Cao and installed Lord Gong again to his former position.[8] Therefore, in reality this state continued to exist for another 150 years before its final annihilation in 487 BCE.[9] As was the case with other historical inaccuracies in the *Zhouxun*, the tragic demise of Cao, which culminated

---

[8] *Zuozhuan*, Xi 28, 474; 429. *Shiji* 35.1572; Nienhauser 2006, 210.
[9] *Shiji* 35.1574; Nienhauser 2006, 212.

in the dismantling of its ancestral temple, is best understood as a poignant reminder of how fatal the ignorance of the text's precepts would be.

Interestingly, there is a similar anecdote in the *Yanzi chunqiu*.[10] It features a dialogue between Lord Jing of Qi 齊景公 (r. 547–490 BCE) and Master Yan about the meaning of a writing that, while having a similar message to the maxim appearing the *Zhouxun*, was recovered in the ruins of the perished domain of Ji 紀 (Wu Z. 1982, 336; Milburn 2016, 326–327). In view of the close resemblance between the two stories as well as their historical background—the state of Ji was abolished in 690 BCE faced with the annexation by the state of Qi, which was justified through an ostensible insult directed at a Qi ruler by the head of Ji generations earlier[11]—a direct link between the two texts appears very likely. Therefore, it seems possible that, in this case, the historical inaccuracy of the *Zhouxun* could stem from applying a story involving Qi and Ji to the conflict between Jin and Cao.

Apart from the general accusations of not heeding ministerial advice, the *Zhouxun* does not specify the exact nature of the Cao ruler's transgressions. Other texts contain more information on this. Namely, according to the *Zuozhuan* and *Shiji*, Lord Gong of Cao did not only treat Chong'er badly, disdaining the remonstrations of his worthy aide Xi Fuji, but also showed appreciation for the "three hundred" unworthy men, by allowing them to "ride chariots," which was the prerogative of officials.[12] Perhaps, Jiufan's interpretation of the wise saying: "do not employ petty people, do not magnify the inhumane," could be understood as directed at this aspect of Lord Gong's rule.

---

[10] For the possible date of composition, see Durrant 1993, 486–487. For evidence of the pre-Qin date of creation as well as the multilayered nature of the text, see Milburn 2010, 10–13.
[11] *Zuozhuan*, Zhuang 4.2, 165; 145 and 146n18.
[12] *Zuozhuan*, Xi 28.3, 453; 411. *Shiji* 35.1574; Nienhauser 2006, 212.

9

Ninth Month

Although the first two slips of this chapter are missing, we can conclude from the remaining parts that the relevant instruction was "delivered" on the first day of the ninth month. We return here to the state of Jin and move on to the events that postdate Lord Wen's conquest of Cao by some twenty years. This time, Lord Zhaowen centers his admonitions around events in the life of the illustrious Jin minister, Zhao Dun (d. 601 BCE), which presumably took place between 610 and 607 BCE. Zhao Dun is also known under his posthumous title Zhao Xuanzi 趙宣子 or Zhao Xuanmeng 趙宣孟,[1] which combines his posthumous title "venerable" (*xuan* 宣) with the cognomen Meng.

As an exemplarily worthy minister, he is associated with a number of reforms in Jin, "reverting to an older order."[2] His dedication to governmental affairs and the wellbeing of the state was such that even his indirect involvement in the assassination of Lord Ling of Jin in 607 BCE did not diminish his fame (Pines 2002, 153).[3] This event exemplifies the rise of the Zhao lineage, which will eventually culminate with their recognition by the Zhou Son of Heaven as leaders of independent polities in 403 BCE. At the same time, it shows that the emphatic revival of Jin achieved by Lord Wen did not last very long and the power of the ruling family declined.

According to the present story, Zhao Dun once saved a Jin officer from starvation, who later sacrificed his life in order to rescue his erstwhile savior from an assassination attempt staged by Lord Ling.

In its recovered version, the chapter comprises twelve slips (111–122), with the first two slips missing. Therefore, we can assume that its original scope was 14 slips. The content can be divided into a narrative dedicated to Zhao Dun

---

[1] *Shiji* "Zhao shijia" 趙世家 (43.1782).
[2] *Zuozhuan*, Wen 6.1, 545–546; 491: 制事典，正法罪，辟刑獄，董逋逃，由質要，治舊洿，本秩禮，續常職，出滯淹，既成，以授大傅陽子，與大師賈佗，使行諸晉國，以為常法。 "He established regulations for official affairs, set straight the application of the laws to crimes, put in order litigation proceedings, controlled fugitives, kept strictly to bonds and contracts, corrected old abuses, stabilized the ritual pertaining to ranks, renewed the customary official duties, and promoted those who had been blocked or obstructed."
[3] For more on Zhao Dun's involvement in the assassination of Lord Ling, see Van Auken 2014, 18, 23.

(111/1–118/24), a moral lesson drawn from historical precedent (119/1–120/20), and an appeal to Prince Gong in the form of a rhetorical question (120/21–121/6). The moralizing conclusion of the story is based on a combination of *shi* and *shu* quotations. As in chapter 7, there is an extensive parallel to the *Lüshi chunqiu*, namely, section 15.4 ("Baogeng"). Therefore, I will again use the relevant passages from the latter to reconstruct the lacunae in the *Zhouxun*.

Translation

【·維歲九月更旦之日，龏（共）大子朝，周昭文公自身貳之，用茲念也。曰：】
[· It was on the first day of the ninth month of the year, when Crown Prince Gong came to court. Lord Zhaowen of Zhou personally enjoined him with these (following) reminders. He said:]

{昔趙宣孟將上之絳，見骩桑之下，有餓人臥不能起者，宣孟止}[4]
{In the past, when Zhao Xuanmeng was on his way up to Jiang, he saw a starving man lying beneath a withered mulberry, unable to rise. Xuanmeng stopped his}[5]

111/1 車，為下飡（飱），搭[6]而餔之，餓人再咽而能視矣。宣孟問之曰：「爾何為[111]而飢若此？」對（對）曰：「臣宦於降（絳），歸而糧絕，羞行气（乞）而曾（憎）自取，故至於[112]若此。」宣孟予之脯二朐，拜受而弗敢食。問其故，曰「臣有老母，將[113]以遺之。」宣孟曰：「斯食之，吾更予女（汝）。」乃賜之脯二束與餘布百，迷（遂）[114]去之上。處三年，晉靈公欲殺宣孟，伏士與房中以侍（待）。發酒，宣孟[115]智（知）之，中飲而出。靈公令房中之士疾追殺之。一人追遽，先及宣[116]孟，見宣孟之面，曰：「欸！君邪！請為君反死。」宣孟曰：「而名為誰？」反走，[117]且對（對）曰：「何以名為？臣，夫委桑下之餓人也。」環（還）鬭（鬪）而死。宣孟迷（遂）生。[118]

---

[4] Reconstructed based on the parallel in the *Lüshi chunqiu* (Chen Q. 2001, 901). The length of the passage is 24 characters, corresponding to the number of characters written on one bamboo slip of the *Zhouxun*.
[5] Compare translation in Knoblock and Riegel 2000, 352.
[6] Unlike the editors of the *Zhouxun*, who interpret the character 搭 as *juan* 涓 "cleanse, making clean," Chen Jian 2016 argues that the graph in question should be read as *qing* 傾 "tilt, pour out." I agree with this interpretation as the object of this action is represented by the graph 飡, which is evidently a variation of the character *sun* 飧/飱, designating a kind of rice porridge that the ancient Chinese kept in a pot when traveling.

chariot and lowered [a pot with] rice porridge. Tilting [the pot], [Xuanmeng] fed it to him. The hungry man choked several times before regaining his vision. Xuanmeng asked him: "What did you do to be starving like this?" The man replied: "Your servant had an office in Jiang[7]. When returning home, my supplies of grain ran out. I was ashamed to beg and resented to steal. So, I ended up in this state." Xuanmeng gave him two strips of dried meat. The man bowed receiving them but did not dare to eat. When asked why, he replied: "Your servant has an aged mother. I am going to give the meat to her." Xuanmeng said: "Eat this and I will give you more." He then presented the man with another two bundles of dried meat as well as [more than] a hundred pieces of cash and then left, resuming his journey up the river. Three years later, Lord Ling of Jin wanted to have Xuanmeng killed. He had knights (*shi* 士) hide in a chamber to await him. When the wine was served, Xuanmeng realized what was happening and left in the middle of drinking. Lord Ling ordered the knights hiding in the chamber to quickly chase after and kill him. One man quickly pursued Xuanmeng and was first to catch up with him. [But] when he saw Xuanmeng's face, he said: "Oh! It is your lordship! I ask for permission to go back and die on your lordship's behalf." Xuanmeng asked: "What is your name?" Turning to go, the man replied: "What difference would my name make? Your servant is the man who was starving beneath the withered mulberry." Returning, he fought and died. As a consequence, Xuanmeng was able to survive.

119/1 此《書》之所謂也,「德幾無小」者也。故壹德一士,猶生其身,兄(況)德萬【119】人庠?故《詩》曰「赳赳武夫,公侯之干城」,「濟濟多士,文王以甯(寧)」。120/20

This is what a Document expresses in saying: "There is almost no such thing as a small kindness." And so, if by being once kind to a single *shi*, one could keep his own life, how much greater [would the result be of] being kind to ten thousand men? And so, an Ode says: "Valiant are the warriors, shield and wall of lords and marquesses. Awe-inspiring are the many *shi*, with them King Wen achieved peace."

120/21 人君其胡【120】可以毋務愛士?121/6
How can a ruler not devote himself to caring for his men of service?

121/7 已學(教)大子用茲念,斯乃受(授)之書,而自身屬(囑)之曰:【121】女(汝)勉毋忘歲九月更旦之馴(訓)。【122】

---

[7] Jiang was the Jin capital at that time. Qian 2001, 498.

Having instructed the crown prince with these reminders, [Lord Zhaowen] gave him the text [of his speech] and personally cautioned him, saying: "Strive not to forget the instructions from the first day of the ninth month of the year."

Comments

Zhao Dun is first portrayed as travelling from, most likely, the allotment of the Zhao lineage to the then capital of Jin, Jiang (Chen Q. 2001, 904–905n10). On his way, he encountered a man who had an office in Jiang but was returning home and ran out of provisions. Regardless of his exact occupation, this was evidently a man of high moral standards for he preferred slow death through starvation to "begging" or "robbing." Possibly, Zhao Dun's generous treatment of the starving man was prompted by the latter's exemplary attitude, which was only reinforced through his evident care for his aged mother. We encounter this man for the second time already as a *shi* 士 in the service of Lord Ling, a term that is difficult to translate due to its multiple connotations.[8] In the current chapter, I find the translation "knight" fitting because the task this man is given, to assassinate Zhao Dun, evidently requires some martial skills. Such understanding of the term *shi* is also suggested by the summary part, which deploys military imagery. Just as he was ready to sacrifice his life for his moral principles when running out of food, the man repays Zhao Dun's goodness by sacrificing his life to protect the latter. The timespan of three years that passed between the two events, only serves to emphasize the depth of his gratitude.

The summary of the narrative contains several noteworthy points. First, a Document quotation suggests to the reader that the narrative should be understood as exemplifying the nature and working of *de* (virtue, kindness). Notably, this is the first appearance of the term *de* in chapter 9. Next, a citation of an Ode makes clear that the *shi*, who appeared in the anecdote, should be primarily understood as a warrior (*wufu* 武夫). Third, the *Zhouxun* connects the two authoritative sources by introducing a bridging passage containing common terminology, *de* 德 and *shi* 士 (line 3).

```
1    此《書》之所謂也,
2    「德幾無小」者也。
3    故壹德一士,
4    猶生其身,              真
5    況德萬人庫?            真
6    故《詩》曰
```

---

[8] For a detailed treatment of this term during the period on question, see Chan 2004, 59–116 and Pines 2009, 115–135.

```
 7    「赳赳武夫,
 8    公侯之干城」,                                    耕
 9    「濟濟多士,
10    文王以寧」。                                     耕
```

As for the two quoted sources, the *shu*-line has parallels of varying degrees of closeness in several transmitted and excavated early works[9]. These suggest that its affiliation with the documentary literature cannot be confirmed and reflects its authors' understanding of the genre. The *shi* quotation is even more interesting because it corresponds to two different poems in the received *Shijing*.[10] The first poem (lines 7–8) is "Tuju" (Mao 7) from the "Guofeng" section and the second (lines 9–10) is "Wenwang" (Mao 235), the opening poem of the "Daya" section.

This is quite remarkable given the stark difference in the alleged circumstances of the creation, the initial function as well as the main themes and concerns of the "Guofeng" and "Daya."[11] Both poems seem to have been carefully chosen because they demonstrated such common characteristics as meter, rhyme (group: *geng* 耕), and opening reduplicatives. However, it is open to discussion whether the authors really wanted to create the impression of citing from one and the same poem. After all, with the publication of the first volume of the Anhui University collection, we know that a complete version of "Tuju" existed well prior to the unification of China through Qin.[12] And different parts of "Wenwang" are also attested in several excavated materials (Kern 2003, 34).

The concluding rhetorical question reaffirms that the anecdote should be read to the effect that it is absolutely necessary for a ruler to show respect and

---

[9] See *Mozi* "Ming gui xia" 明鬼下 (Sun Y. 2001, 249; Compare translation in Johnston 2010, 303): 得璣無小,滅宗無大。"There is no small obtaining of a pearl, there is no great extermination of a lineage."; Mawangdui manuscript *Er san zi wen* 二三子問 (Shaughnessy 1997, 173): 故曰德義無小,失宗無大,此之謂也。"Therefore, it is said 'Of virtue and propriety there is nothing small, and in losing the ancestral temple there is nothing great,' which is what is meant by this."

[10] When quoting different passages from the same work or from various works that belong to the same genre, the common praxis in early Chinese texts was to separate individual quotations by the phrase "it also says" (*you yue* 又曰) as is demonstrated on multiple occasions in the *Zuozhuan*. The instances of referencing in the style of this fragment of the *Zhouxun* are indeed rare. For two examples, see Xu R. 2014, 154.

[11] Nylan 2001, 73 describes "Guofeng" as focused "on subjects of daily life, including courtship, unrequited love, and the hardships of war." On the other hand, "Daya" are mainly concerned with royal activities, including entertainment and ancestral sacrifice. See also Kern 2010a, 19–20.

[12] For juxtaposition with an early counterpart in the manuscript corpus published by Anhui University, see Anhui daxue Hanzi fazhan yu yingyong yanjiu zhongxin 2019, 157.

care for the *shi*—members of the educated strata of the population, who abide by high morals principles and possess martial skills.

Context

This account belongs among the most popular anecdotes from the pre- and early imperial eras, appearing *inter alia* in the *Zuozhuan* and *Shiji*.[13] According to the *Zuozhuan* and *Shiji*, the banquet incident was only one among several attempts by Lord Ling to have Zhao Dun assassinated.[14] In the *Zuozhuan*'s account, at the banquet, Zhao Dun was saved by two different men: his guard named Shi Miming 提彌明, who recognized Lord Ling's plans to ambush Zhao Dun and helped his master escape the scene, sacrificing his life in the process, and a man called Ling Zhe 靈輒, who, prior to this event, was saved by Zhao Dun from starvation and eventually became Lord Ling's bodyguard. Unlike Shi Miming, Ling Zhe seems to have managed to escape the scene unharmed.[15] The *Shiji*, on the other hand, reports that Shi Miming 示眯明 (sometimes transcribed as Shimi Ming), previously saved by Zhao Dun from starvation, was the only person who rescued the latter at Lord Ling's banquet and who managed to escape (*Shiji* 39.1674; Nienhauser 2006, 350–353). Interestingly, the *Shiji*, like the *Zhouxun*, uses the term *shi* in its account of the events which is absent from the corresponding passages of the *Zuozhuan*.

It is evident that, when compared to the two main sources in early Chinese history, the *Zhouxun* places greater emphasis on how eagerly the (anonymous) man sacrificed his life to repay Zhao Dun's goodness.

---

[13] *Zuozhuan*, Xuan 2, 659–662; 595. For a discussion on whether Ling Zhe escaped the scene, see the commentary in Yang B. 1995, 662. *Shiji* 39.1674; Nienhauser 2006, 350–351.
[14] See, for example, the assassination attempt entrusted to Chu Mi 鉏麑, who, however, preferred committing suicide to killing Zhao Dun. *Zuozhuan*, Xuan 2.3, 658; 595). For the conflict between "trustworthiness" (*xin* 信) and "loyalty" (*zhong* 忠) that informed Chu's decision, see Pines 2002, 151–152.
[15] *Zuozhuan*, Xuan 2.3, 659–662; 595. For a discussion on whether Ling Zhe escaped the scene, see Yang B. 1995, 662.

10

Tenth Month

In the admonition from the tenth month, Lord Zhaowen directs his attention at the first ruler of the state of Wei, Marquis Wen of Wei (r. 424–387 BCE). By so doing, he formally stays in the former Jin area as Wei emerged from the tripartition of this once vast and mighty polity into the states of Wei, Zhao, and Han. The discussion makes a temporal leap of about 200 years past the days of Zhao Dun. Marquis Wen of Wei was a famed individual, coming to prominence for employing the most able men of his era, who spearheaded some of the most radical and ground-breaking political reforms.[1] It was during his rule that the Wei, alongside Zhao and Han, was recognized by the Son of Heaven as an independent polity in the year 403, event which heralded the beginning of the Warring States period (403–221 BCE).

The story presented here unfolds around the dilemma that Marquis Wen faced when deciding which son to establish as his successor and which criteria a contender to the throne should fulfill to qualify as a good ruler. The storyline thus resembles the narrative of the third chapter, in which King Wen of Zhou had to commit to one criterion (worthiness) excluding three other options (nobility, seniority, personal affection).

The passage includes eleven bamboo slips (123–133), although in its initial state it is estimated to have included one more (between 128/129) (*Beida Mss.* 113–114). In addition, slip 128 is damaged at the top with approximately four graphs missing (*Beida Mss.* 21). The discussion consists of the narrative (124/2–128/24), which is concluded by (the now) incomplete summary (129/1–4), and appeal to Prince Gong (129/5–132/22). The latter ends with a quotation from a Document. This deviates from the pattern of concluding historical examples with a quotation from authoritative sources that we observed in most previous cases. In this example, a *shu* line is used, not to summarize a historical precedent but to animate Prince Gong to pursue the correct way of action indicated in the authoritative lore.

---

[1] Lewis 1999a, 649. On Li Kui's reforms, see Lewis 1999a, 604–606. *Shiji* "Wei shijia" 魏世家 (44.1840; For Russian translation, see Vyatkin 1992, 81–84; For French translation, see Chavannes 1967, 53–56).

Translation

123/1 • 維歲十月更旦之日，龏（共）大子朝，周昭文公自身貳之，用茲念也。【123】

• It was on the first day of the tenth month of the year, when Crown Prince Gong came to court. Lord Zhaowen of Zhou personally enjoined him with these (following) reminders. He said:

124/1 曰：昔魏文侯有子二人，曰頎，曰擊。其少長（鈞）均，而頎也愛。以頎為【124】後，而對〈封〉毄（擊）於中山。二子者，長孺子頎愚而不能聽親，中山之君【125】慧而孝以茲（慈）仁。魏文侯曰：「寡人置子，不置慧而置愚，不立孝仁【126】而立無親，則是寡人不貴賢而黨於愛子也。愛子而亡國，其何【127】□□□□，劋（豈）能守祭？置賢而信賢，則父之所貴與所甚愛，其累（矣）」【128】

In the past, Marquis Wen of Wei had two sons, named Qi and Ji. They were [roughly] the same age, but it was Qi whom he loved. So, he made Qi his successor, and enfeoffed Ji in Zhongshan. Of the two sons, the older son Qi was foolish and proved incapable of listening to his father. The Lord of Zhongshan [on the other hand] was wise and filial, showing compassion and humaneness. Marquis Wen of Wei said: "When installing my successor, I did not install the wise one but [rather] the foolish one. I did not establish the filial and humane one, but the unloving one. This shows that I did not value the worthy son but sided with the one I loved." To ruin the state out of love for a son, how …., can the sacrificial offerings [to the ancestors] really be protected? If the worthy [son] is installed and trusted, then what the father values and what he exceedingly loves, how

……129/1 世彌賢也。 129/4

… from generation to generation (the rulers of Wei) have become even worthier.

129/5 今女（汝）能賢，則鄏（鄏）邑雖小，其庸不如三晉之始也？爾為【129】不賢，則周雖千乘，其徒步幾矣。夫從徒步而為千乘，此世之所【130】上（尚）也。夫從千乘而去之徒步，此古之所病也。不徒可病，其於先【131】人有傷。此《書》之所謂曰：「女（汝）毋遺祖巧（考）羞哉」者，其此之謂乎？132/22

Now, if you were able to be worthy, then, although the City of Ru is small, how would it be inferior to the three Jin in their beginning? [But] if you are not worthy, then, although the Zhou have one thousand war chariots, it would almost be as if they merely fought on foot. Now, to start off fighting on foot and end up with one thousand chariots, is something that the world holds in esteem. But to start off with one thousand chariots and forfeit them, ending up fighting on foot, is something that the ancients regarded as disastrous. Not only can it be regarded as disastrous, but it actually harms one's ancestors. This is what a Document expresses in saying: "Do not bring shame upon your ancestors!" Does it [not] give expression to [precisely] this?

131/23 已學（教）【132】大子用茲念，斯乃受（授）之書，而自身屬（囑）之曰：女（汝）勉毋忘歲十月更旦之馴（訓）。【133】
Having instructed the crown prince with these reminders, [Lord Zhaowen] gave him the text [of his speech] and personally cautioned him, saying: "Strive not to forget the instructions from the first day of the tenth month of the year."

Comments

According to the narrative, Marquis Wen of Wei, when choosing his successor, made the mistake of allowing his emotions to influence his decision. Therefore, the slightly younger son, Ji 擊, who stood out through his wisdom, filial piety and other virtues, was enfeoffed with the area of Zhongshan[2], while the "beloved" son, Qi 頎, was made successor to the Wei throne. The latter, however, proved to be foolish and incapable of "listening to his father." Interestingly, we are not given any details as to concrete manifestations of Qi's ineptness and Ji's worthiness. This, again, demonstrates the highly idealistic nature of the *Zhouxun*, which was not concerned with the exact process of moral cultivation and different stages involved therein.

After recognizing the vast gulf between his sons' abilities, Marquis Wen of Wei is depicted as regretting his initial decision. Because of the lacuna between slips 128 and 129, it is not clear whether, in the account of the *Zhouxun*, he undertook any actions to redress the succession issue. However, in view of historical records, in which Ji succeeds Marquis Wen, receiving the posthumous title of Marquis Wu 武侯 (r. 395–370 BCE) (*Shiji* 44.1841), as well as the ending of this chapter, it stands to reason that the initial successor was indeed replaced through Ji. Therefore, I conjecture that this issue must have been discussed in the missing part and I also understand the fragment "…from generation to generation (the rulers of Wei) have become worthier" (*shi mi xian ye* 世彌賢也) (129/1–4) as elaborating upon the positive developments that took place in Wei since Ji's ascension to the throne. As such, it must have belonged to Lord Zhaowen's summary of the reported historical events. We will see summaries of this type in the subsequent chapters.

---

[2] The state of Zhongshan was invaded and given to Ji for "protection" (*shou* 守) in 408 BCE. *Shiji* "Liu guo nian biao" 六國年表 (15.708).

In his appeal, Lord Zhaowen points to the similarity between the small state of Zhou and the "three Jin" (one of which was Wei) at the incipient stage of their development. If Prince Gong manages to live up to the standards of a worthy ruler, claims Lord Zhaowen, then Zhou might take a similar trajectory to Wei. This claim is astonishing for several reasons. First, it disregards the (nominal) preeminence of the Zhou among all the other states in the All-under-Heaven alongside their conventional claims to power. The renunciation of these claims by a representative of the Zhou ruling family, such as Lord Zhaowen, is nothing short of an open declaration of the bankruptcy of the core ideas defining Zhou ideology. In a similar way, the official recognition of the former ministers of Jin as feudal lords of independent polities shook the very foundations of Zhou ritual norms.

Both the historical precedent and personal instruction contain passages constructed by means of two juxtaposed strands. In the narrative part, this structure is predicated upon the different character traits of the two sons, while in the personal appeal to Prince Gong, it is used to demonstrate that any deviations from the propositions would bring disastrous consequences. As a result, we are dealing with yet another sophisticated example of a quasi-historical writing. However, the rhyme and meter in the present chapter are characterized by inconsistent patterns. Below are some examples thereof:

Opening (124/2–125/7)

1	昔魏文侯有子二人，	真	In the past, Marquis Wen of Wei had two sons,
2	曰頎，曰擊。		named Qi and Ji.
3	其少長均，	真	They were [roughly] the same age,
4	而頎也愛。		but it was Qi whom he loved.
5	以頎為後，		So, he made Qi his successor,
6	而封擊於中山。	元	and enfeoffed Ji in Zhongshan.

Characterization of the Two Sons (125/8–126/6)

7	二子者，		Of the two sons,
8	長孺子頎愚而不能聽親，	真	the older son Qi was foolish and proved incapable of listening to his father.
9	中山之君慧而孝以慈仁。	真	The Lord of Zhongshan was wise and filial, showing compassion and humaneness.

General Principles of Action Espoused by Lord Zhaowen (131/3–132/3)

10	夫從徒步而為千乘，	蒸	Now, to start off fighting on foot and end up with one thousand chariots,
11	此世之所│尚也。	陽	is something that the world holds in esteem.
12	夫從千乘而去之徒步，		But to start off with one thousand chariots and forfeit them, ending up fighting on foot,
13	此古之所病也。	陽	is something that the ancients regarded as disastrous.
14	不徒可病，	陽	Not only can it be regarded as disastrous,
15	其於先│人有傷。	陽	but it actually harms one's ancestors.

Evidently, while in the narrative part the negative connotations are mentioned first (line 8), in Lord Zhaowen's personal appeal to Prince Gong the opposite is the case (lines 10 and 11).

Lord Zhaowen uses a *shu* saying: "Do not bring shame upon your ancestors!," to urge his successor to develop a "worthy" character. This is the second example of a demonstratively didactic application of a Document. As for the affiliation of this line with the *shu* compilations, no transmitted source from that tradition has parallels to it. However, there is a close counterpart in the Tsinghua manuscript *Huang men* 皇門.[3] Significantly, the relevant sentence: "Do not bring shame upon your ancestors!" (毋作祖考羞哉), appears in the concluding appeal to the addressee of the text.[4] And, thematically, there is a certain overlap between the *Huang men* and the *Zhouxun* too.[5]

Context

In the present chapter, the *Zhouxun*, once again, shows significant deviations from other sources. The *Shiji* does not mention another successor to Marquis Wen but Ji, who is always treated as the rightful heir apparent, eventually succeeding the Wei throne as Marquis Wu 武侯 (?–370 BCE) (*Shiji* 44.1841). The future Marquis Wu is shown there as having been involved in several successful large-scale military operations and received Zhongshan as his allotment in the seventeenth year of his father's reign (408 BCE). In Zhongshan, he was accompanied by Cang Tang 倉唐 as advisor by his side (*Shiji* 44.1838; Vyatkin 1992, 82). Unlike Sima Qian's account, the *Han Shi waizhuan* and *Shuoyuan* contain a

---

[3] For transcription, see Li X. 2010, 163–172.
[4] Li X, 2010, 165, slip 13. Intriguingly, the last part of this sentence is absent from the transmitted *Huang men*, which is a chapter of the *Yi Zhoushu*. Li X. 2010, 172.
[5] On the depiction of Zhou as a small state in the *Huang men*, see Li J. 2011, 65–66.

version of the anecdote that addresses Marquis Wen's succession. However, the two works also differ from the *Zhouxun* in presenting Ji as the older offspring, whose installation took place largely due to the wise assistance of Cang Tang and not because of another candidate's shortcomings.[6] Moreover, a great role in Ji's installation is attributed to his alleged knowledge of the Odes. Marquis Wen, an enthusiastic supporter of the Ruist doctrine, and a student of the famous disciple of Confucius, Zixia 子夏 (*Shiji* 44.1839; Vyatkin 1992, 82), is shown to have been deeply moved by Ji's ability to express his grief (enacted by Cang Tang) about the long separation from his father by means of the *Shijing*. This sentiment and ability to present it in a culturally sophisticated way manifested Ji's filial piety and worthiness. While the demonstration of Ji's worthy character leads to the demotion of the younger descendant in both texts, it is only in the *Shuoyuan* that his abilities are contrasted with Marquis Wen's ostensible "love" for his younger son.[7] In this way, the *Zhouxun* and *Shuoyuan* are similar in making this story involve a decision in favor of either a beloved or a worthy throne contender. The overview of Wei's constant successes ensuing from Marquis Wen's choice of the worthy Ji provided by Lord Zhaowen is ignorant of the fact that already in the wake of Ji's, that is, Marquis Wu's, death, a major succession crisis occurred in the state of Wei, which almost brought this state to the brink of extinction (*Shiji* 44.1843; Vyatkin 1992, 84–85).

---

[6] *Beida Mss.* 137n1. The younger son has the personal name Su 訴 in the *Han Shi waizhuan* "Juan ba" 卷八 (Xu W. 1980, 297–281; Hightower 1952, 261–264) and Zhi 摯 in the *Shuoyuan* "Feng shi" 奉使 (Xiang 1987, 296–298; Henry 2021, 702–707).

[7] *Shuoyuan* "Feng shi" (Xiang 1987, 298; Henry 2021, 707): 夫遠賢而近所愛，非社稷之長策也。 "Putting worthy men at a distance and drawing close to those you are fond of is not a policy that will be of long-term benefit to the altars of the grain and soil."

11

Eleventh Month

The instruction delivered on the eleventh month contains two historical references, which we have only previously encountered in chapter 2. Their resemblance goes beyond just the number of stories. Like in the second chapter, here, the anecdotes are also mentioned in the reversed order of their alleged occurrence in time. The main protagonist of the first story is Lord Xian of Qin (r. 384–362 BCE), who preceded Lord Zhaowen by only a few decades, whereas the second account features the champion of abdication, the legendary emperor Yao, as well as his minister and successor Shun, whose activities mark the beginning of Chinese history (at least, according to the *Shangshu*). Therefore, from the perspective of the *Zhouxun*, the chronological distance between the two stories addressed in chapter 11 covers the entire span of Chinese history.

The main character of the first story, Lord Xian of Qin, was a sovereign under whose rule and with whose reforms began the inevitable ascendancy of Qin to superpower status.[1] By choosing Lord Xian as the next exemplary Qin ruler after Lord Mu, the authors present a treatment of Qin history reminiscent of the *Shiji*.[2] In fact, an order issued by Lord Xian's son, the illustrious Lord Xiao 秦孝公 (r. 361–338 BCE), in the first year of his rule, emphasizes their affinity in no uncertain terms, by commemorating Lord Xian specifically as restoring and continuing Lord Mu's great enterprise.[3]

The account is centered around the gruesome practice of human sacrifice. While human sacrifice during funerals was a common phenomenon in the entire Zhou world, there was a widespread (biased) perception in preimperial China that Qin have implemented this practice with particular severity and cruelty.[4] The

---

[1] Among Lord Xian's most influential political measures was the organization of commoners into five family units (*wu* 伍). *Shiji* "Qin Shihuang benji" 秦始皇本紀 (6.289). For archeological evidence, see Hsing 2014, 162–163.
[2] On the possible reasons behind this pattern in the "Basic Annals of Qin," see Pines 2005/2006, 33–34.
[3] *Shiji* 5.202; Nienhauser 1994a, 108: 獻公即位，鎮撫邊境，徙治櫟陽，且欲東伐，復繆公之故地，修繆公之政令。"After Duke Xian acceded to the position, he guarded and calmed the borders, moved the capital to Yueyang, and prepared to launch an expedition east in order to recover Lord Mu's former territory and to implement Lord Mu's orders [there]."
[4] According to Falkenhausen 2004, 129, the perception of Qin's mortuary customs as particularly severe and ruthless regarding human sacrifice is biased. In reality, when it comes to

fourth century BCE witnessed a significant dwindling of this practice throughout the Zhou cultural sphere. In Qin, these changes were heralded by Lord Xian, who prohibited the custom of burying people alive together with the dead in the first year of his rule (*Shiji* 5.201; Nienhauser 1994a, 107).

In the story, Lord Xian, from his sickbed, requested from his (otherwise unknown) heir apparent Zhong Jingzi 仲敬子, to not have his funeral performed according to the old Qin custom, which allegedly required burying several sons by concubines alive alongside their deceased father. Because Zhong Jingzi refused to grant his father's request and discarded the latter's humane rationale behind it, effectively approving the murder of his five half-brothers, he was demoted as successor to the throne and possibly fell victim to his own proposition, having to accompany his father to the netherworld instead of his siblings.[5]

The second historical account of this chapter marks the first appearance of the legendary emperors Yao and Shun in the text. In this account, Yao advises Shun that worthiness should be used as the only criterion for establishing one's successor. The connection to the story about Lord Xian and Zhong Jingzi is not immediately clear, until we take into consideration their appearance in chapter 14, where they are represented as attempting to reform their sons, Dan Zhu and Shang Jun respectively, but ultimately failing in this task, given the great moral shortcomings of their progeny. As a result, the two inept sons are demoted, giving way to the worthy Shun and Yu. In the manuscript, the two accounts appear to share the common motif of the original heir's demotion, which is precipitated by their inability to obey their fathers. Moreover, Lord Zhaowen's appeal to Prince Gong points to the same theme.

The passage comprises fourteen bamboo slips (134–147), and two additional slips (between 140/141) appear to be missing (*Beida Mss.* 114). Thematically, the text shows a more complex arrangement than in the previous cases. It opens with Lord Zhaowen's quotation of a brief stanza from the "Daya" 大雅 section of the *Shijing* (135/5–12), which corresponds to the poem "Yi" (Mao 256).[6] This quote is imbedded into further explanations to Prince Gong, which likewise can be regarded as the free paraphrasing of "Yi" (135/13–136/4), showing a shared concern for the self-cultivation of a young throne contender and his amiable relation to the people for the sake of preserving power.[7] The subsequent narrative about Lord Xian (136/6–144/2) concludes with a brief summary

---

archeological evidence for such practices, Qin tombs from that period do not differ much from the contemporaneous burial sites found elsewhere in the Zhou cultural sphere. On evidence for human sacrifice in the various states of the Zhou confederacy; see Falkenhausen 2006, 181n28.

[5] Han 2015, 293. In this case, the text would be coming very close to suggesting that even physically removing an unable heir apparent is legitimate under special circumstances.

[6] For translation, see Legge 1879, 413–417.

[7] For more information, see Legge 1879, 413.

(144/3–19) and a plea to Prince Gong (144/20–145/13). The short second account featuring Yao and Shun (145/14–146/9) is followed by a rhetorical question addressing Prince Gong (146/10–21).

Translation

134/1 • 維歲十一月更旦之日，龏（共）大子朝，周昭文公自身貳之，用茲念也。【134】
• It was on the first day of the eleventh month of the year, when Crown Prince Gong came to court. Lord Zhaowen of Zhou personally enjoined him with these (following) reminders.

135/1 稱於大雅曰：「於（嗚）乎（呼）！小子、未智（知）臧否」[8]。余故畢告女（汝）於得國失國，廢【135】興之所以。136/4
Calling upon the "Daya," he said: "Ah well! My son! You do not yet know what is good and what is not." Thus, I am going to fully reveal to you how states are gained and lost, and what causes [one's] dismissal or rise to power.

136/5 曰：昔秦獻公有疾，乃召其嗣中（仲）敬子，而自身謂之曰：【136】「秦國之故，適有大喪，必從群薛（薛）。今寡人適為下游，而欲無使從，【137】其可得乎？」中（仲）敬子曰：「秦國有故，其何可變易？」公曰：「為人君者，其【138】臣有罪，剴（豈）可而毋敗（赦）？罪獸（猶）有敗（赦），而皇（況）無罪乎？無罪而強殺之，吾【139】弗忍也。其命尚未竆（窮），而欲其亟終，剴（豈）可謂德？且已去其民矣，而【140】尚獸（猶）有不惠之名，其何以彌久而侖思於百姓？子其敬聽，毋逆......」【141】......入，乃謂夫人曰：「女（汝）有子六人，寗（寧）利一人而亡五人乎？其寗（寧）利五【142】人而亡一人乎？」夫人對（對）曰：「寗（寧）利五人。」於是果亡一人而已，不眾【143】所害。144/2
He said: In the past, when Lord Xian of Qin became ill, he summoned his heir Zhong Jingzi and personally told him: "According to an old custom of the state of Qin, on the occasion of the ruler's funeral, a number of his sons by concubines must follow him into the grave. Now I am about to leave for the netherworld and wish that no one is made to follow me there. Can this be achieved?" Zhong Jingzi said: "This is an old custom of the state of Qin, how can it be altered and changed?" The lord said: "If a ruler has a subordinate who commits an offence, can he really not pardon him? And even if an offender is [occasionally] pardoned, how much more so [should it be the case with] the innocent one? Recklessly

---

[8] Unlike the editors, I set quotation marks around the quote from Mao 256.

killing innocent people, is something I cannot bear to do. [For] if a person has not yet reached his allotted span of life, and I wish it to end abruptly, – can that really be called virtue? So, [even long] after leaving my people [in such way], I would retain the reputation of being unkind. What would then be the point of my [longstanding] concern for the [wellbeing of] the "hundred surnames" that grew with every passing season [of my life]? My son, listen respectfully, and do not oppose…" … entered, then he said to his consort: "You have six sons. Would you rather sacrifice five sons to benefit one, or would you rather sacrifice one son to benefit five?" His consort replied: "I would rather benefit five sons." Therefore, he indeed decided to make one son perish, diminishing the number of people hurt.

144/3 故中（仲）敬子之所以述（遂）不得為後者，不聽親也。144/19
Thus, the reason why Zhong Jingzi did not become successor was because he did not listen to his father.

144/20 今女（汝）無孝而【144】難聽親，則周唯（雖）小國，其庸可得有？ 145/13
Now, you are not filial and dislike listening to your father. Thus, although Zhou is a small state, how could you obtain it?

145/14 昔堯貳舜曰：「置嗣無宜，以賢為【145】宜，立後無正，以賢為命。」 146/9
In the past, Yao enjoined Shun, saying: "In installing one's heir, no [method] is appropriate, [other than making] worthiness your standard. In establishing one's successor, no [way] is orthodox, [other than making] worthiness your imperative.

146/10 夫賢之臣不賢，久矣，剴（豈）乃今哉？ 146/21
Now, long has it been the case that that ministers of worthy [rulers] are not themselves worthy. Why should it be different today?

146/22 已學（教）大【146】子用茲念，斯乃受（授）之書，而自身屬（囑）之曰：女（汝）勉毋忘歲十一月更旦之馴（訓）。【147】
Having instructed the crown prince with these reminders, [Lord Zhaowen] gave him the text [of his speech] and personally cautioned him, saying: "Strive not to forget the instructions from the first day of the eleventh month of the year."

Comments

In view of the complexity of the chapter, I analyze each section separately.

1. Lord Zhaowen's First Address to Prince Gong (135/1–136/4)

This is the only example in the *Zhouxun* where a poem is referred to not by its generic term *shi* but by the designation of the section of the *Shijing* in which it appears: "Daya" or "Major Court Hymns." While other "Daya" pieces appear in the *Zhouxun,* they are not explicitly identified as such. It makes sense that, at this point, "Lord Zhaowen" invokes the poem's title to accentuate the solemn character and significance of his admonition and, possibly, to create a connection between his instructions and the court activities of the early Zhou kings.

Building on a quote from the poem "Yi," the *Zhouxun* also borrows its rhyme *zhi* (Cheng and Jiang 1999, 865):

```
1    「嗚呼！小子、           之
2    未知臧否。」              之
3    余故畢告汝
     於得國失國，              職
4    廢興之所以。              之
```

However, by not indicating the end of the quote, Lord Zhaowen treats the source very freely. This *shi*-quote appears in the beginning of the chapter, setting the tone for subsequent passages. This is different from other instances of such quotations in the text, where they function as either summarizing historical precedents or lending authority to Lord Zhaowen's admonitions to Prince Gong. While the poem belonged to the most frequently quoted poetic sources in Chinese antiquity (Goldin 2005, 147–148), the *Zhouxun* seems unique among the available texts in invoking this particular couplet.

2. Account of Lord Xian and Zhong Jingzi (136/6–144/19)

The causes for [one's] dismissal or rise to power announced in the introductory part are elucidated in the anecdote about Lord Xian of Qin. Lord Xian is depicted here as wishing to abandon the old Qin funerary custom lest he becomes responsible for the deaths of several innocent (*wuzui* 無罪) people. Even though the people in question are his own sons, Lord Xian resorts to public discourse by appealing to the relation between ruler and subordinates, and not that between father and son(s).⁹ Through this expansion of the frame of reference, the heir apparent, Zhong Jingzi, is effectively required to forfeit the privileged status he enjoys within his lineage.¹⁰ Moreover, in this setting, his wish to implement the Qin's ancient funerary custom becomes tantamount to willfully demanding capital punishment for five innocent people. The demand ought to be rejected not only for its legal unsoundness but also because Lord Xian declared the welfare of the people as his main priority. Considering this, Zhong Jingzi appears to have been eventually demoted and lost his life. Lord Zhaowen contends, however, that the Qin prince was dismissed primarily because he failed to heed his father on the importance of treating the people with kindness.

As for the rhetorical characteristics of this narrative, while its beginning contains no rhymed passages, Lord Xian's speech becomes intermingled with rhymes when he starts to justify his wish to abandon the conventional funerary practices of Qin. At this juncture, the text operates mainly with the rhyme groups *dong* 冬, *geng* 耕 and *zhen* 真:

Reasons for Wishing to Abandon the Custom (140/3–16)

1	其命尚未窮,	冬	[For] if a person has not yet reached his allotted span of life,
2	而欲其亟終,	冬	and I wish it to end abruptly, –
3	豈可謂德?		Can that really be called virtue?

Consequences of Following the Custom (140/17–141/24)

4	且已去其民矣,	真	So, [even long] after leaving my people [in such way],
5	而|尚猶有不惠之名,	耕	I would retain the reputation of being unkind.
6	其何以彌久而侖思於百姓?	耕	What would then be the point of my [longstanding] concern for the [wellbeing of] the "hundred surnames"?
7	子其敬聽,	耕	My son, listen respectfully,
8	毋逆|		and do not oppose…"

---

⁹ Possibly, there is a pun involved here, because, according to the *Liji* "Yu zao" 玉藻 (Yang T. 2004, 388), the sons by concubines were supposed to refer to themselves as "your minister, the shoot from the stock" (*chen nie* 臣孽).

¹⁰ On the preeminent position of the heir apparent in the old ritual tradition of the Zhou, see *Zuozhuan*, Min 2.7, 268; 243.

Lord Xian's Dialogue with the Consort (142/1–143/14)

9	……入，乃謂夫人曰：	真	… entered, then he said to his consort:
10	「汝有子六人，	真	"You have six sons.
11	寧利一人而亡五人乎？	真	Would you rather sacrifice five sons to benefit one,
12	其寧利五｜人而亡一人乎？	真	or would you rather sacrifice one son to benefit five?"
13	夫人對曰：		His consort replied:
14	寧利五人。	真	"I would rather benefit five sons."

Outcome (143/15–144/2)

15	於是果亡一人而已，	真	Therefore, he indeed decided to make one son perish,
16	不眾｜所害。		diminishing the number of people hurt.

Synopsis (144/3–144/19)

17	故仲敬子之所以遂不得而後者，		Thus, the reason why Zhong Jingzi did not become successor
18	不聽親也。	真	was because he did not listen to his father.

As can be seen, rhymes render Lord Xian's arguments more cohesive and, moreover, help organize his speech thematically. The synopsis is connected to the preceding text by means of rhyme to stress the necessity of listening to one's father's advice.

3. Second Address (144/20–145/13)

This topic also constitutes the main tenor of Lord Zhaowen's next address to Prince Gong. Rhyme is used here too to imbue Lord Zhaowen's words with more weight and emphasis. Even though thematically this is a new unit, rhyme *zhen* 真 connects it with the previous section:

1	今汝無孝 而｜難聽親，	真	Now, you are not filial and dislike listening to your father.
2	則周雖小國，	職	Thus, although Zhou is a small state,
3	其庸可得有？	之	how could you obtain it?

Accordingly, the only way for Prince Gong to inherit the Zhou throne was to heed Lord Zhaowen's instructions.

4. Account of Yao and Shun (145/14–146/9)

In the second historical precedent presented in this chapter, we, at last, encounter the earliest figures to be mentioned in the text, the famous antique champions of abdication Yao and Shun. This passage is formulated as a stanza consisting of four tetrasyllabic lines, to reinforce its admonishing character:

1	置嗣無宜，	歌	In installing one's heir, no [method] is appropriate,
2	以賢為宜，	歌	[other than making] worthiness your standard.
3	立後無正，	耕	In establishing one's successor, no [way] is orthodox,
4	以賢為命。	耕	[other than making] worthiness your imperative.

Accordingly, worthiness should be used as the only criterion for establishing one's successor, and kinship ties should play no role in this process. However, Yao's maxim is qualified in the very next sentence.

5. Rhetorical Question (146/10–21)

At this juncture, Lord Zhaowen expresses his doubts about the feasibility of the transfer of power to a worthy minister under existing conditions. His doubts are emphasized by means of common end-rhyme 之 *zhi*.

1	夫賢之臣不賢，久矣，	之	Now, long has it been the case that that ministers of worthy [rulers] are not themselves worthy.
2	剴（豈）乃今哉？	之	Why should it be different today?

The reason for this situation is identified in the diminishing moral aptitude of ministers. In fact, the only two ministers who were ever able to cope with power were Shun and Yu. Therefore, the only viable option to uphold their principles was to establish a successor from among one's own progeny, who would come closest to the ideal of worthiness. This message echoes the rhetorical question in chapter 2, which Lord Zhaowen asks of his successor: "from the ancient times on, was it ever permissible to entrust an unworthy person with the state?"

Context

As was the case with all previous chapters, also here, the *Zhouxun* provides a very unusual view of early Chinese history. For instance, neither Zhong Jingzi nor the fact that Lord Xian had six sons are mentioned in the *Shiji*.[11] It is very likely that this particular number served the purpose of making Zhong Jingzi look especially hard-hearted. After all, by ignoring his father's request he showed readiness to sanction the death of no less than five siblings.

The way in which the *Zhouxun* juxtaposes Lord Xians's five other sons to Zhong Jingzi is relevant against the background of the ode "Huang niao" 黃鳥 (Mao 131). There, the inhabitants of the Qin capital voice their grievance about the loss of three able dignitaries to the custom of human sacrifice implemented at Lord Mu's funeral.[12] If only conventions allowed, so claims the anonymous writer, these worthies would have been rescued by sacrificing in their place a hundred other (presumably, less talented) men.[13] As presented in this chapter, Lord Xian would have dismissed such practice as outright inhumane. The people's abilities should not decide in matters of their life or death, this is the purview of each individual's span of life or destiny.[14] In a sense, the manuscript might be redressing the (biased) view of Qin as especially callous in this chapter.

The *Zhouxun* proclaims that the gruesome funerary custom was applied to a ruler's sons by concubines, whereas the *Zuozhuan* and *Shiji* name representatives of other lineages as people who had to accompany the deceased ruler.[15] This shows, yet again, that the *Zhouxun* constructs its narrative to emphasize certain points. The relevance of sons by concubines and general concern for the wellbeing of the population seem to be the major focal point of this "historical" account. That the *Zhouxun* mentions Lord Xian as a paragon of good governance, and not his even more illustrious, militarily successful, and reform oriented son, Lord Xiao (still a predecessor to Lord Zhaowen), shows just how much

---

[11] *Shiji* 5.201 does not mention this person. Instead, Lord Xiao is identified as Lord Xian's heir apparent. According to Pines 2005/2006, 31, the part of the *Shiji* dedicated to Lord Xian (and his son Lord Xiao) is "perhaps the most reliable Zhanguo portion of the *Shiji*."
[12] *Zuozhuan*, Wen 6.3, 546; 491.
[13] *Shijing* "Huang niao" (Cheng and Jiang 1999, 352; Waley 1960, 311): 彼蒼者天、殲我良人。如可贖兮、人百其身。 "That blue one, Heaven, Takes all our good men. Could we but ransom him? There are a hundred would give their lives." See also Karlgren 1950a, 84. For a comparison with the early counterpart from the Anhui University collection, see Shaughnessy 2021, 13–17.
[14] On this point, the *Zhouxun* is also different from the *Zuozhuan* where the gentleman bemoans the loss of the "good men" (*shanren* 善人) of the state. *Zuozhuan*, Wen 6.3, 546–548; 491–492.
[15] For the *Zuozhuan*, see the preceding note. For a similar account in the *Shiji* 5.194–195; Nienhauser 1994a, 101–102.

importance its authors attached to abandoning human sacrifice. In their eyes, this measure was a decisive step in the state of Qin towards the ideal of humane rule.

It is also remarkable that the similarity between Lord Xian and Yao concerned not only dismissing unruly heirs apparent, but also their rationale for doing so, at least when we compare the present account of Lord Xian to how Yao is shown to have deliberated his inept son Dan Zhu's dismissal, in the *Shiji* (which, most likely, follows here an earlier source). In both cases, the rulers reached the conclusion that allegiance to their rightful successor would have entailed suffering for a group of people (sons by concubines in the *Zhouxun* and the general population in the *Shiji*).[16] Consequently, by dismissing their heirs apparent, both Yao and Lord Xian opted for a lesser evil. In the narrative of the *Zhouxun*, this decision led to the establishment of a new successor from among the sons by concubines (which is inconsistent with Lord Xiao's pedigree). One is thus left wondering whether the focus on the sons of concubines had a specific meaning for the authors of the *Zhouxun*. Were they trying to suggest that by establishing a successor from among this group of offspring, a ruler was following in the steps of the great Yao?

---

[16] *Shiji* 1.30; Adopted from Nienhauser 1994a, 10–11: 授舜，則天下得其利而丹朱病；授丹朱，則天下病而丹朱得其利。堯曰：「終不以天下之病而利一人」，而卒授舜以天下。 "Giving it to Shun, the people of the world would have the benefit of it and Dan Zhu would be displeased. If he gave Dan Zhu the world, then the people of the world would be displeased and Dan Zhu would have the benefit of it. Yao said, "In the final analysis, I will not displease the people and benefit a single man." And, in the end, he gave Shun the world."

12

Twelfth Month

In his last instruction of the regular year, Lord Zhaowen first returns to the model laid out in the first chapter. He begins by presenting a series of general admonitions which are constructed as chain argument and concluded with a rhetorical question. Unlike in chapter 1, however, no authoritative sources are quoted here to support the argument. Following that, Lord Zhaowen provides two historical precedents to substantiate his general instructions. Both examples belong to well-known stories in the corpus of early Chinese literature. The first example recounts how King Cheng of Zhou (r. 1042/35–1006 BCE) refused to believe slander about the Duke of Zhou[1] and, therefore, was able to become a great ruler. The second example shows how Lord Huan of Qi (r. 685–643 BCE) became a hegemon due to the wise assistance of Guan Yiwu 管夷吾 (?–645 BCE), whom he promoted to the highest administrative position in the state of Qi despite their erstwhile conflict[2] and despite criticism of this decision on the part of his other ministers. Both stories suggest that a ruler should make his decisions based only on his personal assessment of a situation. In mentioning two ancient precedents, this instruction resembles chapters 2 and 11. However, in this chapter, the historical events are depicted in chronological order. I argue that doing so was important to the development of the argument: in his concluding appeal to Prince Gong, Lord Zhaowen singles out Lord Huan as a singular model of emulation.

The chapter includes eighteen slips (148–165), and two slips appear to be missing (between 153/154 and 164/165) (*Beida Mss.* 115). With twenty slips, it would have been the third longest unit of the text, after chapters 14 and 1. In terms of its content, it can be divided into four main parts: 1) four general principles of governance (149/2–153/16) (and, possibly, a conclusion (153/17–154/7)); 2) first anecdote (154/8–156/2) and a concluding statement (156/3–156/18); 3) second anecdote (156/19–161/8) and a concluding statement

---

[1] For analysis of the different images of the Duke of Zhou in early sources, see Nylan 2010, 94–128, and Huang 2018, 136–141.
[2] In the *Zuozhuan*, Zhuang 9.5, 180; 159, it was Guan Zhong's early acquaintance Bao Shuya 鲍叔牙, who, being aware of Guan Zhong's worthiness, always treated him graciously despite them serving rivaling brothers and recommended him to Lord Huan.

(161/9–1622/5); and, finally, 4) an appeal to Prince Gong (162/6–164/23), centered around a saying heard by Lord Zhaowen.

Translation

148/1 • 維歲十二月更旦之日，龏（共）大子朝，周昭文公自身貳之，用茲念【148】也。曰：149/2

• It was on the first day of the twelfth month of the year, when Crown Prince Gong came to court. Lord Zhaowen of Zhou personally enjoined him with these (following) reminders. He said:

149/3 俟國者，不可以不寬，不寬則無以容眾。眾之為君而弗能容，其何【149】以守國？國不守而城空虛，危孰大焉？150/14

He, who is waiting [to inherit] a state, must not fail to be lenient. If he fails to be lenient, he will have no means to be tolerant to the masses. Ruling the masses, yet being unable to be tolerant to them, how could he protect his state? When a state is unprotected and its cities are empty and weak, what is more dangerous than this?

150/15 有土地者，不可以不惠，不惠則無【150】以來民。【民】之使而莫骨〈肯〉來，其誰與處國？151/14

He, who possesses land and territory, must not fail to be kind. If he fails to be kind, he will have no means to entice the people to come [to his state]. [Being in the position to] employ the people, yet having no one willing to come, who then will dwell with him in his state?

151/15 君百姓者，不可以不信，不信則【151】無以致遠近。遠近莫至，將誰為主？152/11

A lord over the "hundred surnames" must not fail to be trustworthy. If he fails to be trustworthy, he will have no means to command the support of those distant or near. If neither those distant nor near come, whose ruler will he be?

152/12 守宗廟者，不可以信讒。信讒則苛，苛則怒，怒【152】則傷心，心傷則氣不平，氣不平則百疾生。百疾生，將安得𦜔（壽）？153/16

He, who protects the ancestral temple, must not trust slanderers. If he trusts slanderers, he will be harsh. If he is harsh, he will be angry. If he is angry, he will harm his heart[-mind]. If he harms his heart, his vital energy will be unbalanced. If his vital energy is unbalanced, the "hundred diseases" will emerge. If the "hundred diseases" emerge, how can he attain longevity?

153/17 故為人君而能行之【153】……154/1 子信讒，反以為慝。154/7
And so, if a ruler is able to carry these [four] out...... [if] you trust slanderers, [you] will, on the contrary, turn [the situation] to [your] detriment.

154/8 昔周公旦東從〈征〉，三年不歸，有惡之於周成王【154】者，其志盈車。成王既弗信也，而積其志以侍（待）周公。已視（示）周公，乃【155】燔之。156/2
In the past, the Duke of Zhou, Dan, went on a punitive expedition to the East and did not return for three years. Someone vilified him in front of King Cheng of Zhou, with enough reports to fill a cart. King Cheng did not believe [these reports], but gathered them, awaiting [the return of] the Duke of Zhou. After showing them to the Duke of Zhou, he burned them.

156/3 故周成王所以能述（遂）成其王者，不信讒也。156/18
And so, the reason why King Cheng of Zhou could consummate his kingship, was that he did not believe slander.

156/19 昔管夷吾為公【156】子起〈赳〉射齊桓公，中其鉤北（背）。及桓公之為君也，論（掄）其賢臣，而智（知）其【157】莫能及管夷吾也，於是召管夷吾於魯而授之相。或進閒（諫）曰：「夷【158】吾之罪大矣，奈何不以為僇（戮）而授之相也？」齊桓公曰：「吾聞之，為【159】人君者，不久臧（藏）怨，論臣之道，取其成功而不苛其小故。」於是述（遂）【160】用管中（仲），使治齊國。161/7
In the past, Guan Yiwu shot Lord Huan of Qi on behalf of the Noble Scion Jiu, piercing through his belt buckle [with an arrow]. When Lord Huan came to power and was assessing his worthy ministers, he realized that no one among them could come up to Guan Yiwu. Therefore, he summoned Guan Yiwu from Lu and offered him the post of Prime Minister. Someone came forward and remonstrated [with him], saying: "Yiwu's crimes are great! Why is he not being executed, but being offered the chancellorship [instead]?" Lord Huan of Qi said: "I have heard it said: 'A ruler does not harbor anger for long. The proper way to assess ministers, is to pay attention to their accomplishments and not to punish harshly their small transgressions.'" Thereupon, he employed Guan Zhong and entrusted him with the governance of the state of Qi.

161/8 故桓公之所以九合諸侯而述（遂）柏（伯）於世者，則【161】管中（仲）之力也。162/5
And so, the reason why Lord Huan [was able to] assemble the regional lords nine times and succeed in becoming hegemon of his age, was because of Guan Zhong's assistance.

162/6 今如能濃桓公之順（訓），去還忿，用賢仇³，聽諫而毋復（覆）【162】過，則而【國】雖小區區，其何患於不逢（豐）侈？吾聞之曰：「人君其強適足【163】以復（覆）過，其智適足以逐（卻）閒（諫），若此者，失國之主也。」其胡可毋慎？ 164/23

Now, if you are able to emulate Lord Huan's lesson, if you do away with repaying anger with anger, if you employ worthy aides, if you heed remonstrations and do not cover up (your) mistakes, then, although your state is small and insignificant, why worry that it will not become rich and prosperous? I have heard it said: "If a ruler's strength is merely sufficient to cover up mistakes, if his knowledge is merely sufficient to reject remonstrations, such a ruler will lose (his) state." How can one not be cautious about this?

164/24 已【164】【學（教）大子用茲念，斯乃受（授）之書，而自身屬（囑）之曰：女（汝）勉毋忘歲十二】月更旦之馴（訓）。【165】

Having [instructed the crown prince with these reminders, [Lord Zhaowen] gave him the text [of his speech] and personally cautioned him, saying: "Strive not to forget] the instructions from the first day of the [twelfth month of the year.]"

Comments

1. Four General Principles (149/2–154/7)

Unlike in the first chapter, here, the addressee of the "theoretical" instructions is referred to by different designations. They are: "he, who is waiting [to inherit] a state," "he, who owns land and territory," "he, who rules over the 'hundred surnames'" and "he, who protects the ancestral temple." These designations highlight different aspects of what being a sovereign entailed in ancient China. The four points respectively highlight the importance of leniency, kindness, trustworthiness, and not believing slander. While the magnanimous treatment of the people is one of the major topics of the *Zhouxun*, the two latter topics come up more sporadically. In the first chapter, a ruler is warned not to believe slander lest his state and cities become deserted. But here the consequences of failing to abide by these warnings are presented as detrimental to personal health and longevity. Most likely, this is because "empty cities" already feature as a negative effect of not being lenient to the people in the first instruction of the chapter.

---

³ Unlike the editors, who read the graph 仇 (162/19) as *chou* 仇, Chen Jian (2015) interprets it as *zuo* 佐 (to assist; assistant). I follow his suggestion, because *zuo* belongs to the rhyme group *ge* 歌, forming a rhymed passage with the graph *guo* 過 at the end of the following sentence.

2. Anecdote about King Cheng and the Duke of Zhou and Summary

In this version of the famous story, King Cheng refused to believe reports vilifying the Duke of Zhou, which were so numerous they could fill a cart. Its connection to the preceding general discussion about "not believing slander" appears rather tenuous, as this story does not make any reference to health discourse. As they stand in the text, it rather seems that they only share the topic of slander. According to the synopsis, King Cheng was able to "consummate" (*cheng* 成) his kingship precisely because he refused to believe the slander against his uncle. The pun involving his posthumous title, "accomplished" (*cheng* 成), and the appraisal of his governance was certainly intended.[4]

3. Anecdote about Lord Huan of Qi and Guan Zhong and Summary

The second anecdote involves Lord Huan and his decision to entrust his erstwhile enemy, Guan Zhong, with the governance of his state. While the topic of slander is absent here, the similarity to the preceding story resides in the emphasis on "rational" decision-making based on the sober assessment of a situation, untainted by one's emotions. The ubiquitous validity of these principles is underscored here by describing them as something that Lord Huan has heard (lines 3–6). The veracity of the saying is further enhanced by the use of regular meter (for the most part) and rhyme.

1	齊桓公曰：		Lord Huan of Qi said:
2	「吾聞之，		"I have heard it said:
3	為｜人君者，		'A ruler
4	不久藏[怒]，	魚	does not harbor anger for long.
5	論臣之道，		The proper way to assess ministers,
6	取其成功		is to pay attention to their accomplishments
	而不苛其小[故]。	魚	and not to punish harshly their small transgressions.'"
7	於是遂｜用管仲，		Thereupon, he employed Guan Zhong
8	使治齊[國]。	職	and entrusted him with ordering of the state of Qi.

Synopsis

9	故桓公之所以九合諸侯而遂伯於[世]者，	月祭	And so, the reason why Lord Huan [was able to] assemble the regional lords nine times and succeed in becoming hegemon of his age,

---

[4] On some early examples of such use, see Khayutina 2021, 158.

10   則|管仲之|力|也。   職   was because of Guan Zhong's assistance.

The saying varies from any other explicitly quoted material mentioned so far in the *Zhouxun*, in that it represents a self-contained textual unit which itself includes several distinct sections.

The text employs the same synopsis: "and so, X is Y," as in the above case, to demonstrate the importance of Lord Huan's decision for his political career.

4. Lord Zhaowen's Personal Address (162/6–164/23)

In his concluding appeal, Lord Zhaowen urges Prince Gong to emulate Lord Huan's treatment of worthy aides, leaving King Cheng aside. This might suggest that the argument in this chapter was presented in a linear fashion, proceeding from one trope to another similar topic, which is somewhat reminiscent of chain arguments.

Interestingly, by referring in his speech to a "heard" saying, Lord Zhaowen himself is shown to emulate the illustrious Qi ruler in heeding others' opinion. This becomes clear when we consider that theirs are the only two instances of referring to a saying by means of *wen zhi* in the entire text. At the same time, the fact that it was "heard" also underscores its validity as the general principle involving the survival or vanishing of a state. Here, the saying is integrated in the larger context of Lord Zhaowen's speech by means of the same vocabulary, meter and rhyme.

1	今如能濬桓公之|訓|，	文	Now, if you are able to emulate Lord Huan's lesson,
2	去還|忿|，	文	if you do away with repaying anger with anger,
3	用賢|佐|，	歌	if you employ worthy aides,
4	聽諫而毋覆|過|，	歌	if you heed remonstrations and do not cover up (your) mistakes,
5	則而國雖小區|區|，	侯	then, although your state is small and insignificant,
6	其何患於不豐|侈|？	歌	why worry that it will not become rich and prosperous?
7	吾聞之曰：		I have heard it said:
8	人君其強適足|以覆|過|，	歌	"If a ruler's strength is merely sufficient to cover up mistakes,
9	其智適足以卻|諫|，	元	if his knowledge is merely sufficient to reject remonstrations,
10	若此者，		such a ruler
11	失國之主也。		will lose (his) state."

| 12 | 其胡可毋慎? | 真 | How can one not be cautious about this? |

Just like the previous "saying," this one also stands out from other quoted sources through its length and complexity. Its structure is particularly interesting: the opening "ruler" refers to both subsequent sentences (lines 8 and 9). Therefore, it can be represented as follows:

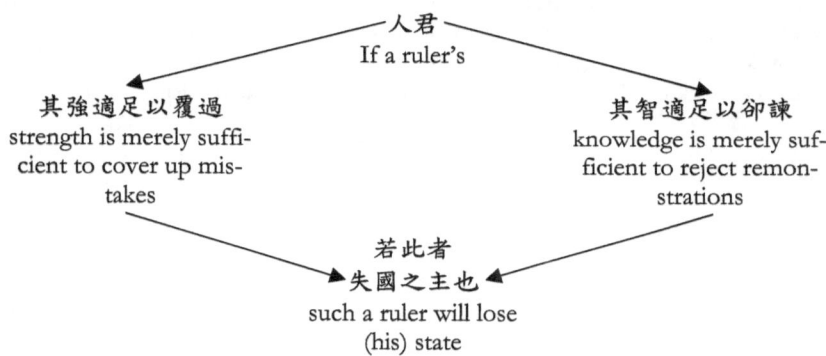

As can be seen, this is a short yet complete passage, developed in several argumentative steps. This also makes it different from the quoted *shu*, *shi* or *yan*.

Context

When compared to other early texts, the *Zhouxun* stands out through its depiction of the ease with which King Cheng of Zhou and Lord Huan of Qi were able to put aside any emotion-based considerations and focus only on the strengths of particular individuals. In most other texts, they are depicted as showing (at least, initially) a much more skeptical attitude toward the Duke of Zhou[5] and Guan

---

[5] Some records suggest that King Cheng might have initially believed slanderers and that he changed his mind after seeing tangible evidence of the Duke of Zhou's innocence in the form of tablets inscribed with the latter's prayer to the Zhou ancestors. See the *Shangshu*-chapter "Jin Teng" 金縢 (Gu and Liu 2005, 1223; Karlgren 1950b, 35–36) and the *Shiji* "Lu Zhou Gong shijia" 魯周公世家 (33.1520; Nienhauser 2006, 137). Michael Nylan 2010, 106, notes that the "Metal-bound Coffer" story does not completely succeed in absolving the Duke of Zhou "from the implicit charges of arrogance, attention-grabbing, and ruthlessness." King Cheng's distrust of the Duke of Zhou is even more prominent in the Tsinghua manuscript *Zhou Wuwang you ji Zhou Gong suo zi yi dai wang zhi zhi* 周武王有疾周公所自以代王之志 (For

Zhong[6], respectively. This difference clearly manifests the idealistic nature of the *Zhouxun*.

At the same time, by discussing the Duke of Zhou and Guan Zhong in the same chapter and in comparable contexts, the authors suggest a close similarity between the two. Therefore, the Duke of Zhou appears here as a subordinate of King Cheng of Zhou. This view is opposed to another early position stating that "the Duke of Zhou had inherited the throne after King Wu and ruled as king" (Gren 2017, 195). There is also no ambiguity about the possible involvement of the Duke of Zhou in the political crisis of the early Zhou dynasty, which was reflected in many other early sources. King Cheng's uncle is presented in an unreservedly positive way in the *Zhouxun* and suspicions regarding him are identified as the work of slanderers, which a wise ruler is expected to dismiss.

---

transcription, see Li X. 2010, 157–162). For translation and discussion of the conflict between these two actors, see Meyer 2014, 937–988 and Meyer 2017b, 243–246. For the analysis of the three versions of the "Jin Teng" story, see Huang 2018, 116–136. For the crucial role of the written documents in this account, see Krijgsman 2019, 104–105.

[6] *Lüshi chunqiu* "Zan neng" 贊能 24.2 (Chen Q. 2001, 1601; Knoblock and Riegel 2000, 609–610). On the accounts of Guan Zhong's assassination attempt, see *Guoyu* "Jinyu si" 晉語四 (Xu Y. 2002, 347) and *Shiji* "Qi Taigong shijia" 齊太公世家 (32.1485–86).

13

Intercalary Month

The next audience takes places on the first day of the "intercalary month."[1] Intercalation by means of an additional thirteenth month was used in early China to synchronize the lunar and solar calendars. In pre-imperial time, intercalary months were customarily inserted at the end of the year (Cullen 2017, 17). Therefore, it is logical to assume that this audience took place in the winter of that year, after the twelfth month. This month shows the comprehensive character of Lord Zhaowen's instructions, who imparted royal guidance to Prince Gong on all possible occasions. It is noteworthy since most years in late pre-imperial China did not include intercalary months,[2] and so there would have been fewer occasions for uttering these admonitions when compared to the precepts associated with other months. This could be interpreted both as a sign of their relative marginality (as something that need not be constantly repeated) and their uniqueness (as something to be imparted on special occasions only). I maintain that the content of chapter 13 embodies both of these two aspects. Its relative marginality shows itself in close parallel to chapter 6 and, above all, chapter 10. As a consequence, all essential messages of the text are conveyed during the regular calendar year. Chapter 13 is unique in echoing the setting of the *Zhouxun* as well as providing a rare description of Lord Zhaowen's self-understanding.

As for the narrative, its main protagonist is a minister of the state of Jin, Zhao Yang 趙鞅 (?–476 BCE), who is also widely known under his posthumous title Zhao Jianzi. Chronologically, we move more than one hundred years ahead of the events around Zhao Dun, the early representative of the Zhao lineage, discussed in chapter 9. Zhao Jianzi is described here as faced with choosing a worthy successor from among his sons, whose number was, conveniently, confined to just two: Lu the Elder 伯魯 and Wuxu 無卹. This is the same predicament in which Marquis Wen of Wei found himself in chapter ten. Also here, the younger candidate eventually gets the upper hand over his elder brother. His

---

[1] For more on intercalation in pre-imperial and early imperial China, see Pankenier 2013, 48n20; Cullen 2017, 12 and 12n18.
[2] As to the frequency of their appearance, Cullen states that: "by some time in the pre-imperial period the tradition had been established that 19 years should contain seven intercalary months" (2017, 16).

depiction has him embodying characteristics which were reminiscent of Lord Wen of Jin as portrayed in chapter 6.

Lord Zhaowen's assessment of his own abilities belongs among the unique traits of the chapter. Accordingly, he was not equal to Zhao Yang just as Prince Gong was inferior to Wuxu. In this, Lord Zhaowen admits that people have different abilities and that the high moral standards of exemplary individuals might remain unreachable for the less talented. This prompts the question as to the minimal requitements for becoming a worthy, but Lord Zhaowen does not broach this matter. However, it seems to follow from chapter 13 that some demonstrable evidence about one's aspirations to achieve self-reformation (regardless of the ultimate success or the practitioner's sincerity) would constitute a necessary precondition for deciding the issue of succession.

The plot of this chapter echoes the setting of the *Zhouxun*: the interactions between Zhao Yang and his two sons are constructed in close parallel to Lord Zhaowen's own instructions of Prince Gong. Zhao Yang is said here to compose an instructive message for his sons, commit it to writing, recite its content for them and, finally, give them copies of his admonition hoping that they will absorb his teachings. Lord Zhaowen can be seen as emulating the same steps while attempting to reform his son.

The passage includes thirteen slips (166–178), and three (at most) slips between 169 and 170 appear to be missing (*Beida Mss.* 140n3). It includes two main parts. The historical precedent (167/2–176/4), which is concluded by Lord Zhaowen's summary (175/8–176/4), and an appeal to Prince Gong (176/5–177/19), which is centered around a quotation from a proverb (176/23–177/6).

Translation

166/1 • 維歲閏月更旦之日，龏（共）大子朝，周昭文公自身貳之，用茲念也。【166】曰：167/1

• It was on the first day of the intercalary month of the year, when Crown Prince Gong came to court. Lord Zhaowen of Zhou personally enjoined him with these (following) reminders. He said:

167/2 昔趙闌（簡）子身書二牘，而親自諴（籀）之。其書之言：「節欲而聽諫，【167】敬賢勿曼（慢），使能勿賤。為人君者能行之三者，其國必彌大，其民【168】弗去散（散）。」已諴（籀）茲書，右手把一以予柏（伯）魯，左手把一以予無邮（卹）。俱【169】……在，柏（伯）魯亡其書，令之口諷之而弗能得。無邮（卹）出其書於左袂，趡（跪）【170】而進之，令口諷誦之而習。闌（簡）子曰：「魯也，不智（知）好學之有賴也，不【171】智（知）從（縱）欲之日敗也，不智（知）自以為少而年已管（暮）也。

不識之三者,其【172】安能守祭?」無卹好學而智(知)貴善言,孝弟(悌)兹(慈)仁而主令弗曼(慢)。令之【173】守祭,其使能使民毋去已罷(遷)。」乃立無卹以為泰(太)子。閒(簡)子已終,無【174】卹即立(位),述(遂)為賢主。175/7

In the past, Zhao Jianzi personally inscribed two wooden tablets and recited the contents by himself. His text read: "Moderate desires and heed remonstrations, respect the worthy and do not treat them contemptuously. Employ the capable and do not look down on them. If a ruler is able to carry out these three points, his state will certainly become ever greater, and his people will not leave him and disperse." After reciting this text, he took one copy into his right hand to give to Lu, the Elder, and took the other copy into his left hand to give to Wuxu. Both... ... to remain. Lu, the Elder, lost his copy, and, when asked to recite it [from memory], was unable to do so. Wuxu [to the contrary] took his copy out of his left sleeve, kneeled down and presented it [to Jianzi]. When asked to recite and chant it, he turned out to be well versed in it. Jianzi said: "Lu, you do not realize that to love learning is advantageous. You do not realize that indulging in desires brings a speedy decline. You do not realize that, although you see yourself as young, you are already in your twilight years. How can someone who does not understand these three points protect our ancestral altars? Wuxu, you are fond of learning and realize that good words are to be valued. You are filial, brotherly, compassionate, humane, and not neglectful of your ruler's orders. If I entrust you with the protection of our ancestral altars, you will be able to prevent people from leaving and moving away." Thereupon, he established Wuxu as crown prince. After Jianzi died, Wuxu ascended the throne, and thereupon became a worthy sovereign.

175/8 故趙是(氏)之所以始也千乘,已而為萬乘者,其【175】二主賢也。176/4

So, the reason why the Zhao lineage began with one thousand chariots and ended with ten thousand, was because of these two worthy sovereigns.

176/5 今我不如趙閒(簡)鞅,而爾有(又)不及襄子無卹。膚(諺)曰:「揜(掩)雉【176】弗得,銀(更)順其風。」今而雖不能及趙襄子,曾不若膚(諺)?177/19

Now, I am inferior to Zhao Jian[zi] named Yang, and you are not as good as [Zhao] Xiangzi named Wuxu. [But] a proverb says: "If, when trying to catch pheasants, you fail, change [your approach] to suit their habits." Now, even though you are not as good as Zhao Xiangzi, can you really not accord with this proverb?

177/20 已學（教）大子用【177】茲念，斯乃受（授）之書，而自身屬（囑）之曰：女（汝）勉毋忘歲閏月更旦之馴（訓）。【178】

Having instructed the crown prince with these reminders, [Lord Zhaowen] gave him the text [of his speech] and personally cautioned him, saying: "Strive not to forget the instructions from the first day of the intercalary month of the year."

Comments

As can be seen, the love of learning which supposedly distinguished Wuxu from Lu, the Elder, manifested itself in his ability to memorize three short lines: "Moderate desires and heed remonstrations," "Respect the worthy and do not treat them contemptuously" and, finally, "Employ the capable and do not look down on them." As Wuxu received instructions directly from his father, it is understandable why his eagerness to learn was discussed here as filial piety. However, it is not clear how his ability to memorize three simple lines was indicative of his brotherly piety, compassion, and humanness.[3] By the same token, Lu the Elder's incapacity, his indulgence in desire and other negative traits do not simply follow from his loss of his father's writing. Neither does his negligence of fatherly admonitions account for him being in his "twilight years." The connection between the moral characteristics of the protagonists and their actions is thus not depicted very convincingly, as everywhere in the manuscript. Moreover, the text is silent on the concrete political measures Zhao Xiangzi undertook when seizing power. The worthiness of father and son Zhao as described here is a concept with strong moral connotations and devoid of any administrative meaning, something prevalent when it was first introduced into philosophical discourse.[4]

Lord Zhaowen expresses hope that Prince Gong, although lacking Zhao Xiangzi's talent, will to the best of his abilities emulate him. Thus, the Zhou could be hoped to follow the same trajectory of development as the state of Zhao previously did. As it was the case in chapter 10, this claim is astonishing for a descendant of the illustrious founders of the Zhou dynasty. By openly admitting his inferiority to Zhao Jianzi, Lord Zhaowen does away with all conventional Zhou claims to power and legitimacy. In his understanding, Zhou is no longer a proud and powerful holder of the Heavenly Mandate but an insignificant and weak domain struggling for survival.

---

[3] As such, Wuxu is portrayed as effectively embodying the same virtues that helped Lord Wen of Jin secure the allegiance of the people of Jin in chapter six. *Beida Mss.* 140, slips 171–175. However, the latter's relationship to his father is not discussed there. Chapter 8 portrays Lord Wen of Jin as possessing an inquisitive mind without referring to the notion "learning."

[4] Initially, the concept of worthiness mainly connoted expertise in administrative tasks (Loy 2013, 208).

Intercalary Month / 177

The historical precedent, especially parts involving direct speech, demonstrates a familiar sophisticated structure that employs large scale juxtapositions of antithetical content and frequent use of rhyme. The juxtaposition is predicated upon the storyline, which portrays Zhao Jianzi's interactions with his two sons as well as their different abilities. The most characteristic passages are:

Zhao Jiangzi's Instruction (167/15–169/3)

1	其書之言：	元	His text read:
2	節欲而聽諫，	元	"Moderate desires and heed remonstrations,
3	敬賢勿慢，	元	respect the worthy and do not treat them contemptuously.
4	使能勿賤。	元	Employ the capable and do not look down on them.
5	為人君者能行之三者，		If a ruler is able to carry out these three points,
6	其國必彌大，		his state will certainly become ever greater,
7	其民弗去散。	元	and his people will not leave him and disperse."

Zhao Jianzi's Appraisal of his Sons' Performance (171/14–174/11)

8	魯也，	魚	Lu,
9	不知好學之有賴也，	月祭	you do not realize that to love learning is advantageous.
10	不知縱欲之日敗也，	月祭	You do not realize that indulging in desires brings a speedy decline.
11	不知自以為少而年已暮也。	鐸	You do not realize that, although you see yourself as young, you are already in your twilight years.
12	不識之三者，		How can someone who does not understand these three points
13	其安能守祭？」	月祭	protect our ancestral altars?
14	無卹好學而知貴善言，	元	Wuxu, you are fond of learning and realize that good words are to be valued.
15	孝悌慈仁而主令弗慢。	元	You are filial, brotherly, compassionate, humane, and not neglectful of your ruler's orders.
16	令之守祭，		If I entrust you with the protection of our ancestral altars,

| 17 | 其使能使民毋去已遷。 | 元 | you will be able to prevent people from leaving and moving away. |

Zhao Jianzi's inscription and his praise of Wuxu are both based on the rhyme *yuan* 元, underscoring the latter's compliance with his father's precepts. While the criticism of Lu, the Elder, mainly involves rhyme group *yueji* 月祭, the name itself builds a separate textual unit through the final particle *ye* 也. Thus, it is made to rhyme, rather ominously, with the word "twilight" (*mu* 暮) from line 11 (the irregular rhyme *yu* 魚 / *duo* 鐸 was very common in the writings of the period). Again, this shows that rhyme is constitutive to the meaning of the text.

The proverb that Lord Zhaowen uses for the final admonition of his designated successor has a verbatim counterpart in the *Huainanzi*.[5] However, there, it is attributed to a Document of Zhou. The attribution appears incomprehensible given the nature-based imagery of these lines. As I argued in the first part of the book, one possible way to explain it is to assume that, at this point, the *Huainanzi* borrowed from the *Zhouxun* and ascribed the alleged genre of the quoted source to the adverbial phrase itself.

Context

Some of Zhao Jianzi's instructions are reminiscent of his portrayal in other sources. The short Tsinghua manuscript *Zhao Jianzi* 趙簡子 depicts the eponymous protagonist as inquiring and receiving instructions from more senior Jin officials and learning from them that political success or failure are decided by the ruler's frugality (*jian* 儉) or wastefulness (*chi* 侈).[6] The *Shiji* portrays him as a man who expected directness and honesty from his subordinates (*Shiji* 43.1792; Vyatkin 1992, 53–54). When it comes to the events surrounding the establishment of Wuxu, the account of the *Zhouxun* has a close parallel in a lost fragment from the *Han Shi waizhuan* as quoted in the *Taiping yulan*.[7] However, the *Shiji* maintains that Wuxu, who as a son by a low-born woman originally did not belong to his father's entourage, replaced the original heir apparent, Lu, not because of his "love of learning" and Lu's own shortcomings, but rather due to his great abilities in planning military affairs (*Shiji* 43.1789; Vyatkin 1992, 52).[8] Moreover,

---

[5] *Huainanzi* "Lanming xun" (He N.1998, 498; Major 2010, 230)

[6] The manuscript comprises eleven bamboo slips and two parts. For transcription, see Li X. 2017, 107–111. On the discussion of frugality and wastefulness in the *Zhao Jianzi*, see Zhao and Shi 2017, 86–88. For a thematic analysis, see Cook 2019.

[7] But also the *Wenxuan* 文選 and *Zizhi tongjian* 資治通鑑 record similar anecdotes (*Beida Mss*.141).

[8] On the other hand, *Huainanzi* "Daoying xun" stresses Xiangzi's ability to endure humiliation (He N. 1998, 12.833).

Zhao Jianzi is said to have realized Wuxu's potential only after a physiognomist, Gubu Ziqing 姑布子卿, brought it to his attention.[9] The *Zhouxun*'s preoccupation with the issues of morality as legitimizing political power yet again comes clearly to light.

Intriguingly, although Zhao Xiangzi had several sons, he returned power to the lineage of his brother Lu, whose son, Zhou 周, he previously enfeoffed with the new conquered territory Dai 代 (*Shiji* 43.1794–1796; Vyatkin 1992, 55–56). To this end, he established his great-nephew, Huan 浣, the future Marquis Xian of Zhao 獻侯, as his crown prince. We see here the same undogmatic attitude towards the installment of a successor that is demonstrated in many stories throughout the manuscript.

---

[9] For an analysis of this story from the standpoint of "a mantic session," see Raphals 2013, 256–257.

14

The Day after the La-Festival

The remaining material was divided by the editors into two different textual units. First, there are the so-called "small chapters" (*xiaozhang* 小章), which include twenty-six slips (179–204) and consist of various short passages that cannot be associated with any particular date or either one of the two "framing" formulas of the *Zhouxun* (*Beida Mss.* 141–144). As such, this material has no direct link to Lord Zhaowen, even though it shares his concerns for the edification of the potential throne contenders.

A number of famous rulers from the early periods of Chinese history are presented here as instructing their sons. All of them have already been discussed in the previous chapters of the *Zhouxun*. These are the legendary emperors Shun and Yu, Kings Tang (of Shang), Wen and Wu (of Zhou), as well as the famous hegemons from the Chunqiu period, Lord Huan of Qi (r. 685–643 BCE), Lord Mu of Qin (r. 659–621 BCE) and King Goujian of Yue (r. 496–465 BCE). Moreover, some fragments lack attribution to any person (179; 201–204).

Secondly, there is a unit comprising seven bamboo slips (205–211) which, unlike the rest of the *Zhouxun*, features deviating formulaic expressions at the beginning and the end (*Beida Mss.* 144). Accordingly, the dates of Lord Zhaowen's instructions were the "day of the year end's food offering ceremony," opening the chapter (205/2–7), and "the day after the La-sacrifice" (211/6–9) of the "new year" closing it (211/10–11).

The editorial team conjectures that these two designations referred to the same day, although different views have also been proposed.[1] I agree with the editors for the following reasons. In pre-imperial China, the La-sacrifice was, despite some regional differences, closely associated with the end of the year (Bodde 1975, 52). It was a religious ritual that consisted of providing "sustenance for divinities and the spirits of the departed during the cold and darkness of winter" (*ibid.*, 55). However, a look at the *Shiji*, "Tianguan shu" 天官書, reveals that,

---

[1] This is the view expressed by the majority of Chinese scholars who investigated this question. See Yan Buke, who maintains that the La-sacrifice took place on the last day of the year (2011b, 33) and Han 2015, 251. Cheng Shaoxuan, on the other hand, holds that *xiang he zhi ri* can be regarded as the New Year's Eve, while *la zhi ming ri* stands for the first day of the new year (2013, 564). In this case, we are dealing with two chapters.

in some calendric systems, the day after this sacrifice signaled both the end of the old year and the beginning of the new year:

臘明日，人眾卒歲，一會飲食，發陽氣，故曰初歲。(*Shiji* 27.1340)
[For some the year begins with] the day after La-sacrifice, the populace ends the year by gathering as one to eat and drink, exciting the *yang materia vitalis*, hence this is said to initiate the year. (Pankenier 2013, 501)

Therefore, it appears very likely that, in this chapter, the *Zhouxun* referred to the same day using different designations. This was, in my opinion, because of the authors' intention to create a sense of transition from the old to the new year. In this way, Lord Zhaowen's instructions were shown to retain their significance and validity even after the beginning of the new cycle of twelve (or thirteen) months.

Considering the character count notation: "grand total: six thousand," which appears at the end of slip 211 (211/14–17), it stands to reason that the chapter comprising slips 205–211 concluded the entire manuscript. Furthermore, that these seven bamboo slips (205–211) originally belonged to the same chapter implies that it must have engaged with several discussion topics. For it starts with the story about the unsuccessful attempts of the legendary Yao to reform his inept son Dan Zhu (206/1–207/25) and ends with a reference to the coup in the state of Qi, when the initial ruling family was replaced through the ministerial lineage of Tian 田 in 485 BCE (209/11–210/3) (Lewis 1999a, 598). It is evident that this chapter must have included even more historical precedents since Lord Zhaowen is said to have invoked the examples of the six kings and five hegemons (210/9–12) in his instructions from "the day after the La-sacrifice."

When considering that most rulers mentioned in the "small chapters" appeared in many versions of the list of the six kings and five hegemons as devised in the pre-Qin time[2], the question arises whether the "small chapters" (179–204) and slips 205–211 originally constituted the same textual unit. Following Chen Jian (2015) and in disagreement with the editors[3], I give an affirmative answer to this question. In fact, the affinity of the relevant fragments follows from several characteristics they have in common. Firstly, and most apparently, they all share the general setting of a royal instruction directed at a designated successor. They are also rather brief, which distinguishes them from comparable material in other chapters. Moreover, use of parallelism and rhyme is more prominent here than in other chapters and they also differ from the rest of the manuscript through

---

[2] For the six kings in the *Lüshi chunqiu*, see Chen Q. 2001, 606n9. For the different lists of the five hegemons, see Khayutina 2006, 22. See also, Durrant, Li and Schaberg 2016, 722n68.
[3] Han 2015, 254, maintains that even though these units are related to each other they belong to the different layers of the *Zhouxun*.

their pronounced "religious" emphasis on the decisive role of higher powers, such as Heaven, spirits, and ghosts, in political affairs.

In Chen Jian's arrangement, the long concluding chapter (14) started with the legendary emperors Yao and Shun, proceeded from there to the dynastic founders Yu, Tang, Wen and Wu and, finally, provided accounts of the five hegemons, closing with a discussion of Lord Huan of Qi. While the other two hegemons appearing in the "small chapters" are Lord Mu of Qin and King Goujian of Yue, the identity of the two missing members of that list can only be guessed. Among other candidates, Lord Wen of Jin and King Zhao of Chu seem most likely given the textual parallels between their accounts in chapters 5 and 6 and the tropes that we find in this concluding chapter.

Among these five illustrious sovereigns, King Goujian was the latest member, considering the time when he lived. Why then does the chapter end with Lord Huan of Qi who preceded Goujian by almost two hundred years, while otherwise attempting to discuss the rulers in chronological order? I conjecture that this arrangement reflects the general significance of the ministerial coup in Qi as a poignant warning to all rulers in the *oikumene* and, moreover and most importantly, the course of the discussion in the twelve chapters, where Lord Huan was included as the last sovereign epitomizing the importance of employing wise aides.

In general, a comparison between the events and activities ascribed to a certain individual in this chapter and elsewhere in the text in most cases suggests the temporal precedence of the present chapter. As I have argued previously, this has to do with the transitional character of this chapter, which constitutes both the end and the beginning of the *Zhouxun*. Therefore, when reading the accounts from this chapter, one should also consider the stories involving the same individuals presented in other chapters.

Following the above, I treat all the remaining fragments of the *Zhouxun* as originally constituting one single chapter. This long chapter consists of thirty-three slips (179–211), forming by far the longest text unit of the book. In my translation, I implement the following arrangement of bamboo slips: 205–207, 179, 180–198, 201–204, 199–200, 208–211. At the same time, it is possible that some stories recorded therein originally appeared in a different succession.

Translation

205/1 • 維歲冬（終）享駕（賀）之日，龏（共）大子朝，周昭文公自身貳之，用茲念也。曰：[205]

• It was on the day of the year end's food offering ceremony, when Crown Prince Gong came to court. Lord Zhaowen of Zhou personally enjoined him with these (following) reminders. He said:

昔堯之所愛子曰丹朱，不好茲（慈）孝，䌛（繇）樂以愉（渝）。堯欲其賢，而弗能【206】教海（誨）乃廢弗立，而吳（虞）舜受是置。於是為篇曰：「子而能茲（慈）仁，則以代【207】其身。為其無親，則不若以國予世之賢人。」[4]【179】

In the past, the son whom Yao loved was Dan Zhu, who was fond neither of compassion nor filial piety and embellished music with excessive emotions. Yao wanted him to become worthy, but was unable to instruct him. Therefore, he dismissed [Dan Zhu], not establishing him. Instead, Yu Shun received this position. Thereupon, [Yao] composed a script [addressing Shun] that said: "If you can be compassionate and humane, then I will use you to replace him. If he treats his father unlovingly, then it is better to give the state to a worthy of the age."

180/1 • 舜之所愛子曰商均，舜啟道（導）之，欲其能賢，學（教）之而不可，乃放遂〈逐〉【180】之，弗使王民。於是為篇曰：「父之愛子也，剴（豈）惡貴之？念予之國，恐【181】以祟之。夫亡國之人，剴（豈）將徒亡國而已？必失其身。」【182】

• The son whom Shun loved was Shang Jun. Shun instructed and guided him, wanting to enable him to become worthy. But it was impossible to instruct him, and so [Shun] expelled and banished him, not letting him be king over the people. Thereupon, [Shun] composed a script that said: "When loving a son, will a father begrudge ennobling him (i.e., making him king)? [But] considering to give him the state, [the father] is afraid to curse him with it. Now, one who destroys a state, does he really destroy just the state? He will certainly lose his life [as well]."

183/1 【•】禹謂啟曰：「丹朱，商均，行兼（義）弗好，寡德少禮，是以不得為堯舜嗣。」【183】

• Yu said to Qi: "Dan Zhu and Shang Jun were not fond of practicing righteousness, and they possessed little virtue and scarce propriety. Thus, they did not get to be successors to Yao and Shun."

184/1 • 湯謂太甲曰：「爾不畏天，其安得見日？爾不事神，將予女（汝）疾，身病【184】而膿（體）痛，剴（豈）能有卹？爾能畏天，則壽（壽）命永長。爾能事神，則無疾央（殃）。【185】禍裞（災）不至，國安而身利。為人主者，其胡可毋好善？【186】

• Tang said to Tai Jia: "If you do not stand in awe before Heaven, how will you get to see the sun? If you do not serve the spirits, they will inflict diseases upon you. With an ailing body and aching limbs, how could you be helped? If you are able to stand in awe before Heaven, your life will be long. If you can serve the

---

[4] The transcription contains no quotation marks at this juncture.

spirits, you will suffer neither diseases nor calamities. With neither misfortune nor disasters looming, your state will be at peace and your body will stand to gain. How could a ruler not be fond of goodness?"

187/1 • 昌謂發曰：「天下之民，爾能愛之，斯而畜也。海內之眾，爾弗能利，【187】斯而讎也。為人主者，茲（慈）惠溫良，其胡可毋好也？」【188】
• Chang said to Fa: "The people of All-under-Heaven! If you are able to care for them, they will yield to you. The masses within the [four] seas! If you are unable to benefit them, they will be your enemy. How can a ruler not be fond of compassion, kindness, warmth, and goodness?"

189/1 • 發謂庸（誦）曰：「天監臨下，日臨九野，爾殺不當，司命在戶，所處不遠，居以視女（汝）。」【189】
• Fa said to Song: "Heaven supervises its subordinates, as the sun oversees the Nine Fields[5]. If your executions [of the people] are inappropriate, [keep in mind that] the Arbiter of Fate is at [your] door[6]. His residence is not far, and he dwells [there] to watch over you."

190/1 • 昔秦穆公臨𨙻谷之水，而身貳其嗣焉，曰：「敬天畏鬼，毋殺無罪。【190】我濃行此，吾故能立柏（伯）於茲泉之上，而命之曰柏（伯）水。爾尚謹承【191】
• In the past, Lord Mu of Qin overlooked the *Shi* valley[7], and personally enjoined his heir there. He said: "Revere Heaven, stand in awe before the spirits, and do not kill the innocent. Because I emulated and carried out these [principles], I was able to establish myself as hegemon [here] at the side of this spring, naming it: 'The Waters of the Hegemon.' Pay attention to being vigilant to inherit…

······192/1 毋重之，必將務治。苟身能治，國家亦治。處上立（位）者，將盈（逞）其志。唯【192】毋身乳（亂），則國家亦乳（亂）。國與身乳（亂），唯（雖）為人主，其安得所願？」【193】
… [if] one attaches importance to it, he will certainly put effort in establishing order. If he can order his person, his state will be ordered as well. [This way] the person in the superior position will freely exercise his will. If one's person is

---

[5] The Nine Fields were nine regions of Heaven corresponding to the nine terrestrial territories. For their shape and arrangement, see Major 1993, 36. See also Pankenier 2013, 270–272.
[6] The Arbiter of Fate was one of the six stars of the "Palace for the Promotion of Civic Virtue" (*Wen chang gong* 文昌宮), see Pankenier 2013, 460. At the same time, it was regarded as a deity determining the length of people's lives. On this, see Waley 1973, 39–40.
[7] According to the editors, this is the Lantian 藍田 valley (*Beida Mss.* 143n2).

disordered, his state will be disordered as well. If state and person are [both] disordered, then, even if one is ruler, how can he attain what he wishes?"

194/1 • 昔越王苟（句）賤（踐）過闔廬之丘，見人發之，歸而貳其嗣曰：「它既可革，唯【194】親不可復得。已不可復得，而為人子者尚猶不能守其骨骸，其【195】若何哉？故發尅（克）殷而為銘於席端曰：『驀（畏）戒！驀（畏）戒！取諫不遠，視而所代！』【196】今越威（滅）干（邗），則剴（豈）獨不可以自為諫？女（汝）試往視闔廬之丘，見其為【197】壑也，而毋輕吾國。」【198】

• In the past, when King Goujian of Yue passed by Helü's burial mound, he saw some people opening it. Upon returning home, he enjoined his heir, saying: "Anything else can be altered, only parents cannot be brought back [after they perish]. But if, after they have left for good, their son is not even able to protect their remains, what could be worse than this? And so, after Fa conquered Yin, he made an inscription at the front edge of his sitting mat that said: 'Beware! Beware! What you [should] take as remonstration is not far, [just] take a look at those whom you have replaced!' Now, Yue has extinguished Han, but are you alone unable to take this as a lesson? Try to go and take a look at Helü's burial mound, see how it has been turned into a gorge, and do not treat my state lightly."

……201/1 主者，唯毋失臣，剴（豈）有（又）尚得復君民？故《詩》曰：『壞（懷）德唯寗（寧），宗子唯城。』【201】女（汝）已為城，而無有壞（懷）德，則城必有陚（隙）。唯毋有陚（隙），其壞也必矣。《書》【202】曰：『木折必節（節），蘠（墻）壞必陚（隙）。』國之安危，必在君世·嗣之述（遂）直（置），必在季【203】歲。女（汝）尚勉德以侍（待）天福，而毋自使廢。【204】

… the sovereign, if he loses his ministers, how will he again obtain the rule over the people? And so, an Ode says: "Cherishing virtue is our only peace; the principal heir is our only [defensive] wall." Now, you are already our wall, but if you do not cherish virtue, the wall surely will have cracks. If there are cracks in the wall, its collapse is certain. A Document says: "Trees are sure to break along the gnarls. Walls are sure to break along the cracks." A state's safety or peril, surely lies in the ruler's heir. The installation of an heir, must take place in the ruler's final year. Pay utmost effort to cultivate virtue, await the blessings of Heaven, and do not cause your own abandonment.

199/1 • 昔齊桓公貳其嗣曰：「膚（諺）有言曰：『生人日飽，死人日肞。』餘[8]剴（豈）能【199】為土，而尚令女（汝）道？夫君民者道，則為人命。

---

[8] I read yu 餘 as a variant for yu 余 "I."

唯毋不道，則人為之【200】輔。民何歸沃？⁹從有道處。暴乳（亂）者亡，鬼神不與。賢主兼國，不宵（肖）無【208】慧，失其疆（疆）士〈土〉，其誰有常所？今女（汝）有民而不能聖，則齊侯之生（姓），剴（豈）【209】必為呂？210/3

• In the past, Lord Huan of Qi enjoined his heir, saying: "A proverb says: 'The living, day by day, gratify appetite; The dead, day by day, putrefy.' Can I, after having turned to soil, still make you [possess] the Way? Now, if a ruler [possesses] the Way, he will command the people. If he does not [possess] the Way, then the people will be his... assistants. Where are the people naturally drawn to as their home? They draw toward the place where the Way is in force. The violent and disorderly will perish, the ghosts and spirits will not support [them]. The worthy ruler conquers other states, [whereas] the unworthy one lacks wisdom and loses his territory. Which one of them will then have a constant place to dwell? Now, you have the people but [if you] are incapable of sagacity, then must the surname of the Marquis' of Qi be Lü?"

210/4 已學（教）大子以六王五柏（伯）之念，斯乃受（授）之書，而自身屬（囑）之【210】曰：女（汝）勉毋忘臘之明日親（新）歲之馴（訓）。大凡六千」【211】

Having instructed the crown prince with the reminders of the six kings and five hegemons, [Lord Zhaowen] gave him the text [of his speech] and personally cautioned him, saying: "Strive not to forget the new year's instructions from the day after the La-sacrifice." Grand total: six thousand [characters].

Comments

There is a clear distinction in the representation of the offspring of the six kings and five hegemons. In the former cases, all sons are identified by their names, whereas the latter always reference unnamed heirs apparent. Moreover, their respective mode of instruction appears to be different. While kings are depicted as resorting to writing or communicating their ideas to their successors by means of "saying," the hegemons engage in stricter sounding "enjoining." However, a specific mode of teaching is ascribed only once to a particular person. For instance, a hegemon who "enjoins" his heir in chapter 14, is depicted as engaging in a different mode of instruction in another chapter. The same goes for the kings.

Furthermore, the discussion of the six kings and five hegemons unfolds according to different formal criteria. In the former group, the introductory formula "in the past" appears only in the first account, while other stories are

---

⁹ The question mark replaced a comma that appears at this juncture in the transcription.

marked with a dot (•). Possibly, this constitutes an attempt to present the six kings as a distinct group. At the same time, when telling the stories of the five hegemons, the text returns to the usual way of invoking the days of yore.

1. Yao and Dan Zhu (and Shun) (206, 207 and 179)

In the interpretation of the editors, the first story of the chapter included only two slips, 206 and 207. However, I believe that Chen Jian (2015) is correct in viewing slip 179 as containing the conclusion of the story recorded on slips 206 and 207. I accept Chen's view for several reasons. First, the verso lines on slips 206, 207 and 179 build a continuous line, implying that, originally, they were placed one after another in that given order (*Beida Mss.* 116 and 117). Moreover, slip 179 contains only sixteen characters and was evidently positioned at the end of a story (*Beida Mss.* 27). Secondly, its content connects smoothly to the storyline as developed in 206 and 207. Finally, the fragment displays the same formal characteristics such as tetrasyllabic lines and characters belonging to the group *zhen* 真.

The rhyming pattern in the passage looks as follows:

1	昔堯之所愛子曰丹朱，		In the past, the son whom Yao loved was Dan Zhu,
2	不好慈孝，		who was fond neither of compassion nor filial piety
3	繁樂以淪。	文	and embellished music with excessive emotions.
4	堯欲其賢，	真	Yao wanted him to become worthy,
5	而弗能教誨，	之	but was unable to instruct him.
6	乃廢弗立，		Therefore, he dismissed [Dan Zhu], not establishing him.
7	而虞舜受是置。	職	Instead, Yu Shun received this position.
8	於是為篇曰：	元	Thereupon, [Yao] composed a script that said:
9	子而能慈仁，	真	"If you can be compassionate and humane,
10	則以代其身。	真	then I will use you to replace him.
11	為其無親，	真	If he treats his father unlovingly,
12	則不若以國予世之賢人。	真	then it is better to give the state to a worthy of the age."

Dan Zhu, otherwise known as an inept and debauched man, is depicted here as the favorite son of his legendary father, Yao. The question of how such a great paragon of virtue as Yao could have ever favored an utterly depraved individual remains unanswered. However, it seems to be a corollary of the juxtaposition of favorite and worthy, which forms the main dilemma for Yao. Even though Yao is portrayed as the loving father of Dan Zhu, he did not hesitate to replace him with a worthy successor, Shun, after recognizing the futility of his own instructional efforts. Yao's text explains the reasons for his actions and is directed at Shun.

In the account about Yao and Shun from chapter 11, Dan Zhu is no longer mentioned. However, that account can be fully understood only against the background of the present passage. This, once again, shows that chapter 14 was not composed after the rest of the text was already completed and was circulating in China.

2. Shun and Shang Jun (and Yu) (180–182)

In accordance with the chronological order of events, the story featuring Yao's successor, Shun, and his son, Shang Jun, must have occupied the second position in this chapter. Like the previous passage, it includes three slips (180–182). Its careful organization is evident in the frequent use of tetrasyllabic lines and rhyme (*zhen* 真 and *wu* 物).

1	舜之所愛子曰商均，	真	The son whom Shun loved was Shang Jun.
2	舜啟導之，		Shun instructed and guided him,
3	欲其能賢，	真	wanting to enable him to become worthy.
4	教之而不可，		But it was impossible to instruct him,
5	乃放逐|之，		and so [Shun] expelled and banished him,
6	弗使王民。	真	not letting him be king over the people.
7	於是為篇曰：		Thereupon, [Shun] composed a script that said:
8	「父之愛子也，	物	"When loving a son,
9	豈惡貴之？	物	will a father begrudge ennobling him?
10	念予之國，		[But] considering to give him the state,
11	恐|以巢之。	物	[the father] is afraid to curse him with it.
12	夫亡國之人，	真	Now, one who destroys a state,
13	豈將徒亡國而已？		does he really destroy just the state?
14	必失其身。」	真	He will certainly lose his life [as well]."

Shun's (otherwise unattested) love for the inept Shang Jun constitutes a clear parallel to the first story. The writing that Shun, like Yao, composed on the occasion of his son's banishment offers a rationale for his decision and is, most likely, addressed to Yu, who remains unmentioned here. For this is the only time in the *Zhouxun* when Shun appears as educator. Were the text addressing Shang Jun, then Yu would not have received a crucial learning opportunity. Shun's writing conveys his worry that by enthroning a beloved inept son the monarch places him in mortal danger. In this way, by banishing Shang Jun, Shun is shown as having saved his son's life, thus, only proving his fatherly love.

3. Yu and Qi (183)

The next ruler-heir pair to be discussed was Shun's successor Yu and his son Qi. As explained previously, most historical sources do not depict Qi as Yu's original successor. The throne was yielded to him only three years after Yu's passing. Therefore, the conversation of the kind recorded here must have appeared rather unlikely even to the early readers of the *Zhouxun*. The passage comprises only one bamboo slip (183) and, just like previous examples, it employs rhyming tetrasyllabic lines (irregular rhyme involving rhyme groups *zhi* 脂, *you* 幽, *zhi* 職, and *zhi* 之).

1	禹謂啟曰：	脂	Yu said to Qi:
2	丹朱，商均，		"Dan Zhu and Shang Jun
3	行義弗好，	幽	were not fond of practicing righteousness,
4	寡德少禮，	脂	and they possessed little virtue and scarce propriety.
5	是以不得	職	Thus, they did not get
6	為堯舜嗣。	之	to be successors to Yao and Shun."

Here, Yu shares with Qi his insight that the reason for Dan Zhu and Shang Jun's dismissal was their failure to shape their characters along the lines of righteousness, virtue, propriety. By referring to the failures of previous rulers' progeny, the text shows some resemblance to the *Shangshu* and *Shiji*, in which Shun uses Dan Zhu's immorality as a pedagogical instrument, to warn his successor, Yu, not to engage in similar behavior.[10] However, unlike in the *Shangshu*, this instruction is directed at the ruler's son, underscoring the preeminence of hereditary transmission in the *Zhouxun*.

This reminder constitutes an indirect threat to Qi of his own impending dismissal should he fail to cultivate fondness for virtue and propriety. Unfortunately, the counterpart in chapter 2 is incomplete so the degree and nature of

---

[10] For the *Shangshu*, see "Gao Yao mo" 皋陶謨 (Gu and Liu 2005, 463; Karlgren 1950b, 11); for the *Shiji*, see 2.80, Nienhauser 1994a, 34–35.

their correspondence cannot be determined. However, the other instruction is framed as an admonition.

4. (Cheng) Tang and Tai Jia (184–186)

The next instruction is dedicated to the ruler-heir pair Tang and Tai Jia from the beginning of the Shang dynasty. As discussed previously, the historicity of this instruction is highly problematic as most sources depict Tai Jia as Tang's grandson, who did not ascend the Shang throne immediately after Tang's passing. Comprising three slips (184–186), the most salient rhetorical feature of the passage consists of the use of argument in two juxtaposed strands (2–7 and 8–13), each of which has a different rhyme pattern (combinations of *zhen* 真 / *zhi* 質 and *zhen* 真 / *yang* 陽).

Introduction:

1	湯謂太甲曰：		Tang said to Tai Jia:

Negative Ramifications:

2	爾不畏天，	真	"If you do not stand in awe before Heaven,
3	其安得見日？	質	how will you get to see the sun?
4	爾不事神，	真	If you do not serve the spirits,
5	將予汝疾，	質	they will inflict diseases upon you.
6	身病﹨而體痛，	東	With ailing body and aching limbs,
7	豈能有卹？	質	how could you be helped?

Positive Ramifications:

8	爾能畏天，	真	If you are able to stand in awe before Heaven,
9	則壽命永長。	陽	your life will be long.
10	爾能事神，	真	If you can serve the spirits,
11	則無疾殃。﹨	陽	you will suffer neither diseases nor calamities.
12	禍災不至，	質	With neither misfortune nor disasters looming,
13	國安而身利。	脂	your state will be at peace and your body will stand to gain.

Rhetorical Question:

14	為人主者，		How could a ruler

15 其胡可毋好 善 ?   元   not be fond of goodness?"

By demonstrating the devastating results of not serving the spirits or standing in awe before Heaven, Tang makes clear that there is no alternative to following his propositions. The argument starts out with the negative strand, underscoring the admonishing character of the passage. Even though goodness does not receive a definition here, by appearing in the concluding rhetorical question, it becomes connected to the practice of serving the spirits and revering Heaven.

The emphasis on Heaven and goodness links this passage to chapter 2, where the same protagonists appear as well. However, the religious implications are much stronger here, as Heaven is treated, alongside the spirits, as something to revere and stand in awe of. The positive outcomes of such behavior include health and longevity.

In chapter 2, Tang is mentioned under his cognomen, the "Militant," which, according to the *Shiji*, he had received in his confrontation with the tyrant Jie. I take this to suggest the anteriority of the events described here.

5. Chang and Fa (187 and 188)

In this section, we move to the two foundational figures of the Zhou dynasty, King Wen and King Wu of Zhou. Called here by his personal name Chang 昌, King Wen advises the future King Wu, likewise referred to by his personal name Fa, about the necessity of caring for and benefitting the people and the masses.

The short passage comprises two slips (187 and 188) and has a similar structure to the account about Tang and Tai Jia. It presents two opposing scenarios (lines 2–4 and 5–7) and concludes with a rhetorical question (8–10). But unlike in the former, the positive strand is mentioned first here. Moreover, all three textual units rhyme with each other. The rhyme falls on the penultimate character of the respective lines. In order to achieve formal coherence, the last part of the rhetorical question was modified to include the final particle *ye* 也.

Introduction:

1 昌謂發曰：   Chang said to Fa:

Positive Ramifications:

2 天下之民，   "The people of All-under-Heaven!
3 爾能愛之，   If you are able to care for them,
4 斯而 畜 也。   覺   they will yield to you.

Negative Ramifications:

5 海內之眾，   The masses within the [four] seas!

6	爾弗能利,			If you are unable to benefit them,
7	斯而讎也。	幽	they will be your enemy.

Rhetorical Question:

8	為人主者,		How can a ruler
9	慈惠溫良,		not be fond
10	其胡可毋好也?	幽	of compassion, kindness, warmth, and goodness?"

The rhetorical question highlights the importance of being fond of compassion, kindness, warmth, and goodness. The structure of the passage highlights these four virtues' association with the central concern of love and benefit for the people.

The Zhou's conquest of Shang and the references to Heaven and its mandate are absent here altogether. The affinity to chapter 3, which presents a more detailed account of King Wen and King Wu, is evident. These are the only two passages in the *Zhouxun* to operate with the notions "All-under-Heaven" and the (people) "within the (four) seas." Moreover, in chapter 3 King Wu is said to have pacified "All-under-Heaven" only after his father's death. Therefore, the account from chapter 14 does not only precede the corresponding story temporally, but it also functions as explanation for King Wu's successes after his enthronement.

6. Fa and Song (189)

In the next instruction, King Wu, still called Fa, makes his son and the future King Cheng (who goes here by his personal name, Song 誦) aware that Heaven constantly supervises people's actions. Therefore, one should not carry out unjust executions.

Also here, individual sentences are connected by means of the same meter and rhyme (group *yu* 魚).

1	發謂誦曰:		Fa said to Song:
2	天監臨下,	魚	"Heaven supervises its subordinates,
3	日臨九野,	魚	as the sun oversees the 'nine fields'.
4	爾殺不當,		If your executions are inappropriate,
5	司命在戶,	魚	the 'arbiter of fate' is at [your] door.
6	所處不遠,		His residence is not far,
7	居以視汝。	魚	and he dwells [there] to watch over you."

Unlike in previous cases, the connection of this theme to chapter 12, where King Cheng appears as a wise ruler dismissing slanderers' accusations of the Duke of Zhou, is less obvious. In contrast to chapter 12, this short instruction introduces the astronomical and religious connotations of Heaven. But it is possible that in the author's understanding King Cheng's actions toward the Duke of Zhou were motivated by his reverence for the "arbiter of fate."

The above instructions were delivered by the "six kings." Despite their problematic historicity, the composition style of these passages shows a certain level of sophistication and organization, achieved through the use of the same meter, rhyme, and parallelism.

7. Lord Mu of Qin and the Heir Apparent (190 and 191)

All extant accounts of the five hegemons open with the familiar reference to the past. The first passage deals with Lord Mu of Qin (r. 659–621 BCE). However, the passage is incomplete, and the editors identified two fragments as belonging to it (*Beida Mss.* 143). The first fragment includes two slips (190 and 191). Here, Lord Mu explains to his unnamed heir the reasons for establishing himself as a hegemon. These are, quite characteristically for this religiously charged chapter, the "reverence of Heaven, awe for spirits" as well as his refusal to "kill the innocent."

As for the rhetorical characteristics of this fragment, we find here a familiar pattern of employing rhymed tetrasyllabic lines.

1	昔秦穆公臨阤谷之水，	微	In the past, Lord Mu of Qin overlooked the *Shi* valley,
2	而身貳其嗣焉，曰：		and personally enjoined his heir there. He said:
3	「敬天畏鬼，	微	"Revere Heaven, stand in awe before the spirits,
4	毋殺無罪。|		and do not kill the innocent.
5	我濞行此，		Because I emulated and carried out these [principles],
6	吾故能立伯於茲泉之上，		I was able to establish myself as hegemon [here] at the side of this spring,
7	而命之曰伯水。	微	naming it: 'The Waters of the Hegemon.'
8	爾尚謹承 ……		Pay attention to being vigilant to inherit…

The connection of this passage to chapter 7, dealing with Lord Mu's kindness towards commoners and his resulting victory over the Jin army, is not very apparent. But one might conjecture that Lord Mu's refusal to punish the commoners who killed and ate his steed expressed the same unwillingness to harm the "innocent."

Interestingly, among all other sovereigns mentioned in the *Zhouxun*, refusal to kill the innocent was attributed only to another Qin ruler, Lord Xian of Qin, namely, in discussing human sacrifice (ch. 11). Lord Mu was notorious when it came to the funeral practice of human sacrifice, as discussed above. So, possibly, this account represents an attempt to disassociate him from this inhuman sacrifice. Consequently, the two Qin rulers discussed in the *Zhouxun* are both characterized by their appreciation of human life.

As for the second fragment (192 and 193), it deviates from Lord Mu's instruction both in terms of the main topic and of rhetorical characteristics. I maintain that it represents a remainder of the passage dealing with Lord Wen of Jin.

8. Lord Wen of Jin and the Heir Apparent? (192 and 193)

This passage differs from the previous one both thematically and formally. Its thematic focus is the importance of good health for effective governance and the correspondence between the principles that regulate the body and the state. As for its formal characteristics, we find here argument in parallel strands which, in addition to depicting the positive (lines 3–6) and negative (7–11) scenarios, are distinguished from each other by means of rhyme (*zhi* versus *yuan*).

1	…毋重之，			[if] one attaches importance to it,
2	必將務治。		之	he will certainly put effort in establishing order.
	Positive Strand:			
3	苟身能治，			If he can order his person,
4	國家亦治。		之	his state will be ordered as well.
5	處上位者，			[This way] the person in the superior position,
6	將逞其志。		之	will freely exercise his will.
	Negative Strand:			
7	唯|毋身亂，			If one's person is disordered,
8	則國家亦亂。		元	his state will be disordered as well.
9	國與身亂，			If state and person are [both] disordered,
10	雖為人主			then, even if one is ruler,
11	其安得所願？		元	how can he attain what he wishes?

The reason why I assume that, originally, it may have featured Lord Wen of Jin is the expression to "freely exercise his will" which, in chapter 6, describes the positive effects of moral excellence presumably obtained by Lord Wen of Jin.

9. King Goujian of Yue and the Heir Apparent (194–198)

The story about King Goujian of Yue instructing his (unnamed) successor includes five bamboo slips amounting to the longest account in chapter 14. This story employs a large number of rhymes (groups *zhi* 之, *zhi* 職 and *yuan* 元), thus resembling chapter 5. The correspondence to that chapter also includes the way in which geographic names are skillfully weaved into the rhyme patterns (lines 13 and 14).

1	昔越王句踐過闔廬之丘，	之	In the past, when King Goujian of Yue passed by Helü's burial mound,
2	見人發之，		he saw some people opening it.
3	歸而貳其嗣曰：	之	Upon returning home, he enjoined his heir, saying:
4	「它既可革，	職	"Anything else can be altered,
5	唯｜親不可復得。	職	only parents cannot be brought back.
6	已不可復得，		But if, after they have left for good,
7	而為人子者	之	their son
	尚猶不能守其骨骸，	之	is not even able to protect their remains,
8	其｜若何哉？		what could be worse than this?
9	故發克殷而為銘於席端曰：	元	And so, after Fa conquered Yin, he made an inscription at the front edge of his sitting mat that said:
10	『畏戒！畏戒！	之	'Beware! Beware!
11	取諫不遠，	元	What you [should] take as remonstration is not far,
12	視而所代！』｜	職	[just] take a look at those whom you have replaced!'
13	今越滅邢，	元	Now, Yue has extinguished Han,
14	則豈獨不可以自為諫？	元	but are you alone unable to take this as a lesson?
15	汝試往視闔廬之丘，	之	Try to go and take a look at Helü's burial mound,
16	見其為｜壑也，		see how it has been turned into a gorge,
17	而毋輕吾國。」	職	and do not treat my state lightly."

As in chapter 5, King Goujian admonishes his heir by using the image of King Helü's ravished tomb. However, while in the former, Goujian communicates the contents of a folk song, here, he is said to witness the terrifying scene personally. In both cases, his personal responsibility for the ignominious treatment of the diseased adversary does not seem to be suggested. By this token, the grisly event appears as the unavoidable consequence of King Helü's own mistakes. Significantly, this admonition is not delivered by King Goujian from his deathbed as it was the case in chapter 5. Therefore, it must have taken place earlier in this ruler's life than the latter event. In both stories, King Goujian expresses concern that his successor will treat the state lightly.

King Goujian's reference to King Wu of Zhou having inscribed a warning at the edge of his sitting mat has a parallel in the "Wuwang jianzuo" 武王踐阼 chapter of the *Da Dai Liji* and a corresponding Shanghai Museum manuscript, which was given the same title (*Beida Mss.* 143n4).[11] But, while in the two latter sources, King Wu produces a series of warning inscriptions, the *Zhouxun* mentions only the one voicing the necessity to learn from the mistakes of one's defeated enemies. At the same time, the exact nature of the transgressions that drove the Shang to ruin is not specified.

Just like chapter 5, this account contains several important elements from Lord Zhaowen's instructions: references to the past, drawing a lesson from historical events, and admonishing the heir in light of these lessons.

10. King Zhao of Chu and the Heir Apparent? (201–204)

Because I assume that slips 199 and 200 belonged to the last story of this chapter, the next fragment to be discussed will be the one formed by slips 201–204. While the line segments on their backs do not form a continuous line,[12] these fragments operate with similar images and can be arranged in a coherent way. They place great emphasis on the importance of the heir apparent by likening him to the defensive walls of a city (*cheng* 城). The great significance of subordinates' support and the exact time of the heir's installation are broached here too. Their formal characteristics also show a high degree of conformity, suggesting that these fragments did, indeed, belong to the same passage. After all, the present passage is built almost exclusively by using rhymed tetra- and pentasyllabic lines.

1	……主者，		… the sovereign,
2	唯毋失臣，	真	if he loses his ministers,

---

[11] For a comparison between these two versions as well as the rhyme patterns, see Zhou 2018, 4–29.
[12] This is true, at least, for the first two slips, 200 and 201. For the reproduction, see *Beida Mss.* 117. For a possible explanation, see *ibid.*, 144n3.

3	豈又尚得復君民？	真	how will he again obtain the rule over the people?
4	故《詩》曰：		And so, an Ode says:
5	『懷德唯寧，	耕	"Cherishing virtue is our only peace;
6	宗子唯城。』	耕	the principal heir is our only [defensive] wall."
7	汝已為城，		Now, you are already our wall,
8	而無有懷德，		but if you do not cherish virtue,
9	則城必有隙。	鐸	the wall surely will have cracks.
10	唯毋有隙，		If there are cracks in the wall,
11	其壞也必矣。	質	its collapse is certain.
12	《書》曰：		A Document says:
13	『木折必節，	質	"Trees are sure to break along the gnarls.
14	墻壞必隙。』	鐸	Walls are sure to break along the cracks."
15	國之安危，		A state's safety or peril,
16	必在君世。	月祭	surely lies in the ruler's heir.
17	嗣之遂置，	職	The installation of an heir,
18	必在季歲。	月祭	must take place in the ruler's final year.
19	汝尚勉德	職	Pay utmost effort to cultivate virtue,
20	以待天福，	職	await the blessings of Heaven,
21	而毋自使廢。	月祭	and do not cause your own abandonment.

The tropes of subordinates' support and regaining power explored here feature prominently in the account about Kind Zhao of Chu in chapter 4, which, uniquely for the manuscript under investigation, uses the quotations of the same *shi*-stanza (Mao 254). Therefore, it seems very likely that this passage originally contained King Zhao's instruction to his unnamed heir.

This instruction is unusual in the context of the current chapter in quoting from the *shi* and *shu* as well as in establishing a connection between these quotations. The bridging passage comprising lines 7–11 contains common terminology, here: "walls" and "cracks." We have already encountered an example of a similarly constructed argument in chapter 9 (only with a different order of *shi* and *shu*-citations). There, it reflects Lord Zhaowen's expertise; here, it demonstrates King Zhao's familiarity with "authoritative" sources. But just like everywhere else in the *Zhouxun*, the association of the supposed *shu*-lines with documentary lore is problematic. While resembling sayings in various early texts (Han 2015, 282), it is only in the *Shangjun shu* 商君書 that they are subsumed under a specific literary genre, namely, the proverb.[13] Such categorization appears stylistically more appropriate, considering the characteristic juxtaposition of imagery coming from the natural world and human craft. What their ascription to *shu* accomplishes is render these images a matter greatly relevant to the political affairs of the state.

11. Lord Huan of Qi and the Heir Apparent (199, 200, 208, 209 and 210)

Lord Huan of Qi, who already made a brief appearance in chapter 12 as a sovereign who excelled at recognizing and employing worthy aides, is depicted on slips 199 and 200 as cautioning his (yet again) unnamed heir apparent. In some instances, the transcription of the editors has been challenged by Chen Jian (2015). His amendments mostly concern the content of the proverb that Lord Huan recites in the beginning of his speech. In the transcription, the proverb reads as follows: 生人曰飽，死人曰朽（孝）. This could be translated as "[What matters] for the living is enough food; [what matters] for the dead is filial piety [i.e. sacrifices]." However, Chen suggests that the graphs 曰 (199/16 and 199/20) should be interpreted as *ri* 日 "sun; day; daily" instead of *yue* 曰. He does not follow the editors in interpreting the graph *xiu* 朽 (199/21) (to putrefy, rotten) as a phonetic loan for *xiao* 孝 "filial piety; sacrifice." Thus, the proverb can be understood as saying: "The living, day by day, gratify appetite; The dead, day by day, putrefy." Moreover, unlike the editorial team, Chen reads the graph 土 (200/5) as *tu* 土 "earth; soil" and not as *shi* 士. This proverbial saying has no counterparts in the extant sources of the period.

I also follow Chen in connecting these two slips to the last fragment of the *Zhouxun* that includes slips 208–211. This fragment contains the admonition part referring to the political situation in the state of Qi (208/1–210/3) and the closing formula of the entire manuscript (210/4–211/14) which is followed by the overall character count (211/15–18). While the editors conjectured that it could be connected to Lord Huan's account (*Beida Mss.* 145n8), Chen Jian went a step further and persuasively demonstrated the thematic unity of the said material. As a result, last instruction of chapter 14 is recorded on slips 199, 200, 208, 209 and 210.

The formal characteristics of the account resemble those seen in previous passages in heavily relying on rhyme and juxtaposition. Chen's suggestion to read *xiu* 朽 (199/21) in its original meaning and 土 (200/5) as *tu* has the advantage that these characters belong to the rhyme groups *you* 幽 and *yu* 魚 respectively.

---

[13] *Shangjun shu* "Xiu quan" 修權 (Jiang 1986, 85; Pines 2017, 196–197): 諺曰：「蠹眾而木折，隙大而牆壞。」There is a saying: "When there are plenty of woodworms, the wood will be broken; when a fissure is large, the wall collapses."

As such, they blend in with the surrounding lines which are dominated by the same rhyme groups.

1	昔齊桓公貳其嗣曰：		In the past, Lord Huan of Qi enjoined his heir, saying:
2	諺有言曰：		"A proverb says:
3	『生人日飽,	幽	'The living, day by day, gratify appetite;
4	死人日殂。』	幽	The dead, day by day, putrefy'.
5	餘豈能為土,	魚	Can I, after having turned to soil,
6	而尚令汝道?	幽	still make you [possess] the Way?
7	夫君民者道,		Now, if a ruler over the people [possesses] the Way,
8	則為人命。		he will command the people.
9	唯毋不道,	幽	If he does not [possess] the Way,
10	則人為之輔。	魚	then the people will be his… assistants.
11	民何歸沃?		Where are the people naturally drawn to as their home?
12	從有道處。	魚	They draw toward the place where the Way is in force.
13	暴亂者亡,		The violent and disorderly will perish,
14	鬼神不與。	魚	the ghosts and spirits will not support [them].
15	賢主兼國,		The worthy ruler conquers other states,
16	不肖無慧,		[whereas] the unworthy one lacks wisdom
17	失其疆土,	魚	and loses his territory.
18	其誰有常所?	魚	Which one of them will then have a constant place to dwell?
19	今汝有民而不能聖,	耕	Now, you have the people but [if you] are incapable of sagacity,
20	則齊侯之姓,	耕	then must the surname of the Marquis' of Qi
21	豈必為呂?	魚	be Lü?"

When reconstructed in this way, the passage broaches several topics, among them the importance of wise assistants who can inform a ruler about the principles of the Way. This is congruent with Lord Huan's portrayal in chapter 12 as an expert in recognizing and employing subordinates' abilities. Hence, this ability appears to be the most salient feature of this ruler as recorded in the *Zhouxun*. Such an image of Lord Huan of Qi was made prominent in the *Guanzi*, and one wonders whether the authors of the *Zhouxun* were familiar with this influential text.[14] If the above arrangement of the slips is correct, then the anecdotes about Lord Huan would have concluded Lord Zhaowen's instructions in both the main body of text (which ends with the twelfth month) and in this chapter. This implies that the authors viewed ministerial assistance and council as a factor of vital importance. We thus see that the *Zhouxun* espouses a twofold view of ministers: on the one hand, they are viewed as potential foes of the ruler, who should be held at arm's length and under constant supervision (ch. 1), but, on the other hand, they are irreplaceable as they can instruct the sovereign in the correct principles of governance and provide a crucial link between the latter and the people of a state (chs. 3, 8, 12, 14).

The identity of the figure making the concluding statement about the change of the Qi rulers' family name (lines 19–21) is uncertain. The editors attribute it to Lord Huan (*Beida Mss.* 145n8). But I maintain that it could be associated with Lord Zhaowen, given that the formula "now, you" is mostly used in his addresses to Prince Gong. In this case, this admonition no longer expresses Lord Huan's intuition about the eventual usurpation of the Qi throne by the Tian lineage (Lewis 1999a, 598), but reflects on historical realities and could be translated as "then did the surname of the Marquis' of Qi have to be necessarily 'Lü'?" Sagacity is named here as the last qualification for the exemplary ruler. Given its close association with auditory perception (Chen N. 2000, 412), it seems likely that this term was chosen to highlight the ability to listen to advice from others, be it from one's subordinates or one's father.

Context

As we have seen, the instructions on the six kings and five hegemons represent two distinct groups that differ in regard to some of their formal characteristics, such as framing the encounters, naming protagonists as well as their length. However, their content does not vary significantly across these two groups, as such, we can assume that their formal variance was simply meant to establish a sense of difference between "kings" and "hegemons."

The records in the two groups stipulate the prevalence of the educational practice of father-rulers instructing their offspring from the earliest periods of Chinese history on. The chapter is of pivotal importance in the context of the whole book, insofar as Lord Zhaowen appears to mold his own admonitions of Prince Gong along the examples set by these "ancient" paragons. In fact, parallels between the two include the frequent use of rhyme, regular meter, parallelism, as well as the overall palpable sense of worry and urgency. By promulgating the ubiquitous character of this practice, the text does not seem to be concerned with the dubious historicity of the accounts presented. To reiterate, to portray

---

[14] For a general introduction, see Rickett 1993, 244–251.

Yu as intending to establish Qi and Tang as personally admonishing Tai Jia, as did the *Zhouxun*, was simply ahistorical, and anachronistic and going against most historical records. Moreover, the effectiveness of this practice is not always demonstrated sufficiently clearly. To take the example of Lord Huan of Qi, we know that a succession struggle broke out in Qi immediately after his death even before he was buried (Hsu 1999, 568),[15] and, most importantly, that eventually the power in this state was usurped by the Tian lineage. How are we then to assess the effectiveness of his instruction depicted here? Are we to assume that Lord Huan failed in his educational endeavor, or was it rather the case that his heir(s) proved to be inept? The text does not provide an answer to these questions. Yet the impression remains that only a worthy person, however his excellence is achieved, will prevail in the incessant political struggles.

---

[15] The ostensible reason for this was his love for women which led to his favorites becoming influential and wanting to install their sons as heir apparent. *Zuozhuan*, Xi 17.5, 375; 337.

Conclusion

As a set of "instructions," the *Zhouxun* belongs to the documentary genre. Yet, it differs from the purported pronouncements of the ancient sovereigns and their worthy aides recorded in the extant *shu*-compendia in a variety of ways. It implements no archaisms even when depicting the most ancient events, it contains a wealth of narrative materials and, most importantly, it is ascribed to a rather obscure ruler who lived in the second half of the fourth century BCE. Still, its indebtedness to the *shu*-tradition is evident. On a more general level, the *Zhouxun* treats writing as the most reliable way to communicate knowledge. On the other hand, the text employs framing techniques characteristic of the "documentary" genre. Considering this and given the dubious historicity of the encounters presented in the text, it can be argued that its authors deliberately chose the "instruction" format to imbue their ideas with a sense of authority and solemnity, which they aimed to derive from this "venerated" genre.

The basic assumption of the *Zhouxun* is that a ruler should be worthy, that the sovereign position required and presupposed excellence of character. The moral exemplarity of the sovereign was postulated in early China long before the *Zhouxun*, so it hardly constitutes its most innovative contribution. What distinguishes this text from earlier works is the vast number of virtues that it expects a ruler to embody. The list of moral characteristics which constitute worthiness is indeed long, highlighting the highly idealistic nature of the text, its eclectic ideological orientation, and its relatively late date of composition. This variegated collage of ethical norms notwithstanding, the concrete manifestation of a ruler's worthiness was, rather conventionally, seen in his popular support and, resulting from that, in the prosperity and military strength of his state.

The notion of worthiness is also connected to another, rather peculiar ideological feature of the text. Namely, that the transfer of power should be determined solely by the abilities (worthiness) of the ruler's offspring. The application of meritocratic principles of succession within the family setting was most likely a response to the abdication discourse that shaped the intellectual life of the Warring States like few other ideas did, as can be witnessed in a great number of works of the period, either transmitted or newly excavated. Intriguingly, by shifting the focus to the sovereign's progeny, the *Zhouxun* turned the tables on the advocates of abdication who promoted the transfer of power to anyone worthy of the throne. The text can also be interpreted as addressing the conflict between "respecting the worthy" (*zun xian* 尊賢) and "loving kin" (*ai qin* 愛親)—a common theme in early China (Allan 2015, 10). By bestowing power upon a virtuous son both the meritocratic and hereditary principles of succession were observed.

Still, the heir's worthiness was, rather conventionally, evidenced by his "filial piety" and respect for his father.

Another striking idea proposed by the *Zhouxun* is that a father-ruler should be personally responsible for the education of his offspring as well as the assessment of their suitability for the throne. The necessity of the parent's personal involvement in the education of his children was seldom stated as radically in early China as was done in the manuscript under investigation. This unusually strong emphasis might, to some degree, reflect accounts found in other *shu*-writings of the period where fathers, through instruction, prepared their sons to receive the Heaven's Mandate. But it is best explained through the internal logic of the text. The assumption seems to be that only a worthy individual can understand what constitutes worthiness and how to instill it in other people. Moreover, fostering an able successor and investing him with power was proclaimed to be in the self-interest of the powerholder, insofar as it guaranteed the continuing existence of his state and, consequently, enabled him to permanently receive sacrificial offerings in posterity.

The ideal practice of the worthy father-ruler inculcating moral values into his offspring and personally determining his successor was promoted by the authors of the *Zhouxun* as the main prerequisite for long-standing political success. To substantiate their claims, they attempted to interpret the entire span of Chinese history in light of this singular principle. Accordingly, the reason why the hereditary dynasties Xia, Shang, and Zhou were founded and could endure was not because their founders obtained the Mandate of Heaven, but rather because, being worthies, they naturally won the allegiance of the people and, most importantly, made efforts to educate their sons and personally determined their succession. Hence the characteristic focus on the interactions between the first and the second generations of rulers in a given dynasty, even if some of them were outright anachronistic. Most alleged encounters between father-rulers and their sons that relate to later periods and various political entities (Yue, Qin, Zhao, and Wei) were likewise meant to prove the effectiveness of this didactic practice but were equally historically problematic. However, dubious historicity was a common phenomenon among the texts of that time as history increasingly came to be used (and distorted) for ideological ends. It is for this reason that the Warring States period is sometimes called "the lowest ebb of the Chinese historiographic tradition" (Pines 2005b, 220). So, the manifold historical incongruities in the *Zhouxun* should not lead us to the assumption that its authors were not familiar with history or were careless with facts. The thoughtful organization of the text is the best evidence that this could not have been the case. Rather, the text's customary deviations from "mainstream" historical knowledge show just how determined the authors were in making their point (Goldin 2017, 50).

I maintain that their main ideological endeavor was, ultimately, to stipulate a ruler's complete freedom of decision in regard to the issue of succession.

Accordingly, the alleged personal involvement of the father-rulers in their sons' education was a means to justify and affirm this freedom. In any case, the didactic content of their speeches did not amount to much, being often confined to commonplace platitudes, while the main criterion for the success of a student's learning remained personal allegiance to their father. Thus, in the end, we may conclude the main goal of the *Zhouxun* was to establish the normativity of enthroning the most loyal (whatever that implied) of the ruler's offspring regardless of the status of their maternal lineage.

The rejection of the rule of primogeniture as the main instrument for determining succession found here might represent an attempt to formulate a theoretical justification for the widespread disregard of this rule, as many powerholders from the Warring States period and earlier ages, for one reason or another, came to dismiss their first-born sons. However, as I have argued above, this central feature of the *Zhouxun* can also be understood as reflecting specific events that took place in the state of Qin after prince Zichu 子楚, a son by a concubine, ascended the Qin throne and came to be known as King Zhuangxiang of Qin (r. 250–247 BCE). To begin with, after coming to power, he grew to become a ruler who stood out through his virtue and kindness and completed the conquest of the Zhou, effectively becoming their successor (*Shiji* 5.219; Nienhauser 1995, 122). But equally intriguing in this context is his chancellor Lü Buwei (292–235 BCE). Not only was Lü Buwei instrumental in the establishment of Zichu as Qin ruler, he also assisted King Zhuangxiang in conquering the Zhou and, moreover, he oversaw the creation of the *Lüshi chunqiu*. To recall, in addition to borrowing from the *Zhouxun*, the *Lüshi chunqiu* was the only work to hail Lord Zhaowen as a worthy ruler and teacher of King Hui of Qin. While the exact correlation between these facts and the *Zhouxun* remains, at least in the current state of the field, a matter of speculation, their manifold correspondences cannot be treated as a mere coincidence. In light of the above, I maintain that this manuscript might very well have been created in the aftermath of the Qin's conquest of the Zhou to assert the superiority of the Qin and praise its king. But even if this was not the case, the manuscript remains a fascinating witness to the variety of the intellectual positions in pre-imperial China worthy of further studies.

Bibliography

Allan, Sarah. 1972–73. "The Identities of Taigong Wang 太公望 in Zhou and Han Literature." *Monumenta Serica* 30:57–99.

———. 2012. "On *Shu* 書 (Documents) and the Origin of the *Shang shu* 尚書 (Ancient Documents) in Light of Recently Discovered Bamboo Slip Manuscripts." *Bulletin of the School of Oriental and African Studies* 75.3:547–557.

———. 2015. *Buried Ideas: Legends of Abdication and Ideal Government in Early Chinese Bamboo-Slip Manuscripts*. Albany: State University of New York Press.

———. 2016. *The Heir and the Sage: Dynastic Legend in Early China*. Revised and Expanded Edition. New York: State University of New York Press.

Ames, Roger. 2003. "*Li* and the A-theistic Religiousness of Classical Confucianism." In *Confucian Spirituality. Vol. One.*, eds. Tu Weiming and Mary Evelyn Tucker, 165–182. New York: The Crossroad Publishing Company.

Anhui daxue Hanzi fazhan yu yingyong yanjiu zhongxin 安徽大學漢字發展與應用研究中心, ed. 2019. *Anhui daxue cang Zhanguo zhujian* 安徽大學藏戰國竹簡, vol. 1. Shanghai: Zhongxi shuju.

Barbieri-Low, Anthony Jerome, and Robin D. S. Yates. 2015. *Law, State, and Society in Early Imperial China: A Study with Critical Edition and Translation of the Legal Texts from Zhangjiashan Tomb no. 247*, Vol. II. Leiden: Brill.

Behr, Wolfgang, and Bernhard Führer. 2005. "Einführende Notizen zum Lesen in China mit besonderer Berücksichtigung der Frühzeit." In *Referate der Jahrestagung 2001 der Deutschen Vereinigung für Chinastudien (DVCS)*, ed. Bernhard Führer, 1–42. Bochum: Projekt Verlag

Beijing daxue chutu wenxian yanjiusuo 北京大學出土文獻研究所. 2011. "Beijing daxue cang Xi-Han zhushu gaishuo" 北京大學藏西漢竹書概說. *Wenwu* 6: 49–57.

———, ed. 2015. *Beijing daxue cang Xi-Han zhushu. san* 北京大學藏西漢竹書.叁. Shanghai: Shanghai guji chubanshe.

Bielenstein, Hans. 1980. *The Bureaucracy of Han Times*. Cambridge: Cambridge University Press.

Blakeley, Barry B. 1999. "The Geography of Chu." In *Defining Chu: Image and Reality in Ancient China*, eds. John S. Major and Constance A. Cook, 9–20. Honolulu: University of Hawaii Press.

Blanford, Yumiko F. 1991. "A Textual Approach to 'Zhanguo Zonghengjia Shu': Methods Of Determining the Proximate Origin Word Among Variants." *Early China* 16:187–207.

Bodde, Derk. 1975. *Festivals in Classical China: New Year and Other Annual Observances During the Han Dynasty, 206 B.C.-A.D. 220*. Princeton: Princeton University Press.

_____. 1986. "The State and Empire of Ch'in." In *The Cambridge History of China, Vol. 01: The Ch'in and Han Empires, 221.B.C.-A.D.220*, eds. Denis Twitchett and John K. Fairbank, 20–102. Cambridge: Cambridge University Press.

Boltz, William G. 2005. "The Composite Nature of Early Chinese Text." In *Text and Ritual in Early China*, ed. Martin Kern, 50–78. Seattle: University of Washington Press.

Brindley, Erica. 2003. "Barbarians or Not? Ethnicity and Changing Conceptions of the Ancient Yue (Viet) Peoples, ca. 400-50 BCE." *Asia Major* 16.1:1–32.

_____. 2015. *Ancient China and the Yue: Perceptions and Identities on the Southern Frontier, c. 400 BCE-50 CE*. Cambridge: Cambridge University Press.

Cao Shenggao 曹勝高 and An Na 安娜. 2012. *Liu tao; Guiguzi* 六韜；鬼谷子. Beijing: Zhonghua shuju.

Chan, Shirley. 2004. *The Confucian Shi, Official Service, and the Confucian Analects*. Lewiston: Edwin Mellen Press.

Chang I-Jen 張以仁, William G. Boltz, and Michael Loewe. 1993. "*Kuo-yü*" 國語." In *Early Chinese Texts: A Bibliographical Guide*, ed. Michael Loewe, 263–269. Berkeley: Institute of East Asian Studies.

Chavannes, Edouard. 1967. *Se-Ma Ts'ien — Mémoires Historiques, tome cinquième*. Paris: Librairie d'Amérique et d'Orient Adrien Maisonneuve.

Chen Jian 陳劍. 2012. "Beida zhushu *Zhouxun* 'fei jue wu dai' xiaokao" 北大竹書《周訓》「非爵勿駘」小考. http://www.fdgwz.org.cn/Web/Show/1857. (accessed April 22, 2022).

_____. 2015. "*Zhouxun* 'sui zhong xianghe zhi ri zhang' de bianlian wenti" 《周訓》「歲終享賀之日章」的編連問題. http://www.fdgwz.org.cn/Web/Show/2628. (accessed April 22, 2022.)

_____. 2016. "*Zhouxun* 'wei xia sun gui er bu zhi' jie" 《周馴》「爲下飡捄而餔之」解. http://www.fdgwz.org.cn/Web/Show/2835 (accessed April 22, 2022.)

Chen, Lai 陳來. 2016. "The Ideas of 'Educating' and 'Learning' in Confucian Thought." In *Chinese Philosophy on Teaching and Learning*, eds. Xu Di and Hunter McEwan, 77–95. Albany: State University of New York Press.

Chen Li 陳立. 1994. *Baihu tong shuzheng* 白虎通疏證. Beijing: Zhonghua.

Chen Longyu 陳隆予. 2005. "Lun *Qi lüe* fenlei sixiang de xingcheng ji qi yingxiang" 論《七略》分類思想的形成及其影響. *Tangdu xuekan* 21.5:9–13.

Chen Mengjia 陳夢家. 1985. *Shangshu tonglun* 尚書通論. Beijing: Zhonghua shuju.

Chen, Ning. 2000. "The Etymology of *Sheng* (Sage) and its Confucian Conception in Early China." *Journal of Chinese Philosophy* 27:4:409–427.

Chen Qiyou 陳奇猷. 2001. *Lüshi chunqiu xin jiaoshi* 呂氏春秋新校釋. Shanghai: Shanghai guji chubanshe.

Chen Peifen 陳佩芬. 2002. "Xishe junlao" 昔者君老. In *Shanghai Bowuguan cang Zhanguo Chu zhushu er* 上海博物館藏戰國楚竹書二, ed. Ma Chengyuan 馬承源, 239–246. Shanghai: Shanghai guji.

Chen Xiyong 陳錫勇. 1992. *Zongfa tianming yu chunqiu sixiang chutan* 宗法天命與春秋思想初探. Taipei: Wenjin.

Chen Yingfei 陳穎飛. 2017. "Lun Qinghua jian *Zifan Ziyu* de ji ge wenti" 論清華簡《子犯子余》的幾個問題. *Wenwu* 6:81–83.

Chen Zhi 陳直. 1963. "Qin Shi Huang liu da tongyi zhengce de kaogu ziliao" 秦始皇六大統一政策的考古資料. *Lishi jiaoxue* 歷史教學 8:26–30.

Cheng Junying 程俊英 and Jiang Beiyuan 蔣見元. 1999. *Shijing zhuxi* 詩經注析. Beijing: Zhonghua shuju.

Cheng Shaoxuan 程少軒. 2013. "Tantan Beida Hanjian *Zhouxun* de jige wenti" 談談北大漢簡《周訓》的幾個問題. In *Chutu wenxian yu gu wenzi yanjiu* 出土文獻與古文字研究, ed. Fudan daxue chutu wenxian yu gu wenzi yanjiu zhongxin 復旦大學出土文獻與古文字研究中心, 5:556–557. Shanghai: Shanghai guji.

Cheng Shude 程樹德, ed. 1990. *Lunyu jishi* 論語集釋. Beijing: Zhonghua shuju chuban.

Chien Tsui-Chen 簡翠貞. 2008. "*Zuozhuan* yin yan tan wei"《左傳》引諺探微. *Xinzhu jiaoyu daxue renwen shehui xuebao* 新竹教育大學人文社會學報 1:2:15–43.

Chu Chieh-fan 朱介凡. 1970. *Yanyu de yuanliu, gongneng* 諺語的源流，功能 (Studies in Chinese Proverbs). Taipei: Dongfang wenhua.

Cohen, Paul A. 2009. *Speaking to History: The Story of King Goujian in Twentieth-Century China*. London: The Regents of the University of California.

Cook, Constance A. 2011. "Education and the Way of the Former Kings." In *Writing and Literacy in Early China: Studies from the Columbia Early China Seminar*, eds. Li Feng and David Prager Branner, 302–336. Seattle: University of Washington Press.

_____. 2017. *Ancestors, Kings, and the Dao*. Cambridge, Mass.: Harvard University Asia Center.

_____, and Barry B. Blakeley. 1999. "Introduction." In *Defining Chu: Image and Reality in Ancient China*, eds. John S. Major and Constance A. Cook, 1-8. Honolulu: University of Hawaii Press.

_____, and Paul R. Goldin, eds. 2016. *A Source Book of Ancient Chinese Bronze Inscriptions*. Berkeley: The Society for the Study of Early China.

Cook, Scott. 2012. *The Bamboo Texts of Guodian: A Study and Complete Translation*. 2 vols. Cornell East Asia Series. Ithaca: Cornell University Press.

_____. (Gu Shikao 顧史考). 2019. "Qinghua jian qi *Zhao Jiangzi* chutan" 清華簡柒〈趙簡子〉初探. *Bulletin of Jao Tsung-I Academy of Sinology* 6:361–375.

Crump, James I. 1970. *Chan-Kuo Ts'e*. Oxford: Clarendon Press.

Csikszentmihalyi, Mark. 2004. *Material Virtue: Ethics and The Body in Early China*. Leiden: Brill.
Cullen, Christopher. 2017. *The Foundations of Celestial Reckoning: Three Ancient Chinese Astronomical Systems*. London and New York: Routledge.
Du Lun. 2007. "Legitimitätsideen in der frühen Zhou-Zeit: Eine Untersuchung anhand der „Zhou-Dokumente" im *Shujing*." *Bochumer Jahrbuch zur Ostasienforschung* 31:143–170.
Durrant, Stephen. 1993. "*Yen tzu ch'un ch'iu* 晏子春秋." In *Early Chinese Texts: A Bibliographical Guide*, ed. Michael Loewe, 490–494. Berkeley: Institute of East Asian Studies.
_____, Li Wai-yee and David Schaberg. 2016. *Zuo Tradition / Zuozhuan: Commentary on the "Spring and Autumn Annals."* Seattle: University of Washington Press.
Falkenhausen, Lothar von. 2004. "Mortuary Behavior in Pre-Imperial Qin: a Religious Interpretation in Religion and Chinese Society." In *Religion and Chinese Society*, ed. John Lagerwey, 109–172. Paris: École Française d'Extrême Orient.
_____. 2006. *Chinese Society in the Age of Confucius (1000-250 BCE): The Archaeological Evidence*. Los Angeles: Cotsen Institute of Archaeology, University of California.
_____. 2011. "The Royal Audience and Its Reflections in Western Zhou Bronze Inscriptions." In *Writing & Literacy in Early China: Studies from the Columbia Early China Seminar*, eds. Li Feng and David Prager Branner, 239–270. Seattle & London: University of Washington Press.
_____ and Gideon Shelach. 2014. "Introduction: Archeological Perspectives on the Qin 'Unification' of China." In *Birth of an Empire: The State of Qin Revisited*, eds. Yuri Pines, Lothar von Falkenhausen, Gideon Shelach, Robin D. S. Yates, 37–51. Berkeley: University of California Press.
Fan Xiangyong 范祥雍. 2006. *Zhanguoce jianzheng* 戰國策箋證. Shanghai: Shanghai guji chubanshe.
Fang Shiming 方詩銘 and Wang Xiuling 王修齡, eds. 1981. *Guben zhushu jinian jizheng* 古本竹書紀年輯證. Shanghai: Shanghai guji.
Fang Chaohui 方朝暉. 2001. *Chunqiu Zuozhuan renwu pu* 春秋左傳人物譜. Jinan: Qi Lu shushe.
Fech, Andrej. 2018. "The *Zhou xun* 周訓 and 'Elevating the Worthy' (*shang xian* 尚賢)." *Early China* 41:149–178.
_____. 2020a. "Meritocracy, Heredity and Worthies in Early Daoism." *Culture and Dialogue* 8:363–383.
_____. 2020b. "The Relationship between the *Zhou xun* 周訓 and *Lüshi chunqiu* 呂氏春秋 in the Context of the Late Warring States Period." *Bulletin of the Jao Tsung-I Academy of Sinology* 7:183–224.
Forke, Alfred. 1907. *Lun-Heng, Part I: Philosophical Essays of Wang Ch'ung*. Leipzig: Harrassowitz.
Foster, Christopher J. 2017. "Introduction to the Peking University Han Bamboo Strips: On the Authentication and Study of Purchased Manuscripts." *Early China* 40:167–239.

Franke, Otto. 2001 [1965]. *Geschichte des chinesischen Reiches: eine Darstellung seiner Entstehung, seines Wesens und seiner Entwicklung bis zur neuesten Zeit*. Bd. 1: *Das Altertum und das Werden des konfuzianischen Staates*. Berlin: de Gruyter.

Galambos, Imre. 2004. "The Myth of the Qin Unification of Writing in Han Sources." *Acta Orientalia Academiae Scientiarum Hungaricae* 57.2:181–203.

Galvany, Albert. 2013. "Beyond the Rule of Rules: The Foundations of Sovereign Power in the *Han Feizi*." In *Dao Companion to the Philosophy of Han Fei*, ed. Paul Goldin, 87–106. New York: Springer.

Goldin, Paul R. 2005. *After Confucius: Studies in Early Chinese Philosophy*. Honolulu: University of Hawai'i Press.

———. 2013a. "*Heng Xian* and the Problem of Studying Looted Artefacts." *Dao* 12: 153–160.

———. 2013b. "Introduction: Han Fei and the *Han Feizi*." In *Dao Companion to the Philosophy of Han Fei*, ed. Paul Goldin, 1–21. New York: Springer.

———. 2017. "Non-deductive Argumentation in Early Chinese Philosophy." In *Between History and Philosophy: Anecdotes in Early China*, eds. Paul van Els and Sarah A. Queen, 41–62. Albany: State University of New York Press.

Graham, A.C. 1991. "Questioning of Hereditary Succession in Ancient China." *Rocznik Orientalistyczny* XLVII, Z.2:63–67.

———. 1993. "*Mo tzu* 墨子." In *Early Chinese Texts: A Bibliographical Guide*, ed. Michael Loewe, 336–341. Berkeley: Institute of East Asian Studies.

Grebnev, Yegor. "The *Yi Zhoushu* and the *Shangshu*: The Case of Texts with Speeches." In *Origins of Chinese Political Philosophy: Studies in the Composition and Thought of the Shangshu (Classic of Shangshu)*, eds. Martin Kern and Dirk Meyer, 249–280. Leiden: Brill.

Gren, Magnus Ribbing. 2017. "The Qinghua "Jinteng" 金縢 Manuscript: What It Does Not Tell Us about the Duke of Zhou." In *Origins of Chinese Political Philosophy: Studies in the Composition and Thought of the Shangshu (Classic of Shangshu)*, eds. Martin Kern and Dirk Meyer, 193–223. Leiden: Brill.

Gu Jiegang 顧頡剛. 1982. *Gushibian* 古史辨, Vol. 1. Shanghai: Shanghai guji chubanshe.

——— and Liu Qiyu 劉起釪. 2005. *Shangshu jiaoshi yilun* 尚書校釋譯論. Beijing: Zhonghua shuju.

Guo Lihua 郭梨華. 2018. "*Tang chu yu Tang qiu, Tang zai Chimen* zhong de HuangLao sixiang chutan" 《湯處於湯丘》、《湯在啻門》中的黃老思想初探. In *Chutu wenxian yu Zhongguo gudian xue* 出土文獻與中國古典學, ed. Fudan daxue chutuwenxian yu guwenzi yanjiu zhongxin 復旦大學出土文獻與古文字研究中心, 292–306.

Guo Qingfan 郭慶藩. 1990. *Zhuangzi jijie* 莊子集釋. Beijing: Zhonghua shuju.

Guojia wenwuju gu wenxian yanjiushi 國家文物局古文獻研究室 [Research group on ancient documents of the state cultural relics bureau], ed. 1980. *Mawangdui*

Hanmu boshu 馬王堆漢墓帛書 [Silk documents from the Han tomb at Mawangdui] (Vol. 1). Beijing: Wenwu chubanshe.

Hanshu 漢書. Beijing: Zhonghua shuju. 1962.

Han Wei 韓巍. 2011. "BeiDa Han jian *Laozi* jianjie" 北大漢簡《老子》簡介. *Wenwu* 6: 67–70.

_____. 2015. "Xi-Han zhushu ruogan wenti tantao" 西漢竹書《周訓》若干問題探討. In *Beijing daxue cang Xi-Han zhushu. san* 北京大學藏西漢竹書. 叁. Shanghai: Shanghai guji chubanshe, 248–298.

Harbsmeier, Christoph. 1998. *Science and Civilization in China* VII.1: *Language and Logic in Traditional China*. Cambridge: Cambridge University Press.

Harper, Donald J. 1999. *Early Chinese Medical Literature: the Mawangdui Medical Manuscripts*. London and New York: Kegan Paul International.

Harris, Eirik Lang. 2016. *The Shenzi Fragments: a Philosophical Analysis and Translation*. New York: Columbia University Press.

He, Jianjun. 2021. *Spring and Autumn Annals of Wu and Yue: An Annotated Translation of Wu Yue Chunqiu*. Ithaca and London: Cornell East Asia Series.

He Jin 何晉. 2011. "BeiDa Han jian *Wang Ji* jianshu" 北大漢簡《妄稽》簡述. *Wenwu* 6:75–77.

He Leshi 何樂士. 1989. *Zuozhuan xuci yanjiu*《左傳》虛詞研究. Beijing: Shangwu yinshuguan.

He Ning 何寧, ed. 1998. *Huainanzi jishi* 淮南子集釋. Beijing: Zhonghua shuju.

He Ruyue and Michael Nylan. 2019. "On Citation Practices in the Guodian Manuscripts." In *Dao Companion to the Excavated Guodian Bamboo Manuscripts*, ed. Shirley Chan, 41–62. Cham: Springer Nature.

Hebei sheng wenwu yanjiusuo Dingzhou Hanmu zhujian zhengli xiaozu 河北省文物研究所定州漢墓竹簡整理小組, ed. 1995. "Dingzhou XiHan Zhongshan Huaiwang mu zhujian *Wenzi* shiwen" 定州西漢中山懷王墓竹簡《文子》釋文. *Wenwu* 12:27–34.

_____. 2001. "Dingzhou XiHan Zhongshan Huaiwang mu zhujian *Liutao* shiwen ji jiaozhu" 定州西漢中山懷王墓竹簡《六韜》釋文及校注. *Wenwu* 5:77–83.

Hein, Anke. 2019. "Concepts of "Authenticity" and the Chinese Textual Heritage in Light of Excavated Texts." In *China and the World – the World and China, Volume 1: Transcultural Perspectives on Pre-modern China*. ed. Joachim Gentz, 37–66. Gossenberg: Ostasien Verlag.

Henry, Eric. 1999. "'Junzi Yue' versus 'Zhongni Yue' in *Zuozhuan*." *Harvard Journal of Asiatic Studies* 59.1:125–161.

_____. 2007. "Submerged History of Yue." *Sino-Platonic Papers* 176:1–36.

_____. 2021. *Garden of Eloquence, Shuoyuan* 說苑. Seattle: University of Washington Press.

Hightower, James Robert. 1952. *Han Shih Wai Chuan: Han Ying's Illustrations of the Didactic Application of the Classic of Songs* (Harvard-Yenching Institute Monograph). Cambridge, Mass.: Harvard University Press.

Ho Che Wah 何志華. 2015. *Lüshi chunqiu guankui* 呂氏春秋管窺. Hong Kong: Chung Hwa Book Co.

———, and Chan Hung Kan 陳雄根, eds. 2004. *Xian-Qin liang Han dianji yin "Shijing" ziliao huibian* 先秦兩漢典籍引《詩經》資料彙編 (*Citations from the Shijing to Be Found in Pre-Han and Han Texts*). Hong Kong: The Chinese University of Hong Kong Press.

Hou Naifeng. 侯乃峯. 2018. "Beida zhushu *Zhouxun* 'fei jue wu ji' jieyi" 北大竹書《周訓》「非爵勿羈」解義. *Zhongguo jianbo xuekan* 中國簡帛學刊:103–108.

Hsing, I-tian. 2014. "Qin-Han Census, Tax and Corvee Administration: Notes on Newly Discovered Materials," trs. Hsieh Mei-yu and William G. Growell. In *Birth of an Empire: The State of Qin Revisited*, eds. Yuri Pines, Lothar von Falkenhausen, Gideon Shelach, Robin D. S. Yates, 155–186. Berkeley: University of California Press.

Hsu, Cho-yun. 1999. "The Spring and Autumn Period." In *The Cambridge History of Ancient China: From the Origins of Civilization to 221 B.C.*, eds. Michael Loewe and Edward L. Shaughnessy, 545–586. Cambridge: Cambridge University Press.

Hu Jiacong 胡家聰. 1998. *Jixia zhengming yu HuangLao xinxue* 稷下爭鳴與黃老新學. Beijing: Zhongguo shehui kexue chubanshe.

Huang Dekuan 黃德寬. 2017. "Anhui daxue cang Zhanguo zhujian gaishu" 安徽大學藏戰國竹簡概述. *Wenwu* 9:54–59.

Huang Hui 黃暉, ed. 1990. *Lun heng jiaoshi* 論衡校釋. Beijing: Zhonghua, 1990.

Huang Kuan-Yun. 2018. "Poetry, "The Metal-Bound Coffer," and The Duke of Zhou." *Early China* 41:87–148.

Hulsewé, Anthony François Paulus. 1978. "The Ch'in Documents Discovered in Hupei in 1975." *T'oung Pao* 64:175–217.

Ivanhoe, Philip J. 2000. *Confucian Moral Self Cultivation*. Indianapolis/Cambridge: Hackett Publishing.

Ji Xu-Sheng 李旭昇. 2004. "*Shang Bo er Xizhe junlao* jianwen tanjiu ji qi yu *Shangshu Guming* de xianguan wenti" 《上博二・昔者君老》簡文探究及其與《尚書・顧命》的相關問題. *Zhongguo zhexue yanjiu jikan* 中國文哲研究集刊:253–292.

Jiang Lihong 蔣禮鴻. 1986. *Shangjun shu zhuizhi* 商君書錐指. Beijing: Zhonghua shuju.

Jiao Xun 焦循. 1987. *Mengzi zhengyi* 孟子正義. Beijing: Zhonghua shuju.

Jingmen shi bowuguan 荊門市博物館, ed. 1998. *Guodian Chu mu zhujian* 郭店楚墓竹簡. Beijing: Wenwu chubanshe.

Johnston, Ian. 2010. *The Mozi: A Complete Translation*. Hong Kong: The Chinese University of Hong Kong.

Karlgren, Bernhard. 1950a. *The Book of Shijing*. Stockholm: The Museum of Far Eastern Antiquities.

_____. 1950b. *The Book of Shangshu*. Stockholm: The Museum of Far Eastern Antiquities.

Keightley, David N. 1999. "The Shang: China's First Historical Dynasty." In *The Cambridge History of Ancient China: From the Origins of Civilization to 221 B.C.*, eds. Michael Loewe and Edward L. Shaughnessy, 232–291. Cambridge: Cambridge University Press.

Kern, Martin. 2000. "*Shi jing* Songs as Performance Texts: A Case Study Of "Chu Ci" (Thorny Caltrop)*." *Early China* 25:49–111.

_____. 2003. "Early Chinese Poetics in the Light of Recently Excavated Manuscripts." In *Recarving the Dragon: Understanding Chinese Poetics*, ed. Olga Lomova, 27–72. Prague: The Karolinum Press.

_____. 2005a. "Poetry and Religion: The Representation of 'Truth' in Early Chinese Historiography." In *Historical Truth, Historical Criticism, and Ideology: Chinese Historiography and Historical Culture from a New Comparative Perspective*, eds. Helwig Schmidt-Glintzer, Achim Mittag, and Jörn Rüsen, 53–78. Leiden: Brill.

_____. 2005b. "Quotation and the Confucian Canon in Early Chinese Manuscripts: the Case of "Zi yi" (Black Robes)." *Asiatische Studien-Études Asiatiques* 59:293–332.

———. 2005c. "The *Odes* in Excavated Manuscripts." In *Text and Ritual in Early China*, ed. Martin Kern. Seattle and London: University of Washington Press, 149–193.

_____. 2009. "Bronze Inscriptions, the *Shijing* and the *Shangshu*: The Evolution of the Ancestral Sacrifice During the Western Zhou." In *Early Chinese Religion: Part One: Shang Through Han (1250 BCE-220 AD)*, eds. John Lagerwey and Marc Kalinowski, 143–200. Leiden: Brill.

_____. 2010a. "Early Chinese Literature, Beginnings Through Western Han." In *The Cambridge History of Chinese Literature*, vol. 1, ed. Stephen Owen, 1–115. Cambridge: Cambridge University Press.

_____. 2010b. "Offices of Writing and Reading in the Rituals of Zhou." In *Statecraft and Classical Learning: The Rituals of Zhou in East Asian History*, eds. Benjamin A. Elman and Martin Kern. Leiden: Brill.

_____. 2015. "Language and the Ideology of Kingship in the "Canon of Yao."" In *Ideology of Power and Power of Ideology in Early China*, eds. Yuri Pines et al., 118–151. Leiden: Brill.

_____. 2019. "Xi Shuai" 蟋蟀 ("Cricket") and Its Consequence." *Early China* 42:39–74.

Khayutina, Maria. 2006. "Die Geschichte der Irrfahrt des Prinzen Chong'er." In *Kritik im alten und modernen China*, ed. Heiner Roetz, 20–47. Wiesbaden: Harrasowitz Verlag.

_____. 2008. "Western "Capitals" of the Western Zhou Dynasty: Historical Reality and Its Reflections Until the Time of Sima Qian." *Oriens Extremus* 47:25–65.

_____. 2015. "King Wen, a Settler of Disputes or Judge? The 'Yu-Rui case' in the *Historical Records* and its Historical Background." *BJOAF* 38:261–276.

———. 2021. "The Beginning of Cultural Memory Production in China and the Memory Policy of the Zhou Royal House During the Western Zhou Period." *Early China* 44:19–108.

Knoblock, John. 1994. *Xunzi. A Translation and Study of the Complete Work*, Vol. III. Stanford: Stanford University Press.

———, and Jeffrey Riegel. 2000. *The Annals of Lü Buwei*. Stanford: Stanford University Press.

Krijgsman, Rens. 2017. "Cultural Memory and Excavated Anecdotes in "Documentary" Narrative: Mediating Generic Tensions in the *Baoxun* Manuscript." In *Between History and Philosophy: Anecdotes in Early China*, eds. Paul van Els and Sarah A. Queen, 301–330. Albany: State University of New York Press.

———. 2019. "Self-Reflexive Praxis: Changing Attitudes towards Manuscript and Text in Early China." *Early China* 42:75–110.

Kuszera, Stanislaw. 2017. *Ustanovlenie Dinastii Dschou (The Institutions of Zhou (Zhou li). Part 1. Heaven Officials. Chapters 1-2)*. Moscow: Nauka —Vostochnaya Literatura.

Kusano Tomoko 草野 友子. 2018. "Pekin daigaku no Kankan *Shūkun* no shisō-shi teki kenkyū – *Shi* no in'yō o chūshin ni" 北大漢簡『周馴』の思想史的研究—『詩』の引用を中心に—. *Kanjigaku kenkyū* 漢字学研究 6:33–46.

———. 2019. "Beida Hanjian *Zhouxun* suo yin *Shi* de sixiang shi yanjiu" 北大漢簡《周馴》所引《詩》的思想史研究. *Jianbo* 簡帛 18:189–198.

Lagerwey, John. 1993. "*Wu Yüe ch'un ch'iu* 吳越春秋." In *Early Chinese Texts: A Bibliographical Guide*, ed. Michael Loewe, 473–476. Berkeley: Institute of East Asian Studies.

Lai Guolong. 2015. *Excavating the Afterlife: The Archaeology of Early Chinese Religion*. Seattle: University of Washington Press.

Lau, D. C. 1991. "A Study of Some Textual Problems in the *Lü-shih ch'un-ch'iu* and Their Bearing on Its Composition." *Zhongguo wenzhe yanjiu jikan* 中國文哲研究集刊 1:45–86.

——— 劉殿爵. 1994. *Shangshu dazhuan zhuzi suoyin* 尚書大傳逐字索引 (A Concordance to the Shangshu dazhuan). Hong Kong: Shangwu yinshuguan.

———. 2003. *Mencius*. Hong Kong: The Chinese University Press.

———, and Chan Fong Ching 陳方正. 1995. *Shangshu zhuzi suoyin* 尚書逐字索引 (A Concordance to the Shangshu). Hong Kong: Shangwu yinshuguan.

Legge, James. 1879. *The Sacred Books of China. The Texts of Confucianism. Part I: The Shû-King. The Religious Portions of the Shih King. The Hsiâo King*. Oxford: Clarendon Press.

———. 1885. *Sacred Books of the East*. Vol. XXVIIÖ *The Texts of Confucianism*. Part III: *The Lî Kî, I—X*. Oxford: Clarendon Press.

Lewis, Mark Edward. 1999a. "Warring States: Political History." In *The Cambridge History of Ancient China: From the Origins of Civilization to 221 B.C.*, eds. Michael Loewe and Edward L. Shaughnessy, 587–650. Cambridge: Cambridge University Press.

_____. 1999b. *Writing and Authority in Early China*. New York: State University of New York Press.

_____. 2005. *The Construction Of Space in Early China*. New York: State University of New York Press.

_____. 2006. *The Flood Myths of Early China*. Albany: State University of New York Press.

Li Bujia 李步嘉. 2013. *Yuejue shu jiaoshi* 越絕書校釋. Beijing: Zhonghua shuju.

Li Feng. 2003. "'Feudalism' and Western Zhou China: A Criticism." *Harvard Museum of Asiatic Studies* 63.1:115–144.

_____. 2006. *Landscape and Power in Early China: the Crisis and Fall of the Western Zhou, 1045-771 BCE*. Cambridge: Cambridge University Press.

_____. 2013. *Early China: A Social and Cultural History*. Cambridge: Cambridge University Press.

Li Junming 李均明. 2011."Qinghua jian *Huang men* zhi junchen guan" 清華簡《皇門》之君臣觀. *Zhongguo shi yan jiu* 中國史研究 1:59–66.

Li Ling 李零. 2002. *Rongchengshi* 容成氏. In *Shanghai Bowuguan cang Zhanguo Chu zhushu er* 上海博物館藏戰國楚竹書二, ed. Ma Chengyuan 馬承源, 247–293. Shanghai: Shanghai guji.

_____. 2003. *Pengzu* 彭祖. In *Shanghai Bowuguan cang Zhanguo Chu zhushu san* 上海博物館藏戰國楚竹書三, ed. Ma Chengyuan, 301–308. Shanghai: Shanghai guji chubanshe.

Li Mengcun 李孟存 and 常金仓 Chang Jincang. 1989. *Jin guo shi gangyao* 晉國史綱要. Taiyuan: Shanxi renmin chubanshe.

Li Shoukui 李守奎. 2012a. "Lun Qinghua jian zhong de Zhao Wang ju Qinxi zhi shang yu Zhao Wang gui Sui" 論清華簡中的昭王居秦溪之上與昭王歸隨. In *Gudai jiandu baohu yu zhengli yanjiu* 古代簡牘保護與整理研究, ed. Qinghua daxue chutu wenxian yanjiu yu baohu zhongxin 清華大學出土文獻研究與保護中心, 209–212. Shanghai: Zhongxi shuju.

_____. 2012b. "Qinghua jian *Zhou Gong zhi qinwu* yu Zhou Song" 清華簡《周公之琴舞》與周頌. *Wenwu* 8:72–76.

_____. 2017. "*Yue Gong qi shi* yu Goujian mie Wu de lishi shishi ji gushi liuchuan" 《越公其事》與句踐滅吳的歷史事實及故事流傳. *Wenwu* 6:75–80.

Li Wai-Yee. 2014. "Poetry and Diplomacy in the *Zuozhuan*." *Journal of Chinese Literature and Culture* 1:1-2:241–261.

Li Xueqin. 1985. *Eastern Zhou and Qin Civilizations*, trans. K.C. Chang. New Haven and London: Yale University Press.

_____ 李學勤, ed. 2000. *Chunqiu Gongyang zhuan zhushu* 春秋公羊傳註疏. Beijing: Beijing daxue.

_____, ed. 2010. *Qinghua Daxue cang Zhangguo zhujian* 清華大學藏戰國竹簡, vol. 1. Shanghai: Zhongxi shuju.

———, ed. 2011. *Qinghua Daxue cang Zhangguo zhujian* 清華大學藏戰國竹簡, vol. 5. Shanghai: Zhongxi shuju.

———, ed. 2012. *Qinghua Daxue cang Zhangguo zhujian* 清華大學藏戰國竹簡, vol. 3. Shanghai: Zhongxi shuju.

———, ed. 2017. *Qinghua Daxue cang Zhangguo zhujian* 清華大學藏戰國竹簡, vol. 7. Shanghai: Zhongxi shuju.

Liao Mingchun 廖明春. 2001a. "Guodian Chu jian yin *Shi* lun *Shi* kao" 郭店楚簡引《詩》論《詩》考. In *Xin chu Chu jian shi lun* 新出楚簡試論, ed. Ding Yuanzhi 丁原植, 45–81. Taipei: Taiwan guji chubanshe.

———. 2001b. "Guodian Chu jian yin *Shu* lun *Shu* kao" 郭店楚簡引《書》論《書》考. In *Xin chu Chu jian shi lun* 新出楚簡試論, ed. Ding Yuanzhi 丁原植, 83–110. Taipei: Taiwan guji chubanshe.

———. 2008. *Boshu Zhouyi lunji* 帛書《周易》論集. Shanghai: Shanghai guji chubanshe.

Liao Qun 廖群. 2018. "Jianbo 'shuoti' gushi yu Zhongguo gudai 'xunyu' chuantong —— yi Beida jian *Zhouxun* wei lie" 簡帛「說體」故事與中國古代「訓語」傳統——以北大簡《周馴》為例. *Zhongnan minzu daxue xuebao* 38.4:73–78.

Liao, W.K. 1959. *The Complete Works of Han Fei Tzu*, vol. II. London: Arthur Probsthain.

Lin Qingyuan 林清源. 2019. "Shi Beida Hanjian (san) *Zhouxun* 'fei jue wu ji' —— bing shi *Shi, Zhaonan, Xinglu* shei wei que wu jiao" 釋北大漢簡（參）《周馴》「非爵勿羈」——兼釋《詩·召南·行露》「誰謂雀無角」. *Wen yu zhe* 文與哲 34:41–82.

Lin Jianming 林劍鳴. 1981. *Qinguo fazhan shi* 秦國發展史. Xi'an: Shanxi renmin chubanshe.

Lin Zhipeng 林志鵬. 2015. "Beijing Daxue cang XiHan zhushu *Zhouxun* yanjiu er ti" 北京大學藏西漢竹書《周訓》研究二題. *Jianbo wenxian yu gudai shi – Di er jie chutu wenxian qingnian xuezhe guoji luntan lunwenji* 簡帛文獻與古代史——第二屆出土文獻青年學者國際論壇論文集, ed. Fudan daxue lishixuexi Fudan daxue chutuwenxian yu gu wenzi yanjiu zhongxin, 192–201. Shanghai: Fudan daxue chubanshe.

Ling Xiang 凌襄. 1974. "Shi lun Mawangdui Han mu boshu *Yi Yin. Jiu Zhu*" 試論馬王堆漢墓帛書《伊尹·九主》. *Wenwu* 11:21–44.

Liu Guozhong. 2016. *Introduction to the Tsinghua Bamboo-Strip Manuscripts*, trans. Christopher J. Foster William N. French. Leiden: Brill.

Liu, Ts'ui-Jung. 2015. *Local Realities and Environmental Changes in the History of East Asia*. London & New York: Routledge.

Liu Xiaogan. 1991. "Wuwei (Non-Action): From *Laozi* to *Huainanzi*." *Taoist Resources* 3.1: 41–56.

———. 2015. "Laozi's Philosophy: Textual and Conceptual Analyses." In *Dao Companion to Daoist Philosophy*, ed. Liu Xiaogan, 71–110. New York: Springer.

Liu Zehua 劉澤華. 2020. *Zhongguo zhengzhi sixiangshi. Xianqin juan* 中國政治思想史. 先秦卷. Hangzhou: Zhejiang renmin chubanshe.

Loewe, Michael. 2010. "Social Distinctions, Groups and Privileges." In *China's Early Empires: a Re-Appraisal*, ed. Michael Nylan et al. Cambridge: Cambridge University Press.

———. 2016. *Problems of Han Administration: Ancestral Rites, Weights and Measures, and the Means of Protest*. Leiden: Brill.

Loy, Hui-Chieh. 2013. "From 'Elevating the Worthy' to 'Intimacy with Officers' in the *Mozi*." In *The Mozi as an Evolving Text: Different Voices in Early Chinese Thought*, eds. Carine Defoort and Nicolas Standaert, 205–236. Leiden: Brill.

Lü Zongli 呂宗力. 2016. *Handai de yaoyan* 漢代的謠言. Hangzhou: Zhejiang daxue chubanshe.

Luo Changpei 羅常培 and Zhou Zumo 周祖謨. 2007. *Han Wei Jin Naibeichao yunbu yanbian yanjiu* 漢魏晉南北朝韻部演變研究. Beijing: Zhonghua shuju.

Luo Xinhui. 2015. "Omens and Politics: The Zhou Concept of the Mandate of Heaven as Seen in the *Chengwu* 程寤 Manuscript." In *Ideology of Power and Power of Ideology in Early China*, eds. Yuri Pines et al., 49–68. Leiden: Brill.

Ma Nan 馬楠. 2017. "*Jin Wen Gong ru yu Jin* shu lüe" 《晉文公入于晉》述略. *Wenwu* 3:90–92.

Major, John S. 1993. *Heaven and Earth in Early Han Thought: Chapters Three, Four, and Five of the Huainanzi*. Albany: State University of New York Press.

———. 2010. "Surveying Obscurities." In *The Huainanzi: A Guide to the Theory and Practice of Government in Early Han China*, eds. John S. Major, Sarah A. Queen, Andrew Seth Meyer, and Harold D. Roth, 207–231. New York: Columbia University Press.

———, and Constance A. Cook. 2017. *Ancient China: A History*. Abingdon, Oxon ; New York, NY : Routledge.

Mao Zhenhua 毛振華. 2011. *Zuozhuan fu Shi yanjiu* 《左傳》賦詩研究. Shanghai: Shanghai guji chubanshe.

Mawangdui Hanmu boshu zhengli xiaozu 馬王堆漢墓帛書整理小組, ed. 1976. *Zhanguo zonghengjia shu* 戰國縱橫家書. Beijing: Zhongguo qingnian chubanshe.

Mazanek, Thomas. 2018. "Righting, Riting, and Rewriting *the Book of Odes* (*Shijing*): On 'Filling out the Missing Odes' by Shu Xi." *Chinese Literature: Essays, Articles, Reviews* 40:5–32.

McLeod, Alexus. 2021. *The Dao of Madness: Mental Illness and Self-Cultivation in Early Chinese Philosophy and Medicine*. Oxford: Oxford University Press.

Meisterernst, Barbara. 2002. "Eine Übersetzung der Yüeh-yü Sektion des *Kuo-yü*." In *Und folge nun dem, was mein Herz begehrt: Festschrift für Ulrich Unger zum 70. Geburtstag*, eds. Reinhard Emmerich and Hans Stumpfeldt, 2:509–542. Hamburg: Hamburger Sinologische Gesellschaft

Meyer, Dirk. 2012. *Philosophy on Bamboo: Text and the Production of Meaning in Early China*. Leiden: Brill.

———. 2014. "The Art of Narrative and the Rhetoric of Persuasion in the '*Jīnténg' (Metal Bound Casket) from the Qinghua Collection of Manuscripts." *Asiatische Studien* 68.4:937–988.
———. 2017a. "Recontextualization and Memory Production: Debates on Rulership as Reconstructed from "Guming" 顧命." In *Origins of Chinese Political Philosophy: Studies in the Composition and Thought of the Shangshu (Classic of Shangshu)*, eds. Martin Kern and Dirk Meyer, 106–145. Leiden: Brill.
———. 2017b. ""Shu" Traditions and Text Recomposition: A Reevaluation of "Jinteng" 金縢 and "Zhou Wu Wang you ji" 周武王有疾." In *Origins of Chinese Political Philosophy: Studies in the Composition and Thought of the Shangshu (Classic of Shangshu)*, eds. Martin Kern and Dirk Meyer, 224–248. Leiden: Brill.
———. 2018. "Patterning Meaning": A Thick Description of the Tsinghua Manuscript "*Tāng zài Chì/Dì mén" (Tāng was at the Chì/Dì Gate) and What It Tells Us about Thought Production in Early China." *Bulletin of the Jao Tsung-I Academy of Sinology* 5: 139–167.
Milburn, Olivia. 2010. *The Glory of Yue: An Annotated Translation of the Yuejue shu*. Leiden: Brill.
———. 2016a. *The Spring and Autumn Annals of Master Yan*. Leiden: Brill.
———. 2016b. "The *Xinian*: An Ancient Historical Text from the Qinghua University Collection of Bamboo Books." *Early China* 39:53–109.
Miller, Harry. 2015. *The Gongyang Commentary on The Spring and Autumn Annals: A Full Translation*. Basingstoke: Palgrave Macmillan.
Nienhauser, William H. Jr., ed. 1994a. *The Grand Scribe's Records Vol. I: The Basic Annals of Pre-Han China*. Bloomington & Indianapolis: Indiana University Press.
———, ed. 1994b. *The Grand Scribe's Records Vol. VII: The Memoirs of Pre-Han China*. Bloomington: Indiana University Press.
———, ed. 2006. *The Grand Scribe's Records Vol. V.1: The Hereditary Houses of Pre-Han China, Part I by Ssu-ma Ch'ien*. Bloomington: Indiana University Press.
Nivison, David S. 1996. *The Ways of Confucianism: Investigations in Chinese Philosophy*. Peru: Open Court Publishing Company.
Nylan, Michael. 2001. *The Five "Confucian" Classics*. New Haven: Yale University Press.
———. 2010. "The Many Dukes of Zhou in Early Sources." In *Statecraft and Classical Learning: The Rituals of Zhou in East Asian History*, eds. Benjamin A. Elman and Martin Kern, 94–128. Leiden: Brill.
Pankenier, David W. 2013. *Astrology and Cosmology in Early China: Conforming Earth to Heaven*. New York: Cambridge University Press.
Pines, Yuri. 2002. *Foundations of Confucian Thought: Intellectual Life in the Chunqiu Period, 722-453 B.C.E.* University of Hawaii Press.
———. 2005a. "Disputers of Abdication: Zhanguo Egalitarianism and the Sovereign's Power." *T'oung Pao* 41:243–300.
———. 2005b. "Speeches and the Question of Authenticity in Ancient Chinese Historical Records." In *Historical Truth, Historical Criticism, and Ideology: Chinese Historiography and Historical Culture from a New Comparative Perspective*, eds. Helwig Schmidt-Glintzer, Achim Mittag, and Jörn Rüsen, 197–226. Leiden: Brill.

_____. 2005/2006. "Biases and Their Sources: Qin History in the *Shiji*." *Oriens Extremus* 45:10–34.

_____. 2009. *Envisioning Eternal Empire: Chinese Political Thought of the Warring States Era*. Honolulu: University of Hawai'i Press.

_____. 2013a. "Between Merit and Pedigree: Evolution of the Concept of 'Elevating the Worthy' in pre-imperial China." In *The East Asian Challenge for Democracy: Political Meritocracy in Comparative Perspective*, eds. Daniel Bell and Li Chenyang, 161–202. Cambridge: Cambridge University Press.

_____. 2013b. "Submerged by Absolute Power: The Ruler's Predicament in the *Han Feizi*." In *Dao Companion to the Philosophy of Han Fei*, ed. Paul Goldin, 67–86. New York Springer.

_____. 2014. with Lothar von Falkenhausen, Gideon Shelach, and Robin D. S. Yates, "General Introduction: Qin History Revisited." In *Birth of an Empire: The State of Qin Revisited*, eds. Yuri Pines, Lothar von Falkenhausen, Gideon Shelach, and Robin D.S. Yates, 1–34. Berkeley: University of California Press.

_____. 2017. *The Book of Lord Shang: Apologetics of State Power in Early China*. New York: Columbia University Press.

_____. 2020. *Zhou History Unearthed: The Bamboo Manuscript Xinian and Early Chinese Historiography*. New York: Columbia University Press.

Qian Mu 錢穆. 2001. *Shiji diming kao* 史記地名考. Beijing: Shangwu yinshuguan.

Queen, Sarah A. 2013. "*Han Feizi* and the Old Master: A Comparative Analysis and Translation of *Han Feizi* Chapter 20, "Jie Lao," and Chapter 21, "Yu Lao."" In *Dao Companion to the Philosophy of Han Fei*, edited by Paul R. Goldin, 197–256. New York: Springer.

_____, John S. Major and Michael Puett. 2010. "Boundless Discourses." In *The Huainanzi: A Guide to the Theory and Practice of Government in Early Han China*, eds. John S. Major, Sarah A. Queen, Andrew Seth Meyer, and Harold D. Roth, 490–526. New York: Columbia University Press.

Raphals, Lisa. 2013. *Divination and Prediction in Early China and Ancient Greece*. Cambridge: Cambridge University Press.

Rickett, W. Allyn. 1993. "*Kuan tzu* 管子." In *Early Chinese Texts: A Bibliographical Guide*, ed. Michael Loewe, 244–251. Berkeley: Institute of East Asian Studies.

Riegel, Jeffrey. 1997. "Eros, Introversion, and the Beginnings of *Shijing* Commentary." *Harvard Journal of Asiatic Studies* 57.1:143–177.

Rohsenow, John S. 2001. "Proverbs." In *The Columbia History of Chinese Literature*, ed. Victor H. Mair, 149–159. New York: Columbia University Press.

Roth, Harold D. 2021. *The Contemplative Foundations of Classical Daoism*. Albany: State University of New York Press.

Sabattini, Elisa. 2009. "Prenatal Instructions and Moral Education of the Crown Prince in the "Xinshu" by Jia Yi." *Oriens Extremus* 48:71–86.

Sawyer, Ralph D. and Mei-chün Sawyer. 1993. *The Seven Military Classics of Ancient China*. Boulder: Westview Press.

Schaab-Hanke, Dorothee. 2010. *Der Geschichtsschreiber als Exeget: Facetten der frühen chinesischen Historiographie*. Gossenberg: Ostasien Verlag.

Schaberg, David. 2001. *A Patterned Past: Form and Thought in Early Chinese Historiography*. Cambridge, Mass.; London: Harvard University Asia Center.

_____. 2011. "Chinese History and Philosophy." In *The Oxford History of Historical Writing, Volume 1: Beginnings to AD 600*, eds. Andrew Feldherr and Grant Hardy, 394–414. Oxford: Oxford University Press.

_____. 2015. "On the Range and Performance of *Laozi*-Style Tetrasyllables." In *Literary Forms of Argument in Early China*, eds. Joachim Gentz and Dirk Meyer, 87–111. Leiden: Brill.

_____. 2017. "Speaking of Documents: *Shu* Citations in Warring States Texts." In *Origins of Chinese Political Philosophy: Studies in the Composition and Thought of the Shangshu (Classic of Shangshu)*, eds. Martin Kern and Dirk Meyer, 320–359. Leiden: Brill..

Schwermann, Christian. 2007. "Feigned Madness, Self-Preservation and Covert Censure in Early China." In *Zurück zur Freude. Studien zur chinesischen Literatur und Lebenswelt und ihrer Rezeption in Ost und West. Festschrift für Wolfgang Kubin*, eds. Marc Hermann, Christian Schwermann, and Jari Grosse-Ruyken, 531–572. St. Augustin, Nettetal: Steyler Verlag.

Schuessler, Axel. 2009. *Minimal Old Chinese and Later Han Chinese: A Companion to Grammata Serica Recensa*. Honolulu: University of Hawai'i Press.

_____ and Michael Loewe. 1993. "*Yüeh chüeh shu* 越絕書." In *Early Chinese Texts: A Bibliographical Guide*, ed. Michael Loewe. Berkeley: Institute of East Asian Studies, 490–493.

Seidel, Anna. 1978. "Der Kaiser und sein Ratgeber. Lao tzu and der Taoismus der Han-Zeit." *Saeculum* 29.1:18–50.

Shaughnessy, Edward L. 1993. "*Shang shu* 尚書 (*Shu jing* 書經)." In *Early Chinese Texts: A Bibliographical Guide*, ed. Michael Loewe, 376–389. Berkeley: Institute of East Asian Studies.

_____. 1997. *I Ching: the Classic of Changes*. New York: Ballantine Books.

_____. 1999. "Western Zhou History." In *The Cambridge History of Ancient China: From the Origins of Civilization to 221 B.C.*, eds. Michael Loewe and Edward L. Shaughnessy, 292–351. Cambridge: Cambridge University Press.

_____. 2015. "Unearthed Documents and the Question of the Oral versus Written Nature of the Classic of Poetry." *Harvard Journal of Asiatic Studies* 75.2: 331–375.

_____. 2021. "A First Reading of the Anhui University Bamboo-Slip *Shi jing*." *Bamboo and Silk* 4.1: 1–44.

Shiji. Beijing: Zhonghua shuju, 1959.

Shuihudi Qin mu zhujian zhengli xiaozu 睡虎地秦墓竹簡整理小組, ed.1990. *Shuihudi Qin mu zhujian* 睡虎地秦墓竹簡. Beijing: Wenwu chubanshe.

Slingerland, Edward. 2003. *Confucius Analects*. Indianapolis/Cambridge: Hackett Publishing Company.

Sommer, Deborah. 2003. "Ritual and Sacrifice in Early Confucianism: Contacts with the Spirit World." In *Confucian Spirituality. Vol. One.*, eds. Tu Weiming and Mary Evelyn Tucker, 197–219. New York: Crossroad Publishing.

Sou, Daniel S. (Suh Sungbin 徐誠彬). 2013. "Shaping Qin Local Officals: Exploring the System of Values and Responsibilities Presented in the Excavated Qin Tomb Bamboo Strips." *Monumenta Serica* 61:1–13.

Smith, Jonathan. 2015. "Sound Symbolism in the Reduplicative Vocabulary of the *Shijing*." *Journal of Chinese Literature and Culture* 2(2): 258–285.

Staack, Thies. 2010. "Reconstructing the *Kongzi shilun*: From the Arrangement of the Bamboo Slips to a Tentative Translation." *Asiatische Studien Studes Asiatiques* LXIV.4: 857–906.

_____. 2015. "Identifying Codicological Sub-units in Bamboo Manuscripts: Verso Lines Revisited." *Manuscript Cultures* 8:157–186.

_____. 2017. "Could the Peking University *Laozi* 老子 Really be a Forgery? Some Skeptical Remarks." http://www.ub.uni-heidelberg.de/archiv/22453. (accessed April 20, 2022.)

_____. 2018. "Single- and Multi-Piece Manuscripts in Early Imperial China: On the Background and Significance of a Terminological Distinction." *Early China* 41: 245–295.

Su Jian-Zhou 蘇建洲. 2017. "Lun *Beida Han jian (san) Zhouxun* de chaoben niandai, diben laiyuan yiji chengpian guocheng" 論《北大漢簡（三）·周馴》的抄本年代、底本來源以及成篇過程. In *Di shijie Handai wenxue yu sixiang ji Zhengda zhongwenxi chuangxi liushi zhounian guoji xueshu yantaohui* 第十屆漢代文學與思想暨政大中文系創系六十週年國際學術研討會, ed. *Guoli Zhengzhi daxue zhongguo wenxue xi* 國立政治大學中國文學系, 229–262. Taipei: Zhengda zhongwenxi chuban she.

Sun Feiyan. 2021. "On the Nature of the Tsinghua Bamboo-Slip Manuscript *Chi jiu zhi ji Tang zhi wu*." Tr. Hin Ming Frankie Chik. *Bamboo and Silk* 4.2:246–270.

Sun Yirang 孫詒讓, ed. 2001. *Mozi xiangu* 墨子閒詁. Beijing: Zhonghua chubanshe.

_____. 2015. *Zhouli zhengyi* 周禮正義. Beijing: Zhonghua shuju.

Svarverud, Rune. 1998. *Methods of the Way: Early Chinese Ethical Thought*. Leiden: Brill.

Taskin, V. S. 1987. *Rechi Tsarstv*. Moscow: Izdatel'stvo Nauka.

Tjan, Tjoe Som195. 2. *Po Hu T'ung: The Comprehensive Discussions in the White Tiger Hall*, Vol. Two. Leiden: Brill.

Tong Shuye 童書業. 2019. *Chunqiu Zuozhuan yanjiu* 春秋左傳研究. Shanghai: Shanghai renmin chubanshe.

Tsai Ying-Ying 蔡瑩瑩. 2020. "*Lun Qinghua jian (qi). Yue Gong qi shi* de ticai jiegou yu renwen wenci" 論《清華簡（柒）·越公其事》的體裁結構與人物文辭. *Taida zhongwen xuebao* 臺大中文學報 71:53–106.

Tu, Wei-Ming. 1998. "Probing the "Three Bonds" and "Five Relationships" in Confucian Humanism." In *Confucianism and the Family*, eds. Walter H. Slote and George A. De Vos, 121–136. Albany: State University of New York Press.

Unschuld, Paul U. 2010. *Medicine in China: A History of Ideas. 25th Anniversary Edition, With a New Preface*. Berkeley: University of California Press

Van Auken, Newell Ann. 2014. "Killings and Assassinations in the *Spring and Autumn* as Records of Judgment." *Asia Major* 27.1:1–31.

———. 2016. *The Commentarial Transformation of the Spring and Autumn*. Albany: State University of New York Press.

van Els, Paul. 2018. *The Wenzi: Creativity and Intertextuality in Early Chinese Philosophy*. Leiden: Brill.

Van Zoeren, Stephen. 1991. *Poetry and Personality: Reading, Exegesis, and Hermeneutics in Traditional China*. Stanford, CA: Stanford University Press.

Vankeerberghen, Griet. 2007. "Rulership and Kinship: the *Shangshu dazhuan*'s Discourse on Lords." *Oriens Extremus* 46:84–100.

Vermander, Benoît. 2022. *Comment lire les classiques chinois ?* Paris: Les Belles Lettres.

Vyatkin, Rudolf V., trans. 1992. *Istoricheskie Zapiski (Shi-czi) [Исторические записки (Ши-цзи)]*, Vol. 6. Moscow: Nauka.

———. 1996. *Istoricheskie Zapiski (Shi-czi) [Исторические записки (Ши-цзи)]*, Vol. 7. Moscow: Nauka.

Wagner, Rudolf. 2000. *The Craft of a Chinese Commentator*. Albany: State University of New York Press.

———. 2015. "A Building Block of Chinese Argumentation: Initial Fu 夫 as a Phrase Status Marker." In *Literary Forms of Argument in Early China*, eds. Joachim Gentz and Dirk Meyer. Leiden: Brill.

Waley, Arthur. 1960. *The Book of Songs: The Ancient Chinese Classic of Poetry*. New York: Grove Press.

———. 1973. *The Nine Songs: A Study of Shamanism in Ancient China*. San Francisco: City Lights Books.

Wang Bo 王博. 1996. "Guanyu *Wenzi* de jige wenti" 關於《文子》的幾個問題. *Zhexue yu wenhua* 哲學與文化 8:1908–1914.

———, ed. 2011. *Zhongguo Ruxue shi. Xian Qin juan* 中國儒學史. 先秦史. Beijing: Beijing daxue chubanshe.

Wang Liqi 王利器. 2002. *Lüshi chunqiu zhushu* 呂氏春秋注疏. Chengdu: Ba Shu shushe.

———, and Wang Zhenmin 王貞珉. 1988. *Hanshu Gujinrenbiao shuzheng* 漢書古今人表疏證. Jinan: Qi Lu shushe.

Wang Li 王力. 2000. *Wang Li gu Hanyu zidian* 王力古漢語字典. Beijing: Zhonghua shuju.

Wang Xianshen 王先慎, ed. 2003. *Hanfeizi jijie* 韓非子集解. Beijing: Zhonghua shuju.

Wang Xianqian 王先謙. 1988. *Xunzi jijie* 荀子集解. Beijing: Zhonghua shuju.

Watson, Burton. 1993. *Records of the Grand Historian: Han Dynasty II*. Hong Kong, New York: Columbia University Press.

———. 2013. *The Complete Works of Zhuangzi*. New York: Columbia University Press.

Wilhelm, Richard. 1971. *Lü Bu We Chunqiu – Frühling und Herbst des Lü Bu We*. Düsseldorf/Köln: Diederichs.

Wolff, Ernst. 1999. "I-wen chih" 藝文志. In *The Indiana Companion to Traditional Chinese Literature*. Vol. 2, ed. William H. Nienhauser, Jr. Taipei: SMC Publishing, 63–68.

Wu Yujiang 吳毓江. 1993. *Mozi jiaozhu* 墨子校注. Beijing: Zhonghua shuju.

Wu Rongzeng 吳榮曾. 1995. *Xian Qin Liang Han shi yanjiu* 先秦兩漢史研究. Beijing: Zhonghua shuju.

Wu Hsueh-ju 巫雪如. 2019. "Cong ruogan zi yongfa tan Qinghua jian *Xinian* de zuozhe ji wenben goucheng" 從若干字詞用法談清華簡《繫年》的作者及文本構成. *Tsing Hua Journal of Chinese Studies* 清華學報 49.2:187–227.

Wu Zeyu 吳則虞. 1982. *Yanzi chunqiu jishi* 晏子春秋集釋. Beijing: Zhonghua shuju.

Xiang Zonglu 向宗魯, ed. 1987. *Shuoyuan jiaozheng* 說苑校證. Beijing: Zhonghua shuju.

Xing Wen 邢文. 2016. "Beida jian 'Laozi' bianwei" 北大簡《老子》辨偽. *Guangming ribao* 光明日報, August 8.

Xu Renfu 徐仁甫. 2014. *Gushu yinyu yanjiu* 古書引語研究. Beijing: Zhonghua shuju.

Xu Tanhui 許錟輝. 2009. *Xian Qin dianji yin Shangshu kao* 先秦典籍引《尚書》考. Yongheshi: Huamulan wenhua chubanshe.

Xu Weiyu 許維遹, ed. 1980. *Han Shi waizhuan jishi* 韓詩外傳集釋. Beijing: Zhonghua shuju.

Xu Yuangao 徐元誥. 2002. *Guoyu jijie* 國語集解. Beijing: Zhonghua shuju.

Xu Zaiguo 徐在國. 2017. "Anhui daxue can Zhanguo zhujian *Shijing* shixu yu yiwen" 安徽大學藏戰國竹簡《詩經》詩序與異文. *Wenwu* 9:60–62.

Yan Buke 閻步克. 2011a. "Beida zhushu *Zhouxun* jianjie" 北大竹書《周馴》簡介. *Wenwu* 2011.6: 71–74.

———. 2011b. "'Wei sui dong xiang jia zhi ri' yu 'lang zhi ming ri' xiao kao" 「維歲冬享駕之日」與「䏩之明日」小考. *Zhongguo wenhua* 中國文化 33:30–34.

———. 2012a. "'Bu kuang bu long', 'Da zhi si kuang' kao" 「不狂不聾」、「大智似狂」考. In *Gudai jiandu baohu yu zhengli yanjiu* 古代簡牘保護與整理研究, ed. Qinghua daxue chutu wenxian yanjiu yu baohu zhongxin 清華大學出土文獻研究與保護中心, 299–308. Shanghai: Zhongxi shuju.

———. 2012b. "Shi shi 'fei jun wu jia, fei jue wu (tai)' jian lun 'wo you hao jun, wu yu er mi zhi—Beida zhushu *Zhouxun* zhaji zhi san'" 試釋「非駿勿駕,非爵勿(駘)」兼論「我有好爵,吾與爾靡之」——北大竹書《周訓》札記之三. In *Gudai jiandu baohu yu zhengli yanjiu*, ed. Qinghua daxue chutu wenxian yanjiu yu baohu zhongxin, 309–324. Shanghai: Zhongxi shuju.

Yan Zhenyi 閻振益 and Zhong Xia 鍾夏, ed. 2000. *Xinshu jiaozhu* 新書校注. Beijing: Zhonghua shuju.

Yang Bojun 楊伯峻, ed. 1995. *Chunqiu Zuozhuan zhu* 春秋左傳注. Beijing: Zhonghua shuju.

Yang Kuan 楊寬. 2001. *Zhanguo shiliao biannian jizheng* 戰國史料編年輯證. Shanghai: Shanghai renmin chubanshe.

Yang Tianyu 楊天宇, ed. 2004. *Liji yizhu* 禮記譯注. Shanghai: Shanghai guji chubanshe.

Yates, Robin D. S. 1997. *Five Lost Classics: Tao, Huanglao, and Yin-yang in Han China*. New York: Ballantine Books.

_____. 2002. "Slavery in Early China: A Socio-Cultural Approach." *Journal of East Asian Archaeology* 3.1–2:283–331.

Yin Guoguang 殷國光. 2008. *Lüshi chunqiu cilei yanjiu* 呂氏春秋詞類研究. Beijing: Shangwu yinshuguan.

Yuan, Ai. 2022. "Rhetorical Questions in the *Daodejing*: Argument Construction, Dialogical Insertion, and Sentimental Expression." *Religions* 13.3: 252; https://doi.org/10.3390/rel13030252.

Yuan Qing 袁青. 2017. "Lun Beida Han jian *Zhouxun* de HuangLao xue sixiang" 論北大漢簡《周訓》的黃老學思想. *Zhongguo zhexue shi* 中國哲學史 3:69–74.

_____. 2020. "Qinghua jian *Yue Gong qi shi* yu xian Qin HuangLao xue de zhengzhi sixiang" 清華簡《越公其事》與先秦黃老學的政治思想. *Zhengzi yu wenhua* 哲學與文化 47.6:181–194.

Zhang Fengqian 張豐乾. 2007. *Chutu wenxian yu Wenzi gongan* 出土文獻與文子公案. Beijing: Shehui kexue wenxian chubanshe.

Zhang Hanmo 張瀚墨. 2017. "Yujing, xiuci yu guodu chanshi: 'rei jue wu' 'wo you hao jue' yiji yi niao ming guan de zhengzhi shenhua" 語境、修辭與過度闡釋:「非爵勿𩨬」「我有好爵」以及以鳥名官的政治神話. *Dongfang luntan* 東方論壇 1:49–61.

Zhang Jusan 張居三. 2020. *Guoyu wenxian yanjiu* 《國語》文獻研究 (The Academic Literature Study of Guoyu). Beijing: Zhongguo shehui kexue chubanshe.

Zhang Shuangdi 張雙棣. 1986. *Lüshi chunqiu yizhu* 呂氏春秋譯注. Changchun: Jilin wenshi chubanshe.

_____. 2008. *Lüshi chunqiu cihui yanjiu* 《呂氏春秋》詞彙研究. Beijing: Shangwu yinshuguan.

Zhang Xiancheng 張顯成. 2006. *Jianbo wenxianxue tonglun* 簡帛文獻學通論. Beijing: Zhonghua shuju.

Zhao Huacheng 趙化成. 2011. "BeiDa cang Xi Han zhushu *Zhao Zheng shu* jianshuo" 北大藏西漢竹書《趙正書》簡說. *Wenwu* 6:64–66.

Zhao Pingan 趙平安 and Shi Xiaoli 石小力. 2017. "Cheng Zhuan ji qi yu Zhao Jianzi de wendui — Qinghua jian *Zhao Jianzi* chutan" 成鱄及其與趙簡子的問對: 清華簡《趙簡子》初探. *Wenwu* 3:85–89.

Zhou Boqun. 2018. "A Translation and Analysis of the Shanghai Museum Manuscript *Wu Wang Jian Zuo," *Monumenta Serica* 66:1:1-31.

Zhou Shengchun 周生春. 1997. *Wu Yue chunqiu jijiao huikao* 吳越春秋輯校彙考. Shanghai: Shanghai guji chubanshe.

Index

"All-under-Heaven" (*tianxia*), 14, 29, 33-34, 69, 97, 101-02, 152, 182, 184, 191-92
Anhui University collection, 38, 147
"arbiter of faith" (*siming*), 184
Ban Gu, 74
Battle at Hanyuan, 127, 131-32
Beida manuscripts, *Fan Yin*, 1; *Laozi*, 1; *Wang Ji*, 1; *Zhao Zheng shu*, 1
brotherly piety (*ti*), 43-44, 57, 90-91, 175-76
Cang Tang (Ji's aide), 153-54
Cao (domain), 136, 141-42
chain argument (rhetorical figure), 32, 81, 165, 170
Chen Jian, 5, 181-82, 187, 198
Chengzhou (Zhou capital), 13-15, 19, 90, 95
Chu (state), 8, 26, 105, 108-11
Chu-Wu conflict, 105-11
Chunqiu, 130
Chunqiu, the Spring and Autumn Period, 50, 119, 180
City of Ru, also Jiaru (capital of the West Zhou), 13-14, 16, 90, 95, 150
clairvoyance (*ming*), 43-44, 66, 80, 85-86, 90, 93
commoners (*shuren*), 133, 193-94
compassion/parental love (*ci*), 34, 43-44, 50, 56, 120-21, 124-25, 150, 152, 175-77, 183-84, 187, 192
Confucianism (ruism), 59, 154
Confucius, 40, 82, 154
Da Dai Liji, 122
Dai (area in Zhao), 179

Dan Zhu (Yao's inept son), 26, 50-52, 54, 59, 156, 163, 181, 183, 187, 189
dark virtue (*xuan de*), 45
Daoism, 45, 72-74
"day of the year end's food offering ceremony" (*suizhong xianghe zhiri*), 11, 180, 182
Di tribes, 109
Dingzhou Bajiaolang manuscripts, 5
Documents (*shu*), education and: 057, 202; quotations of, 36-39, 62, 65-66, 68-70, 73-74, 79-84, 88, 90, 94-95, 120-24, 131-32, 134, 144-47, 149, 151, 153, 171, 178, 185, 197-98; *shu* genre and the *Zhouxun*, 12, 70, 202; *Zhouxun* accounts in the context of other *shu*, 98, 203
Du He (East Zhou official), 15
"earth pounder convicts" (*chengdan*), 7, 113, 115
East Zhou, 14, 16-21
(vital) energy (*qi*), 46, 78, 166, 181
Fengze meeting, 17-18
filial piety (*xiao*), 43-44, 50-51, 57, 60, 90, 102, 116, 151, 154, 176, 183, 187, 198, 203
"five hegemons," identity of, 28-29, 182, 193
ghosts (*gui*), 43-45, 181, 186, 199
good(ness) (*shan*), 43-44, 56, 59, 78, 89-92, 96, 113, 121, 125, 130, 175, 177, 184, 191
Gu Sou (Shun's father), 54-55
Gubu Ziqing (physiognomist in Zhao), 178-79
"Guming" (*Shangshu* chapter), 12

225

Guan Zhong, also Guan Yiwu (Qi official), 47, 67, 165, 167, 169-70
Guanzi, 74, 199
Guoyu, 40, 108
Ji (domain), 142
Jiang (Jin capital), 144-46
Jie (tyrant, last ruler of the Xia dynasty), 52, 97, 191
Jin (state), 26-27, 47, 49, 59, 119-20, 122, 126-29, 131, 142-43, 149
Jiufan, aka Zifan, aka Hu Yan (Jin dignitary), 47, 137, 139-40, 142
Han (state), 27, 60, 149
Han (dynasty), 6-7, 74
Han Chengdi, 70
Han Fei, 67, 86-87
Hanfeizi, 18, 20, 64-68, 74
Han Shi waizhuan, 108, 154, 178
Hanshu, 70, 72-74, 117; "Yiwenzhi," 72, 74
Han Wei, 2, 6, 21
Han Wudi, 5
Heaven (*tian*), 60, 66, 80, 83, 86, 89, 90-92, 95, 97, 121, 125, 129, 181, 183-85, 190-93, 197
heredity, 71, 189, 202
hereditary dynasties, 28, 95, 203
Hong Yao (Zhou dignitary), 47, 99-100
Hu Tu (Jin dignitary), 128
Huainanzi, 15, 69-70, 178
HuangLao (doctrine), 74
"Huang niao" (Mao 131), 163
human sacrifice (Qin funerary custom), 131, 155, 157, 163, 194
humanness (*ren*), 43-44, 50, 56-57, 89, 90-91, 120-25, 135, 139, 150, 152, 175-77, 183, 187
"hundred surnames" (*baixing*), 46-47, 90, 94, 120, 122-23, 158, 160, 166, 168
kindness (*hui*), 34-35, 43-44, 90, 120, 123, 133-34, 158, 160, 166, 168, 184, 192

King An of Zhou, 19
King Cheng of Zhou, 26-27, 165, 167, 169-72, as Song, 192-93
King Ding of Zhou, 19
King Fuchai of Wu, 111-14, 116-18
King Goujian of Yue, 26, 28-29, 32, 111-18, 180, 182, 185, 195-96
King Helü of Wu, 105-07, 111-17
King Hui of Qin, 17-18, 72, 204
King Kao of Zhou, 19
King Lie of Zhou, 19
King Nan of Zhou, 19-21
King Ping of Chu, 117
King Shenjing of Zhou, 20
King (Cheng) Tang of Shang, 26, 28-29, 33-34, 88-93, 96-98, 180, 182-83, 190-91, 201
King Weilie of Zhou, 19
King Wen of Zhou, 26-29, 48, 60, 69, 99-101, 103-04, 145, 149, 192, as Chang, 191-92
King Wu of Zhou, 26, 28, 69, 99, 101-04, 172, as Fa, 191-92
King Xian of Zhou, 20
King Zhao of Chu, 26, 28-29, 36, 105-09, 182, possibly: 196-98
King Zhuangxiang of Qin, 71-72, 204
La-sacrifice, 180; the day after, 11, 180-81, 186
Laozi, 1, 67, 73-74
Li Ji (Lord Xian of Jin's consort), 119, 127
Liye documents, 8
Lin Zhipeng, 21
leniency (*kuan*), 25, 43-44, 90, 132, 134-35, 166, 168
Ling Zhe (Jin official), 148
Liu Bang, 7
Liu Xiang, 72, 74, 117
Liu Xin, 74
Liutao, 74
longevity (*shou*), 45-46, 78, 81, 166, 168, 191

"looted" manuscripts, problematic status of, 1-2
Lord Gong of Cao, 26, 136-37, 139-42
Lord Jing of Qi, 142
Lord Huai of Jin, 127-28, as Yuzi 120, 122-24, 126-27
Lord Huan of Qi, 26, 29, 36, 165, 167-71, 180, 182, 186, 198-201
Lord Huan of West Zhou, 18-19
Lord Hui of Jin, 127-28; as Yiwu, 120, 122-24, 126-28
Lord Hui of East Zhou, 18-21
Lord Hui of West Zhou, 18-21
Lord Ling of Jin, 129, 143, 145-46, 148
Lord Mu of Qin, 26-27, 29, 48, 62, 127-28, 130-35, 155, 163, 180, 182, 184, 193-94
Lord Wei of West Zhou, 19
Lord Wen of Jin, 26-29, 62, 119, 122, 128-30, 136-141, 173, 182, possibly: 194-95; as Chong'er 120, 124
Lord Wen of West Zhou, 20
Lord Wu of West Zhou, 20-22
Lord Xian of Jin, 119-20, 122, 127
Lord Xiang of Jin, 129
Lord Xiao of Qin, 18, 155, 163-64
Lord Zhaowen of Zhou, 9-12, 13-018, 20-22, 23-28, 31, 32, 34-36, 39, 41, 43, 56-61, 62-63, 65, 71-72, 77, 81, 87, 88, 93-96, 99-102, 105-09, 111-12, 116, 119-20, 122, 124-26, 129, 130-31, 134, 136-37, 139, 141, 143-44, 149-54, 155-57, 159-63, 165-66, 170, 173-74, 176, 178, 180-82, 196-97, 200, 204
love/care (*ai*), 43-44, 50, 52, 54, 150-52, 154, 183-84, 187-89, 191-92
loyalty (*zhong*), 45
Lü Buwei, 71-72, 204
Lü Cang (East Zhou minister), 15

Lüshi chunqiu, 8, 15-19, 33, 35, 63-64, 68-72, 91, 116-17, 127, 131, 144, 204; sections of, "Ai shi," 63; "Baogeng," 15-16, 18-19, 21-22, 63, 144; "Shenda," 68; "Shiwei," 68-69
madness (*kuang*), 65, 73, 79, 82, 84
mandate of Heaven (*tian ming*), 22, 60-61, 71, 104, 176, 192, 203
Marquis Wen of Wei, 26, 30, 149-54, 173
Marquis Wu of Wei, 151, 153; as Ji (Marquis Wen's son) 150-54 ; as Lord of Zhongshan, 150-52
Marquis Xian of Zhao, 179
masses (*zhong*), 34, 46-47, 69, 90, 94, 120-25, 166, 184, 191
Mencius (philosopher), 129
Mengzi, 60
meritocracy, 12, 50, 55, 71, 202
Mount Qi, 100-01, 109
Mozi, 7
naturalness (*ziran*), 45, 74
"nine fields" (*jiuye*), 184
Noble Scion Jiu (Lord Huan of Qi's brother), 167
non-action (*wuwei*), 45, 74
Odes (*shi*), quotation of, 36-39; 062, 65-66, 68, 70, 73-74, 79-86, 105, 107-08, 144-47, 156-57, 159, 171, 185, 197
officers (*shi*), 17, 46-47, 71, 112, 115, 144-46
parallelism (antithetical), 33-35, 38, 84-86, 125, 152, 177-78, 181, 190-92, 194, 200
Pengzu, quotations of, 36, 39, 78, 81, 83
people (*min*), 35, 46-47, 54, 56, 64, 69, 78-79, 89, 91, 94, 106-09, 116, 112-13, 120-21, 123, 125-26, 130, 157, 160, 166, 174-75, 177-78, 183-86, 188, 191, 196, 199
Pi (corrupt Wu official), 117

Pines, Yuri, 50, 67
primogeniture, 14, 30, 46, 49, 204
Prince Gong, 9-12, 13-16, 18, 20-22, 23-25, 27, 34-35, 39, 41, 45, 56-59, 71, 77, 88, 93-95, 98, 100, 105-07, 112, 120, 124-25, 129, 131, 136-37, 139, 144, 149-50, 152-53, 156-57, 159, 161, 165-66, 170, 173-74, 176, 182, 200
propriety/ritual (*li*), 43-44, 101, 183, 189
proverbs (*yan*), 36, 38-39, 62, 65, 81-87, 174-75, 178, 186, 198-99
Qi (Marquis Wen of Wei's favorite son), 150-52
Qi (Yu's son), 26, 29, 55, 88-89, 92-93, 97-98, 183, 189, 201
Qi lüe, 74
Qin (dynasty), 6-7
Qin (state), 8, 17-18, 22, 26-27, 30, 49, 71-72, 108, 119, 120, 127-28, 130-35, 155-57, 159-60, 162-64, 193-94, 203-04
Qin Shi Huangdi, 71-72
Qing Zheng (Jin official), 135
rhetorical questions, 24, 35, 63, 92, 99, 101-02, 105, 107-08, 131, 134, 144, 147, 157, 162, 165, 190-92
rhymes, 32-33, 38, 91, 93-94, 102, 107, 114, 122, 124-26, 134, 139, 147, 152, 159-62, 169-70, 177-78, 181, 187-200
righteousness (*yi*), 43-44, 89-91, 183, 189
Rong tribes, 130
Ruo (capital of Chu), 108
"rustics" (*yeren*) from Qin, 131-135
sagacity (*sheng*), 43-44, 90, 93, 101, 186, 199, 200
san Jin, "three Jin," 8, 150, 152
Shang (dynasty), 26, 33, 51-52, 60, 81, 88, 95, 98, 190, 196, 203; as Yin, 195

Shanghai Museum collection, 1-2
Shang Jun (Shun's inept son), 26, 54, 59, 156, 183, 188-89
Shangdi, Lord on High, 97
Shangjun shu, 197
Shangshu, 11, 25, 37, 50, 60, 96, 122, 155, 189
Shenzi, 82
Shi Miming (Jin official), 148
Shi valley, 184
Shiji, 15-16, 18-22, 103-04, 108, 126, 128, 135, 141-42, 148, 153, 155, 162-64, 178, 180, 189, 191; chapters of, "Tianguan shu," 180
Shijing, 37-38, 60, 68, 82-83, 108, 147, 154, 156, 159; quoted poems: "Ban" (Mao 254), 38, 108, 197; "Bozhou" (Mao 26), 38, 83; "Jingzhi" (Mao 288), 38, 83, 86; "Tuju" (Mao 7), 38, 147; "Wen-wang" (Mao 235), 38, 147; "Yi" (Mao 256), 38, 156
Shun (sage king), 26, 28-29, 50-55, 59, 71, 155-57, 158, 161-62, 180, 182-83, 187-189
Shuoyuan, 154
Sima Qian, 18, 135
"six kings and five hegemons" (*liuwang wuba*), 11, 28-31, 181-82, 186, 200
"small chapters" (*xiao zhang*), 180-82
sons by concubine (*nie*), 71, 156-57, 163-64, 204
"Son(s) of Heaven" (*tianzi*), 14, 18-19, 142, 149
spirit(s) (*shen*), 33-34, 43-45, 180-81, 183-84, 186, 190-91
Staack, Thies, 7-8
Su Jian-Zhou, 7
subordinates (*xia*), 46-47, 64-66, 78-81, 84, 86, 120, 122-23, 126-27, 136, 184

Tai Jia (King Tang's successor), 26, 29, 33-34, 88-91, 96, 98, 183, 190-91, 201
Taiping yulan, 82, 178
Tian lineage, usurping power in Qi, 181, 200-01
trustworthiness (*xin*), 34-35, 121, 125, 166, 168
Tsinghua University collection, 1-2, 83, 118, 153, 178; *Baoxun*, 12; *Huang men*, 153; *Xinian*, 118, 127; *Yue Gong qi shi*, 118; *Zhao Jianzi*, 178; *Zhougong zhi qinwu*, 83
virtue(-inspired gratitude) (*de*), 17, 43, 49, 78, 90, 94, 107, 120, 123, 128, 132, 134, 145-46, 158, 160, 183, 185, 189, 197
Way (*Dao*), 44, 46, 66-67, 74, 137, 141, 186, 199
Wei (state), 26-27, 30, 49, 60, 149-52, 155, 203
Weili zhidao (excavated manuscript), 82
West Zhou, 14, 16, 18-21
wisdom (*zhi*), 43-44, 47, 65, 73, 79, 81-82, 84, 120, 123
worthies (*xian*): ministers, 17, 28, 47, 50, 55-56, 97-99, 128, 130, 136-36, 139, 142-43, 156, 167-68, 170, 177, 198, 202; rulers: 42, 45-47, 57, 80, 85-86, 137, 140, 158, 162-63, 175, 186, 199, 201-02, 204; sons/successors: 14, 30-31, 41-42, 45, 48, 50, 53-54, 56, 59-60, 65, 68, 93, 96, 98, 100-01, 104, 150-54, 173, 183, 187, 202
worthiness (*xian*), 30, 43-44, 48-49, 51-53, 56, 60, 71-72, 101, 103-04, 149, 151, 154, 156, 158, 162, 174, 176, 202
Wu (state), also called Han after its capital, 7, 70, 105-12, 114-15, 185, 195

"Wuwang jianzuo" (*Da Dai Liji* chapter), 196
Wu-Yue conflict, 70, 116-19
Wu Qi (official in a number of Zhanguo states), 67
Wuxing (excavated manuscript), 86, 93
Wu Zixu (Wu minister), 117
Xi Fuji (Cao official), 136, 142
Xiqi (Lord Xian of Jin's son), 119-20, 122-24, 126-27
Xizhe junlao (excavated manuscript), 12, 67
Xia dynasty, 26, 28, 51-52, 60, 88, 95, 97, 203
Xiang (Shun's younger brother), 55
"Xiaomin" (Mao 195), 38, 68, 83, 86
"Xiaoya" (*Shijing* section), 83
Xinshu, 109
Xun Xi (Jin minister), 127
Xunzi (philosopher), 52
Yan (Jin Diviner), 128
Yanzi, Master Yan (Qi official), 142
Yanzi chunqiu, 122, 142
Yao (sage king), 25-26, 29-30, 50-55, 71, 155-58, 161-64, 181-83, 187-89
Yellow Emperor (Huangdi), 74
Yi (Yu's minister), 55, 97-98
Yi Zhoushu, 69, 122
Yikao the Elder (Bo Yikao; King Wen's eldest son), 103-04
Yi Yin (Shang minister), 67, 96
Ying (Chu capital), 105-09
Yu (legendary founder of the Xia dynasty), 26, 28-29, 54-55, 59, 88-89, 92-93, 97-98, 156, 162, 180, 182-83, 188-89, 201
Yue (state) 7, 26, 29, 70, 108, 111-18, 119, 195-96, 203
Zhanguo, the Warring States Period, 7-8, 12, 25, 27, 30, 50, 61, 103, 111, 118, 134, 149, 202-04
Zhanguo ce, 8, 15-16, 22

Zhang Yi (Qin minister), 15, 17-18
Zhao (lineage; state), 26-27, 30, 49, 56-57, 59-60, 173, 175
Zhao Dun, also Zhao Xuanzi or Zhao Xuanmeng, 26-27, 30, 62, 143-145, 148, 149, 173
(Zhao) Bolu (Zhao Yang's eldest son), 173, 175-78
Zhao Xiangzi, 30, 56-59, 175-76, 179; as Wuxu, 56-59, 173-78
Zhao Yang, also Zhao Jianzi (head of the Zhao lineage), 26-27, 30, 56-59, 173-79
Zhong Jingzi (Lord Xian of Qin's heir apparent), 156-63
Zhongshan (area in Wei), 150-53
Zhou (dynasty), 14, 19, 26, 37, 47-48, 58, 60-61, 72, 95, 99, 105, 172, 176, 191, 196, 203; split in, 19-21
Zhou (tyrant, last ruler of the Shang dynasty), 52, 103-04

Zhou Gong, the Duke of Zhou, 69, 103, 165, 167, 169, 171-72, 193
Zhou Taiwang, also Grand King, Father Dan, or Ancient Duke, Father Dan, 109
Zhouxun, calligraphic style, 5; chapter structure, 23-25; (main) ideas, 41-46; linguistic characteristics, 6-8; overall structure, 25-31; protagonists, 13-22; rhetorical strategies, 32-40; (original) scope, 3-5; setting, 8-12; transcription, 2-3; "Yiwenzhi" entry, 72-73
Zhuangzi, 8, 73, 108
Zhuozi (Lord Xian of Jin's son), 120, 122-24, 126-27
Zixia (disciple of Confucius), 154
Zuozhuan, 35, 40, 48-49, 62, 86, 103, 108, 126, 128, 130, 135, 141-42, 148, 163

www.ingramcontent.com/pod-product-compliance
Lightning Source LLC
Chambersburg PA
CBHW020650230426
43665CB00008B/384

9781931483728